The Governing Crisis

About the Author

W. Lance Bennett (Ph.D., Yale University) teaches political science at the University of Washington. His work on communication and politics has appeared in leading scholarly journals, and his research has been supported by the National Science Foundation, the Ford Foundation, the Social Science Research Council, the Spencer Foundation, and the Fulbright Commission. He is the author of *News: The Politics of Illusion,* and co-editor of *Taken by Storm: The Media, Public Opinion, and U.S. Foreign Policy in the Gulf War.* He was co-recipient of the 1994 Donald McGannon Research Essay Award for Social and Ethical Relevance in Communication Policy.

The Governing Crisis
Media, Money, and Marketing in American Elections

SECOND EDITION

W. Lance Bennett
University of Washington

St. Martin's Press
New York

Managing editor: Patricia Mansfield Phelan
Project editor: Diana Puglisi
Production associate: Melissa Kaprelian
Art director/Cover designer: Lucy Krikorian

Library of Congress Catalog Card Number: 94-74762

Manufactured in the United States of America.

0 9 8 7 6
f e d c b a

For information, write:
St. Martin's Press, Inc.
175 Fifth Avenue
New York, NY 10010

ISBN: 0-312-11615-2

To Murray Edelman

Preface

Writing a second edition of a book titled *The Governing Crisis* is not something to be undertaken lightly. Yet the crisis goes on in the view of most citizens and growing numbers of politicians, journalists, and scholars. This edition provides a more comprehensive look at what is now a more fully developed set of problems. As the title suggests, this is a book about politics, people, and government in the contemporary United States, with the focus on that great engine of government, the election process. It is also a book about communication and politics, with a focus on how new communication technologies are undermining the collective wisdom of democracy.

In the United States, national political contests are moments of opportunity for defining public problems, exploring new directions, evaluating the character of aspiring leaders, and dreaming about the future. Elections are the centerpieces of the civic culture. Yet these grand occasions for stock-taking, consensus-building, and renewal are being squandered on a regular basis. The news brings daily evidence that politicians are unwilling to think or speak before consulting with their pollsters and media consultants. These failings not only fuel voters' disdain for public officials, but they also contribute to a fundamental breakdown in the political process that links the people with their government.

Voters can still make their presence felt, as they did in 1994 by installing the first Republican Congress in forty years. The question remains, however, whether either party can build the consensus required to set a new course for government. This is an age of independent voters choosing independent candidates based on electronic images created through marketing research. This electronic democracy seems to leave few solid traces from the voting booth to the legislative process. Parties and politicians shift the balance of power in Washington with the aid of polls, focus groups, and advertising campaigns. But what is the point of winning political power in this fashion? Average people feel that the elections held for their benefit do not translate into benefits from government.

Solutions to our national governing breakdown require insights that are not readily available in the press. The media are easily distracted by the spectacle of politics, dazzling their audiences with the daily exploits of the personalities that dominate the television screen.[1] The media—both news and advertising—have also become the battlegrounds on which those political personalities struggle for power. The degree of media foolery required for politicians to survive in the current climate of hostility toward politics has contributed greatly to the breakdown of government itself.

Important issues facing government are increasingly the targets of media wars. For example, an important factor contributing to the Republican landslide of 1994 was the Clinton administration's failure to deliver on its promise of national health care reform. Even though more than 70 percent of the public favored reform, fewer than half that number supported the Clinton plan by the time the propaganda barrage had finished with it. The political breakdown around such an important issue is all the more instructive because the failure was not due to divided party government; the electorate of 1992 had entrusted both the White House and Congress to the Democrats. Yet members of the ruling party broke ranks with their president, backing numerous alternative plans, thereby feeding public confusion and anger at the spectacle in Washington. The case of health care illustrates how the popular mandate of the last election can easily be lost as elected officials defend the interests of their political backers and jockey for advantage in the next election.

The slippage between an election that promised health reform and the elected government that failed to deliver it points up another prominent feature of the governing crisis: the power of highly organized interests. The efforts of health care interests—from drug and insurance companies to doctors—helped defeat government action with intense lobbying, massive campaign contributions to lawmakers on key congressional committees, and a record-setting advertising campaign. Communication scholar Kathleen Hall Jamieson looked at the health care campaign as it approached the election: "We are witnessing the largest, most sustained advertising campaign to shape a public policy decision in the history of the Republic. . . . [T]he dollar amount spent on producing and gaining an audience for ads will exceed that expended on ads by Bush and Clinton combined in 1992."[2]

Policy failures and dis-connections between elections and government actions are signs of a system in disarray. As voters grow angrier with elected officials, incumbents hold onto their offices by outspending opponents and bombarding voters with ever more fearful and fantastic media images. Many candidates are driven out of the running by the daunting prospects of raising enough money to run competitive races, as happened with Republican notables William Bennett, Dan Quayle, and Jack Kemp in the preliminary stages of the 1996 presidential race. The great turnovers in Congress associated with the 1992 and 1994 elections were due not so much to voters throwing the incumbents out as to incumbents retiring from office. Many talented lawmakers could no longer stand to raise huge sums of money, only to campaign before hostile constituents, just to return to the frustrations of Washington. Even when politicians with the zeal for such campaigning replace the old guard in this upside-down system, they find it almost obligatory to proclaim their disdain for government and affirm their dread of Washington. When Michael Flanagan won the Illinois House seat of Democratic power broker Dan Rostenkowski (who ran for reelection in 1994 despite being under indictment for corruption), Flanagan announced a self-imposed term limit of ten years, saying of Washington: "That city could corrupt Saint Francis."[3]

One of the dangers in this age of cynicism is that easy explanations abound, and frustrated people often settle for them. Popular support for solutions such as term limits has been described by political scientist Thomas Mann as "a primal scream" from an angry and seemingly powerless public.[4] Majorities in opinion polls are expressing support for a third political party for the first time in the modern era.[5] Are term limits and third parties viable solutions or frustrated responses? This book is dedicated to exploring more challenging explanations of the crisis in order to discover workable solutions.

ROOTS OF THE CRISIS

Three broad organizing themes appear throughout the book to help explain the governing crisis: **media, money,** and **marketing.** It is possible to begin with any one of the three and work toward the other two.

Let's begin with *marketing.* Since the marketplace of ideas has grown unresponsive to the demands of political consumers, politics has increasingly become a marketing challenge. When viewed as marketing rather than a way of life, democracy takes on a different tone: above all, an election is not held for the benefit of all the people, or even most of the people, these days. The political consultants who now run election campaigns will tell you in moments of candor that citizen withdrawal is a blessing in disguise. Political marketing maxim number one: the fewer people voting, the easier it is to sell a candidate. The electorate these days is sized up in much the same way that a market is tested and analyzed prior to the release of a new breakfast cereal or an underarm deodorant. With any luck, a small segment of that market can be identified as the key group whose votes could swing the outcome of the contest. And so, a whole campaign may be pitched in subliminal images that play in Peoria, or wherever that target audience is found. Moving candidates off the shelves these days—even to reduced numbers of voters—is still often a "hard sell." Making this sell has driven the costs of campaigning through the roof.

Money has thus become a doubly troublesome ingredient of the new American politics, fueling the very campaigns that leave voters disillusioned, while exacting the steep price of political loyalty from politicians who take the funds. Many political ideas that might attract voter interest have already been bought and taken off the market by the "political investors" who finance candidates. In the chapters ahead, we will explore the arcane world of political action committees (PACs) and other finance mechanisms that funnel huge amounts of money to candidates and sustain that support after they are elected. The sums of money required to launch a credible bid for office usually come with strings attached, leaving government in many important issue areas something of a mad crosswise pull of power.

The *media* take us into this upside-down world where Madisonian ideals have been traded for Madison Avenue methods. The communication challenge in today's politics is not to inspire and mobilize the great and diverse masses of people, as a romantic notion of democracy might lead us to hope. Rather, the challenge of electronic politics is to persuade the target groups isolated by the marketers to go out and pull their levers in response to test-marketed images and slogans such as tax and spend liberals, corporate welfare, balanced budgets, big government, prayerless schools, tax-paid abortions, weekend rapists on prison release programs, or immigrants who use tax-supported services. The nervous systems of target audiences twitch more violently if the weekend rapist is black or the immigrants are illegal. These media campaigns are more effective if competing messages and other distracting "noise" can be minimized in the daily news. Thus, the media component of the governing crisis also includes the growing array of techniques for keeping a growling press pack at bay. Since news organizations are increasingly owned by large corporations that run them for profit, not for public service, journalists are less likely to act as public watchdogs, settling instead for news as a kind of daily political melodrama. The resulting media spectacle favors scandals and personalized "attack politics" over crusades for serious reforms in the system.

The origins and workings of this electoral system will be explored in detail as the book develops. Part I provides an introduction to the new American politics, highlighted by an overview of the governing crisis, as well as analyses of the 1988 and 1992 presidential campaigns. Part II examines the origins and workings of the crisis, including historical comparisons with earlier periods. Part III looks at the cultural roots of the crisis, from the transformation of elections into increasingly empty rituals to the short-circuiting of the character and leadership tests that are so crucial to American politics. Part IV investigates the policy–election–leadership connection, with analyses of the 1994 midterm elections, a look at various government breakdowns, and a discussion of needed reforms. A more detailed overview is found at the end of Chapter 1.

A NOTE TO THE READER

The ideas in *The Governing Crisis* touch some very personal subjects: what this country should be, who should decide its future, and the rules that we as a people should play by. Out of respect for these important concerns, this book neither hides from controversy nor drains the political life from its subject. A lively, realistic look at our nation's politics is required to think productively about problems that large majorities of the people continue to cite as deep concerns. In grappling with the arguments in the book, the following guidelines may be useful for keeping them in perspective:

- The crisis described in these pages is not of the author's invention, but is something on which most Americans—and increasingly, most of their elected representatives—agree.
- In the spirit of understanding the core problems with the system, constructive criticism is aimed at both the major parties and their leaders. Not even political independents will find an easy endorsement in this book.
- Finally, this realist's perspective is backed by a commitment to the bipartisan reforms outlined in the final chapter.

The moral of this story is that ideas matter in politics. Our continued national creativity requires a political system that permits free discussion and productive communication aimed at keeping democracy working for all.

Acknowledgments

To the teachers, students, concerned citizens, and journalists who responded to the first edition, I offer this second in hopes that I have framed the issues more clearly and have provided more cogent recommendations for resolving the crisis. My thanks go to the many people who have engaged with the argument and offered criticisms and ideas that contributed to this revision. First on the list is Regina Lawrence, who read every chapter in draft form, pointing out arguments that needed more development and providing valuable research assistance throughout the project. All writers should be blessed with such helpful critics. Extremely useful criticism also came from Robert McChesney, who encouraged me to expand and clarify the role of the media in the governing crisis. I hope the changes in this area are apparent. Encouragement to broaden the discussion of voter psychology came from various participants at the conference on the Clinton presidency organized by Stanley Renshon at the City University of New York in November of 1993. Jerry Manheim has been a rich source of ideas about political marketing and strategic communication. Bill Haltom and Steve Livingston have helped me think about ways to make this material teachable as well as readable.

Murray Edelman, to whom this book is dedicated, has continued to impress upon me the importance of thinking critically about how we use political symbols and how to evaluate various popular solutions to our political discontents. My appreciation of the importance of ideas in politics has also been enriched through many exchanges with Erik Åsard, a scholar who remains concerned with culture and language in this electronic age. And my Wednesday night seminars with Don Morrissey have clarified many issues.

I am indebted to Larry Makinson of the Center for Responsive Politics for the sharing of data and ideas about campaign finance and candidate spending patterns. The folks at the Federal Election Commission have also been extraordinarily responsive to requests for data. They have succeeded in making their bureaucracy a user-friendly place.

A special thanks goes to Don Reisman, executive editor and editor extraordinary, who gave me his best advice and then left me alone to write the best book I could. I would also like to thank several reviewers who covered the broad intellectual landscape on elections and democracy: Bruce E. Gronbeck, University of Iowa; Kenneth L. Hacker, New Mexico State University; Nancy Maveety, Tulane University; and Jeremy Rabkin, Cornell University. This book is better for trying to reconcile the range of their input. Thanks, too, for the wonderful copy editing by Betty Pessagno and the contributions of project editor Diana Puglisi.

I cannot fully express my gratitude to Ann Buscherfeld, who has processed the text and produced final manuscripts on two editions of this book. She makes Herculean tasks seem effortless, and short deadlines manageable.

Finally, thanks to the many readers who have responded directly with feedback and suggestions. To the journalists and the citizens' groups who have invited me to talk with them, the stirring of concern and the signs of change at the grass roots are encouraging. Above all, thanks to the many students, who, through the encouragement of their instructors, have communicated their reactions to the first edition. This second edition is aimed most of all at communicating more clearly with you who are interested in learning how to make the most of your experiences as citizens.

W. Lance Bennett
SEATTLE

Contents

The Governing Crisis

PART I

The New American Politics

CHAPTER   1

The Governing Crisis

People talk as though our political system had been taken over by alien beings. *—Kettering Foundation Report on the American Electorate*

Most Americans know the governing crisis as a familiar refrain in the news: Voters are angry, politicians are scared, and government seems unable to cope with the nation's problems. These symptoms of a widely perceived rift between the government and the people have come to dominate both election campaigns and the stretches of politics in between. For the current generation of citizens, the inability to harness the government through the electoral process has become the overriding issue of the age, as measured in opinion polls and other indicators cited throughout this book. In less angry times, voting may have been regarded more as a civic duty and less as a way of sending blunt messages to public officials. More complacent generations of Americans may have encountered the link between voting and government as an abstract civics book lesson. By contrast, Americans coming of age in recent years are likely to form their impressions of elections and government through angry voices on talk shows, electronic town halls, and voting booth rebellions like the 1994 election that produced the first Republican Congress in forty years. As House Speaker Newt Gingrich talked about fulfilling the Republican "Contract with America," and President Bill Clinton proposed a "middle-class bill of rights," pundits began buzzing about the 1996 campaign before the close contests of 1994 had all been settled.

In this dizzying political climate, the election–government connection (widely seen as a dis-connection) has become a tangible, personal issue for citizens, politicians, and journalists alike. It is common to hear questions such as the following raised in settings as different as dinner table conversations, political party strategy meetings, and reports on the nightly news:

- Are major pieces of legislation held hostage by politicians' calculations about the next election?
- Will that next election finally produce leaders who can inspire skeptical citizens and cut through the political squabbling in Washington?
- Will the squabbling and political maneuvering in government—commonly known as gridlock—yield to voter demands to curb organized interests and the careerism of professional politicians?
- Do solutions to the governing crisis lie in term limits, constitutional amendments, third parties, social movements, or other dramatic departures from routine election politics?

Political scientists, politicians, media pundits, and the talk show chorus of average citizens all have varying views on these matters. In this politically charged atmosphere, it pays to think through the problems and the proposed solutions carefully, both to avoid personal confusion and to ensure that chosen courses of action may actually have positive effects on problems that are far from simple in nature. For example, some observers believe that gridlock can be solved simply by sending more public-spirited representatives to Washington—citizen-solons who are free of "special interest" obligations and personal career ambitions. From another view, gridlock offers protection against unwelcome acts by partisan factions who cannot agree on what the broad public interest really is. A leading view from the academy is that something like "gridlock" is precisely what the Constitution was designed to produce when there is little political consensus among the people and acrimonious political factions try to rule the land.

Some scholars are not even sure that government has suffered an actual decline in productivity or responsiveness in recent times. For example, political scientist David Mayhew challenges the common wisdom that divided party control of Congress and the White House (a common feature of contemporary American politics) is responsible for gridlock. He points to measures of bills passed and hearings held as evidence that government is no more active or productive during periods of single-party dominance than during times of divided party rule.[1] The less-than-spectacular legislative success of the Democrats during their brief ascendancy to power between 1993 and 1994 would seem to support this argument.

While it always pays to remember the chilling effects of a constitutional system of limited powers, magnified by historically weak political parties, there is more to the story than this. We must somehow explain the high levels of citizen distress and the large numbers of talented public officials who have left public life voluntarily in recent years out of frustration with the system. Simple counts of the numbers of laws passed or hearings held do not begin to describe the coherence or, in the view of many observers, the incoherence of the political process. Similarly, raw activity counts do not measure the degree to which truly important legislation has failed or been hopelessly compromised—as happened to the Democrats with their promise of health care reform in 1994—while relatively minor political initiatives succeed. Finally, the effects of interests and their money on the nation's politics are as evident as they are hard to quantify.

The above factors are among the many that are routinely cited to support the popular consensus that something has gone badly wrong with government these days. They bear investigating. Just the simple fact that so many people in a democracy have lost faith in government, in politicians, and in the electoral process may qualify as a sign of serious trouble. A major aim of this book is to discover the nature of our contemporary political breakdown and explore the ways in which this breakdown may be different from any that has gone before.

OLD POLITICS, NEW PROBLEMS

In addition to thinking carefully about the origins and possible solutions to the current crisis, it pays to remember that this is neither the first, nor is it likely to be the last, period of friction between the people and their government. Indeed, eras such as the expansion of the Western frontier in the 1830s, the Civil War and the reconstruction of the nation afterward, and the Great Depression of the 1930s make the current period seem relatively tame. History can teach us a lot about what is new and what is old in the present political situation. We will discover in this analysis, for example, that while such things as negative campaigning and periods of distrust in government are fairly common interludes in American history, in the current era the levels of sophistication in opinion polling, marketing, and strategic political communication are unprecedented. The resulting domination of poll-taking, image-making, advertising, and news management in contemporary politics creates the ironic result of ever-more-sophisticated and personally accessible communication that fails to clarify issues or provide the kind of information that is useful for solving problems. What passes these days for political ideas are calculated appeals to short-term voter moods. Such messages leave little lasting imprint on voter consciousness beyond the immediate feeling elicited by electronic images, and the eventual anger at broken promises and shattered expectations.

Government by marketing, polling, and image-making may represent a threat to democracy that the designers of the system never imagined.

Focusing so much attention on the whims and poorly articulated fears of the people and making elected representatives constantly accountable to those continuously aroused emotions would have represented the worst of all political worlds to most of the nation's founders, Federalist and Anti-Federalist alike. Indeed, it was just such a system of popular passions and political pandering that a constitutional design team led by James Madison most feared, and labored hard to avoid.

THE RISE OF ELECTRONIC DEMOCRACY

The core of the current crisis in government may be a superficial brand of democratic accountability that appeals to individual emotions rather than fosters the development of broad, stable public interests. Michael Wines, a journalist covering the 1994 election campaign, noted this possibility with an ironic formulation that would surprise those who believe that the trouble with government these days is its distance from the people:

> Washington is more open, less corrupt, more responsive and more accountable than at any time in history. Its principal problem is not that it listens too little, but that it listens—and is shouted at—too much. The insular, tone-deaf town assailed in hundreds of campaign commercials this autumn died about the time Richard Nixon left office.
>
> Modern Washington is wired for quadrophonic [sic] sound and wide screen video, lashed by fax, computer, 800 number, overnight poll, FedEx, grassroots mail, air shuttle, and CNN to every citizen in every village. . . . Its every twitch is blared to the world . . . and its every misstep is logged in a database for the use of some future office-seeker.
>
> American government is in touch with everyone, moving in synch with the opinion of the moment as gracefully as blackbirds rising in unison from a field. The blackbirds, of course, often go nowhere. Sure, many of the changes in political morals and technology may be good— who wants an unaccountable government?—but the cumulative effect has been to turn a somewhat slow and contemplative system into something more like a 500 channel democracy, with the clicker grasped in the hand of the electorate. As a result, modern politicians have become slaves to public opinion, and what voters profess to want—the unpopular [legislative] vote, made out of conscience—has become an immensely difficult act.[2]

This assessment may exaggerate the responsiveness of government in order to challenge the conventional wisdom that the governing crisis is a result of insensitive politicians who ignore the desires of the people.

What Wines has missed, of course, is that a vicious cycle is at work. Namely, the opinion that bombards Washington and that descends upon candidates at election time is not always the spontaneous outpouring of millions of individuals living and thinking in pristine isolation. Rather, their opinions are researched, shaped, and occasionally whipped into a frenzy through well-orchestrated political communication campaigns run by interest organizations, parties, candidates, and even the same public officials who are subsequently faxed, phoned, E-mailed, approval-rated, voted upon, and otherwise bombarded with said opinion. In this world of "electric rhetoric," as communication scholar Bruce E. Gronbeck terms it, people are spoken to from afar, in terms calculated to elicit less than thoughtful responses, and are not encouraged to think—or act—outside of the categories that are offered by the thirty-second spot, the news sound bite, or the talk show pundit.[3] In the view of political scientist Benjamin Ginsberg, we have entered the era of a "captive public" that is continually subjected to polling and marketing efforts designed either to calm unruly tendencies or, alternatively, to stir up outbursts during spells of unwanted complacency.[4]

The image of a captive public is a useful corrective to Wines's notion of democracy gone to the other extreme, but it, too, may be a bit exaggerated. In weighing the degree to which publics can be seen alternatively as prisoners or as prime movers in the evolving electronic democracy, it helps to work through two important points. First, a certain amount of direct, unprogrammed experience surely accounts for a measure of public opinion. People, after all, are neither fools nor media dupes. However, they may also lead frustrated, isolated political existences in which images, promises, and slogans are often as close as they get to political reality. Walter Lippmann's famous dictum about the average person's experience of political reality may contain even more caution for the current electronic age than it did for the print age in which he wrote: "The only feeling that anyone can have about an event he does not experience is the feeling aroused by his mental image of that event."[5] In other words, people may weigh all the information available to them and make up their own minds, but the information contained in carefully constructed electronic images can be as seductive as it is deceptive. For example, today's citizens may play eyewitness to wars, famines, or revolutions without much capacity to judge whether their living room experience bears any connection to the realities at the scene. Similarly, people may feel that they know candidates or politicians without experiencing any more intimacy than what carefully rehearsed news events or political advertisements offer.

Second, and more importantly, neither the interests behind the scenes nor the factions in government that wage the battles for public opinion are so broad or so ideologically coherent that the public is held captive in large majorities for extended periods of time. Indeed, if the latter situation prevailed, the majority of people might well share the delusion that everything was just fine in government and that they, the people, were properly in charge. More than a decade of increasingly negative opinion polls about government, organized interests, and politicians suggests that most people are adept at loosening the electronic bonds that hold them in short-term alliances around particular issues or candidates. If that is the good news, the bad news is that when people return to the state of freethinking independence, their political feelings and identifications become largely negative ones. For example, as reported in a 1994 Times Mirror survey, only 33 percent of those polled agreed that "most elected officials care what people like me think," down from 47 percent in 1987.[6] Or, to put it in the negative terms that are more familiar to poll-watchers these days, fully 66 percent of those polled disagree with the idea that elected officials care what people like them think. And therein lies another key to understanding the governing crisis: majorities these days are more likely to form around negative attachments than stable positive identifications (a prospect fueled by negative campaigning at election time) and around everyday political appeals to fears, insecurities, racial tensions, and economic uncertainties in society.

Publics in this evolving electronic democracy appear as short-term captives in fragmentary, often isolated electronic networks of opinion. When their chosen positions on the issues fail to materialize in hoped-for policies, or when their latest electoral picks turn out to look or act like all the rest, they may join the ranks of the disenchanted majority. These "virtual publics" are brought to us by the modern science of *strategic communication*. As political communication scholar Jarol Manheim explains it, strategic communication is often driven by short-term political goals that are served by mobilizing precisely targeted and socially disconnected segments of the general population.[7] Intense media wars are waged for the attention and short-term support of these constantly shifting target populations. If there is a danger in this dawning age of electronic democracy, it may lie in the permanent fragmentation of publics. Or, as Robert Entman describes the crisis, the social isolation and shallowness of the media experience may be creating a "democracy without citizens."[8]

Indeed, the very idea of some general, encompassing body called the American public may be a chimera. If this was true when Walter Lippmann wrote of "the phantom public" at the dawning of mass communication earlier in this century, it is even more evident today at the dawning of a new age of personalized electronic communication in which publics can be assembled and shaped through highly individualized appeals.[9] While still quite useful in everyday political rhetoric and as the mythical centerpiece of the election ritual, *The Public* dissolves as quickly as the electronic bonds from which it is created are disconnected. New publics are targeted for the next issue, the next candidate, or the next image campaign. Thus, there are merits to both views of publics as captives of an increasingly managed political system and as the most feared and potentially volatile forces on the political landscape. Yet neither account, by itself, adequately explains their inherent fragmentation or instability, or the growing isolation of the individuals who make them up.[10]

What is important to understand is how all of this pulse-taking, image-making, influence-peddling, and opinion-expressing—with added potboiling from the media—has invaded the electoral process in fundamental ways. Accordingly, several broad issues facing the American political system are explored in depth throughout this book:

- *The Media Spiral.* The systematic transformation of election campaigns into high-tech strategic communication processes has undermined the capacity of elections to serve as stable guidance mechanisms for government. The mass-mediated democracy—for all its talk shows, pollster pulse-taking, up-close-and-personal news coverage of politicians' daily movements, and glitzy political advertising—has created a short circuit in the electronic picture of government. There is no mechanism for turning all the shouting, show-business hype, and celluloid promises into the sustained political power needed to get anything important done in this unwieldy constitutional system. The possibility must be considered that what has been lost in this noisy communication process is the capacity to build the consensus needed to mobilize power of, by, and for the people in the American democracy.
- *The Marketing Syndrome.* Citizens in this system are increasingly like consumers who expect the products they buy to fulfill the personal fantasies promised in the advertising. Heavy bombardment by ever more sophisticated propaganda has left citizens cynical and, perhaps more importantly, selfish. People increasingly expect personal payoffs from government, with little regard for the good of society. At the same time, there is equally little hope that government will actually be able to keep the personalized promises made by candidates and politicians through the magic of marketing research.
- *The Money Chase.* Meanwhile, the unprecedented amount of money required to sustain this communication-driven political process—both during elections, and in the governing periods in between—magnifies the destabilizing influence of organized interests on parties, on the public issue agenda, on election campaigns, and, ultimately, on the capacity of elected officials to carry out the basic ideal of government by the people.

AN ELECTION SYSTEM IN DISARRAY

The media spiral, the marketing syndrome, and the money chase in contemporary politics have undermined the connection between elections and government in the United States. As noted above, the focus of our story is an evolving electoral system in which politicians govern with one eye on the polls and the other on the next election. It is important to consider that we as a people have been affected profoundly by the ways in which we communicate. As we have seen, communication can either mobilize or inhibit the positive formations of power needed to make government work. At a deeper level, communication can also corrupt individuals who are told whatever they want to hear by politicians.

When the next election rolls around in this fragile electronic environment, candidates face often daunting levels of voter dissatisfaction with politicians and government. In some cases, the mighty are toppled, as when Speaker of the House Thomas Foley was defeated in 1994 in a well-financed campaign to "De-Foleyate" Washington, making him the first sitting Speaker to suffer electoral defeat in 134 years. In most cases, however, the incumbents are spared simply because they raise and spend more money than their challengers. Even in the sweeping Republican upset in the 1994 midterm elections, incumbents were returned to office at an 86 percent rate in the House and an 87.5 percent rate in the Senate.

There is little consolation in knowing that the average margins of victory have become slimmer over the past several elections. In the process, the costs of campaigning have risen proportionately. At the same time, voters are more fickle and more likely to wait until the last minute to make up their minds. The growing ranks of independent voters are blind to party labels, one time swinging toward the Democrats, another time toward the Republicans; and, increasingly, these voters are prepared to go with independent candidates. In 1992, for example, a whopping 19 percent of the vote went to independent candidate Ross Perot, who pulled large segments of voters away from George Bush, and, in the process, helped Bill Clinton walk into the White House. In 1994, the independent "Perotistas" swung the other way in overwhelming numbers, delivering Congress to the Republicans. Thus, as elections have become more competitive, they have also become—in this system—less coherent.

In this volatile climate, it is understandable why candidates seek constant guidance from media consultants, pollsters, and image experts. Indeed, candidates who succeed in this system may be better at getting elected than at governing afterward. Many discover that they must bring their campaign teams into office along with them simply to communicate effectively with constituents, and remain viable for the next election. As a result, politics increasingly becomes a media spectacle, as political scientist Murray Edelman describes it, with all sides jockeying for public approval, pointing the finger of scandal and corruption at opponents, and adopting the appearance of high-mindedness and freedom from the influence of interests.[11]

As these spectacles go, the campaign of 1994 witnessed novel forms of what communication scholars Dan Nimmo and James Coombs refer to as "mediated political realities"—those political experiences that exist only in the imaginary world of carefully researched, scripted, staged, and edited media events and productions.[12] For example, some thirty Republican congressional candidates combined market research revealing low support for President Clinton with video-morphing techniques made famous in Hollywood movies and shaving commercials to turn their Democratic opponents into Bill Clinton right before the viewers' eyes. The sound tracks and on-screen titles for these ads cued the transforming facial images with phrases such as "tax and spend politicians," "liberal," "Washington insider," and "Democrat."[13] For their part, large numbers of Democratic candidates used similar polling information to distance themselves from the president and their own party. Many went so far as to declare their opposition to Clinton on various issues and to remove the word "Democrat" from campaign literature and advertising.

Perhaps the award for the most innovative campaign appeal of 1994 should go to Martha Whitehead, the Democratic candidate for Texas state treasurer. She promised, if elected, to eliminate her own office! One of her television commercials opened with a shot of the candidate superimposed next to the Texas state capitol with the words "State Treasurer" appearing underneath her name. She then began to speak these words: "I've decided to do what no Texas politician has ever done before— abolish an entire state agency and my own job." Her image began to dissolve slowly as her final words reached the viewer: "Fewer bureaucrats, less waste, starting with me." And suddenly, she was gone, leaving only her name and an expansive image of the capitol and its lovely grounds on the screen.[14]

A Changing Political Communication Process

The point of these examples is not to be awestruck by the uses of advancing technology or by the politicians' sometimes absurd pandering to voters' moods. Shocking images and pandering politicians have long been part of the political landscape. However, earlier image campaigns were neither as pervasive nor as scientific as today's strategic political communication. Consider some differences between two political ads, one early and one more recent. Something of a political advertising legend has grown around the infamous "daisy girl" ad in Lyndon Johnson's 1964 presidential campaign against Barry Goldwater, in which a young girl holding a flower disappeared in a flash and a nuclear blast filled the screen, implying that Goldwater was too dangerous to control the nuclear trigger in a tense cold war world. A notorious example in more recent years is the signature piece of the 1988 George Bush campaign, the "Willie Horton" commercial. That ad, together with other related crime and "prison release" commercials, implied that Bush's opponent Michael Dukakis was so soft on crime that as the governor of Massachusetts he personally and routinely released murderers and dangerous felons on prison furlough programs. Just imagine, as many voters were invited to do, a bleeding-heart liberal Democrat willingly unleashing crime sprees—including a rape committed by Horton—on innocent victims. Communication scholar Kathleen Jamieson analyzed this ad in *Dirty Politics,* an appropriately titled book on contemporary election rhetoric. As she pointed out, not until his television debut in a cameo role supporting George Bush had William Horton ever been called Willie. The name "Willie" simply flowed more easily with the political script and elicited better reactions from focus groups on which the commercial was tested.[15] These and other examples of political communication methods are discussed in more detail in the election case studies later in the book. For now, several points about these evolving communication forms illustrate how our political discourse has changed.

First, while Johnson's daisy girl was regarded as too offensive to air regularly during the 1964 campaign, the Horton and crime commercials, though controversial, were shown regularly in the 1988 contest. The point here is that there are fewer limits on what is regarded as fair play in the mediated reality game that has come to dominate American politics today.

Second, today's attacks on opponents are not as personal or as crude as the historical name-calling and character insults that have always been part of American elections, but they are much more insidious in another way. As products of market research into the fears and emotions of targeted segments of the electorate, such images cannot be dismissed as easily as a name or a derogatory label. Today's political appeals are aimed at voters' doubts, anger, and insecurities—so-called hot buttons—creating subliminal understandings and feelings that are hard to identify and even harder to counter or erase. Such communication is not the high-minded sort to which a healthy polity might aspire, and it is exclusionary and divisive in ways that hinder broad democratic participation. Political messages these days are often targeted at rather small numbers of key voters, leaving large numbers—often the majority—of citizens feeling left out of the national conversation. Indeed, this communication has left substantial numbers of Americans feeling victimized. For example, was the Horton ad featuring a black man who raped a white woman a racist appeal to white middle-class fears and prejudices, as many black leaders and media critics charged? If so, politicians and their consultants may want to heed the counsel of analysts like Jamieson: namely, anyone who values civility and the hope for harmony in an already divided society should avoid (or be made to avoid?) such appeals as the basis for motivating voters. Yet politicians in their all-consuming desire to win tend to listen to their highly paid consultants who tell them to go with whatever succeeds, or find another line of work. And so, most carefully crafted hot-button appeals and images employ subtle editing and language choices to provide "plausible deniability" against charges of overt lying or prejudice. Meanwhile, the political messages work their subliminal effects at deeper psychological levels.

Third, sophisticated strategic communication no longer occupies the secondary or marginal role in our politics that it did in the earlier era in which the daisy girl ad was shelved as offensive and tasteless. Today these carefully crafted and highly personalized emotional appeals dominate our national political discourse, both during elections and in the periods in between. Moreover, when the now-familiar mix of canned images, sensationalism, and conventional wisdom fails to dominate the political scene, none other than the nation's journalists are the first to excoriate the hapless politician who utters a spontaneous thought or attempts to promote a complex idea. Journalists expect politicians to hire media experts who know how, among other things, to manipulate the press and manage the news. Politicians who suffer bad press because they are poor manipulators encounter little sympathy from the nation's journalists. Research by political scientist Thomas Patterson shows that negative news coverage of politicians has increased dramatically over the last twenty-five years.[16] When politicians fail to master the art of the sound bite and the slick appearance, one can almost hear the press pack grumbling aloud about the need to hire a better press relations officer, pollster, image consultant, or media team. Indeed, that muttering has turned into open criticism of two recent presidents, Bush and Clinton, who, after being elected, failed to exploit the science of political communication as thoroughly as the team that helped make Ronald Reagan into the Great Communicator.

Following these generalizations, a central argument in this book is that there has been a subtle but sure transformation of the American political system into an electronic democracy that serves neither the demands of representation nor the process of political deliberation very well. The electronic democracy is driven by information and communication processes that are more weighted toward personalized psychological images and less accessible to open public exploration of ideas than ever before. Even seemingly open forums such as radio talk shows can be heard to recycle and reinforce the slogans and common wisdom manufactured in the political image factories, while placing a premium on short, angry exchanges among callers that reduce public debate to the level of trash talking in professional sports. And when people, whether politicians or ordinary citizens, attempt to break out of this noisy system of shallow thinking, an opportunistic opponent or a journalist is always ready to stir the political pot, making them wish they had stuck with the conventional wisdom or hired a better media consultant instead.

A Cautionary Example

The transformation of national politics is most apparent in the electoral arena because there the increasingly dysfunctional relations between citizens and their leaders are on regular display. Perhaps the recent campaign that best illustrates some of these communication-driven trends in electoral politics is the 1994 California Senate race between Democratic incumbent Dianne Feinstein and Republican challenger Michael Huffington. This race was not particularly distinguished by slick new video techniques such as morphing or by absurd promises to abolish a California Senate seat if elected. Rather, the campaign was distinguished by two related factors that have come to define our contemporary politics: candidates (1) doing little in the way of spontaneous communicating with the public (leaving virtually everything to be researched, scripted, and marketed by technical advisors), and (2) spending huge amounts of money to get their contrived messages across to ever more skeptical and cynical voters.

In the process, the California contest set a new Senate race spending record of over $40 million. For reference, the total spending in an average Senate race is just over $6 million, with the average price of a seat for the winner going at just over $4 million.[17] Indeed, $40 million is more than most other democratic nations spend on all the races for all the elected offices in national elections. For example, the 1994 election in Sweden, involving six national parties and lists of candidates for parliament and other levels of government, cost an estimated $15 million.[18]

For Dianne Feinstein, this was the second time she had participated in a record spend-fest: she was on the losing side in a $40 million governor's contest against Pete Wilson in 1990. Feinstein, like her opponent Michael Huffington, Ross Perot, and many others, represents a growing trend of rich candidates who write their own checks to get into office. Although Feinstein won narrowly in 1994, the political object lesson in this example is Huffington, who poured an estimated $27 million of his personal fortune into a campaign that followed the new rules of the political game with nearly religious dedication. (Huffington's expenditure eclipsed the previous record of $18 million held by Jesse Helms in the 1990 North Carolina Senate race.) Most of this staggering sum went into waging an intense "air war" (as the media portions of election campaigns are called these days) that nearly defeated his opponent in an election so close that votes were still being counted more than a week after election day.

Huffington's overriding policy position on most issues was summed up in a rare press interview with *Time* magazine in which he issued the breathtaking dictum: "I want a government that does nothing."[19] The Huffington campaign took the rules of the new election-politics game to the extreme:

- Avoid spontaneous public appearances.
- Avoid all possible direct contact with the press.
- Communicate primarily through advertising.
- Use the news to reinforce the images and messages of campaign ads.
- Minimize traditional political labels such as party and ideology.
- Maximize independence, outsiderism, and lack of experience.
- Tag one's opponent with negative labels at every opportunity (in this case: pro-government, Washington insider, liberal Democrat, Clinton supporter, professional politician).
- Find the fear and anger hot buttons—psychological wedges to drive between voters and the opponent. (In this case, feelings about immigrants, crime, and welfare recipients worked well.)
- Offer oneself to voters as a blank slate onto which they can project hopes and dreams (above all, promise them what they want to hear).
- Spend, spend, spend (beginning with hiring the best media advisors money can buy).

It is less amazing that Huffington—a virtual unknown and newcomer to California politics—eventually lost the race than that he came so close to unseating the experienced, politically savvy, well-financed, and relatively popular (as incumbents go these days) Feinstein. Win or lose, the campaign stands as an exemplar of the contemporary political consultant's chapter and verse: keep voters and reporters at maximum distance and administer a measured daily dosage of commercial imagery that pushes the fear buttons against the opponent, while offering the candidate as a safe, even amorphous alternative. In the view of journalist Sidney Blumenthal, who covered the Huffington campaign,

These commercials are more than the typical tools used in the selling of a candidate: they are the sum total of Michael Huffington's existence in the public mind in this Senate campaign. . . . With the exception of occasional appearances at carefully controlled events, Huffington is visible exclusively in thirty- and sixty-second segments. The video reel is the man. . . .

In midterm elections notable all over the country for an extraordinary level of voter alienation, Michael Huffington is the purest candidate of all—almost untouched by experience. In the House of Representatives, he has been a tabula rasa for almost two years. . . . His very blankness appeals to the unsure. . . . For an electorate that has come to regard politics itself as the problem, he seems to be a godsend.

Huffington stands at a confluence of fear, disillusionment, and rage among the electorate. . . . The Huffington campaign has produced a "statement of purpose" (included in a press packet) which is the candidate's fullest expression of policy. . . . It includes only four issues: crime, the economy, illegal immigration, and welfare. . . . In every case, the statement blames Democrats and "government" for the problems. . . .[20]

The Rise of the Selfish Voter

With such an outpouring of media hype and financial excess characterizing contemporary politics, it is easy to overlook the possibility that the objects of it all—namely, American citizens—are themselves contributing to the problem. If this idea seems puzzling, it is probably because the press (and wary politicians) have come to take voter anger as natural and justified—an independent political variable, as it were. Yet if we are to understand the transformation of American politics, we will have to examine the origins of the public mood as carefully as we examine the other elements of the surrounding political process.

Consider the possibility that the angry state of the citizenry may be contributing to the breakdown of the system. This is not to deny people their right to proper disgust when pandered to by celluloid candidates who spend millions to say nothing. More disturbing, however, is the possibility that much of the anger has become self-serving, providing people with an easy excuse to expect government to cater to their needs personally and to avoid thinking about more demanding solutions—particularly solutions that might entail an element of sacrifice.

In the end, the drift toward political independence that characterizes so many voters and candidates in recent times must be understood as a conflicted political position. That is, for many citizens political independence serves at once as a refuge from organized politics that disappoint and as a justification for a me-first, self-centered politics of the personal. One tragic result is that voters are equally likely to punish both the politicians who lie and deceive them and the politicians who attempt to explore national problems with depth, realism, or subtlety.

In such a political system, none of the players end up looking very good, the voters included. As Jay Rockefeller, Democratic senator from West Virginia, told a group of reporters after the 1992 election:

> Voters . . . are angry with politicians like me. And they are angry with you in the media. Well, let me tell you something, the voters are no bargains, either.[21]

To carry this idea a step further, consider the possibility that by paying so much attention to individual feelings and demands, politicians have created a political fantasy world, filled with promise and drama but, ultimately, offering little chance of bringing the fantasies to life. In such an atmosphere, it is no wonder that voters become self-centered. After all, politicians are promising them everything that they want to hear. At the same time, it is little wonder that people grow angry and skeptical when such promises invariably prove empty. At what point should citizens recognize and reject this easy seduction by personalized politics in favor of more challenging political programs and ideas that may involve making some sacrifices for the good of all? Addressing this question, communication scholar Roderick Hart talks about the decline of political virtue and the rise of facile, self-serving ideas in a book aptly titled *Seducing America.*[22] Reaching back into the political culture to locate one of the founding virtues, he calls for a "new Puritanism" that will restore personal discipline, will, and recognition of the greater good of the community. This may be an impossible ideal in this age of instant gratification and easy anger. Even so, it pays to think about why discipline, community, and the avoidance of easy solutions seem to be such foreign ideas in a culture that once promoted these values among its citizens.

THE FOUNDATIONS OF THE CRISIS

It is easy to see why the governing crisis continues despite the increasing levels of turbulence and voter unrest with each election. Serious political reforms, including many of those proposed in this book, require courage and leadership abilities above and beyond those that most politicians possess these days. Moreover, effective national problem solving requires more attention and willingness to listen to one another than average citizens seem prepared to offer. It is not easy to hold national deliberations about complex problems when quick fixes and slogans are rampant. Yet other periods in the nation's history have witnessed great political reform and ferment—even eloquent national debates in which politicians presented reasoned views and citizens listened. What is more, those times occurred with a population considerably less educated and decidedly less wired for communication than the present generation of Americans.

To start thinking about more substantial solutions we must recognize that a *system* of political factors is involved. Begin with a government made unwieldy by constitutional design and made more so by the prominent and relatively unrestrained role of organized interests in the system. Add the money channeled by interests into elections (and into various policy battles in between), and even more of the problem emerges. Now put that money together with relatively little regulation of political communication, particularly with regard to how the public airwaves are used. Finally, add a culture that is deeply suspicious of regulation and governmental restrictions on the electoral process. When members of that culture respond to the crisis as isolated individuals rather than as organized groups, it is easy to see how this system could spiral out of control. Using case studies of contemporary elections and politics, this book explores these and other roots of the governing crisis.

A Simple Framework for Analysis

Looking at such a complex system of political relations could be daunting. Therefore, throughout the book, we will return to a simple framework of ideas that captures the key elements of the crisis that have been discussed thus far and that can be used to trace the development of our current problems with government. Recalling our basic themes of money, marketing, and media, we find that the following three behind-the-scenes factors have dominated contemporary elections in recent years.

The first factor is campaign financing. For reasons explained in later chapters, candidates and parties have been driven into stiff competition for the huge sums of money required to win elections in a system that has fewer restrictions on spending, advertising, and funding than in any other Western industrial democracy. One view of campaign finance has gone so far as to describe elections as investment opportunities for organized interests, particularly big business. This political investment thesis, advanced by political scientist Thomas Ferguson and sociologist Joel Rogers, argues that Democratic candidates have been leveraged steadily to the right in order to compete with Republicans for campaign dollars from their own former backers.[23] As a result, the range of meaningful political difference between candidates has decreased steadily, moving both parties out of line with the majority of voters and leaving candidates with little to offer those who remain interested in politics.

Scholars disagree about how much unity of interest exists (or ever has existed) among political backers. Our explanation does not require establishing this difficult-to-document point. Assume that there is little common interest and even less conspiracy among the diverse range of political party backers. The problem is that individual candidates at all levels, from president and Congress down to the state governments, have been separated from their party loyalties by an elaborate system of individual funding from interest groups. Congress, for example, has been so carved up by the finance system that it now makes sense to talk about two levels of representation: patchwork representation, in which sundry blocs of politicians align issue by issue to represent the legislative agendas of various national interests, and strategic district representation, which strives to deliver service and "pork barrel" projects to the folks back home. There is precious little room left for thinking about—much less, acting on—any issues of broader public interest. The result is a system that virtually prevents broad coalitions from taking concerted action on complex issues. There is little chance that presidents—as Bill Clinton found out rather painfully in his attempt to reform the health care system—can even mobilize their own congressional parties on broad legislative agendas that might generate real public enthusiasm. What has developed instead is a veto system in which the faction of the day, either in Congress or the White House, is likely to block any sweeping initiatives contemplated by more visionary public officials. Not surprisingly, politicians as a group have declined in popularity.

The task of selling these damaged politicians and their ideas brings us to the second factor: the systematic marketing of candidates. Image-making and hype have always been part of American politics, but never with the all-consuming importance they have attained in contemporary campaigning. Candidates whose inventory of ideas has been reduced by the stiff competition for campaign financing have become overwhelmingly dependent on marketing experts and image consultants to manufacture content for otherwise empty campaigns. Scientific techniques for audience analysis and product development have enabled campaigns to compensate for content deficiencies by targeting key groups of voters who respond to manufactured, test-marketed images in sufficient numbers to tilt the electoral balance.

The third pillar of the new politics is the perfection of techniques for controlling the news media while finding more effective ways to communicate with political audiences. In recent years, this has often amounted to bypassing the news altogether and reaching the public through advertising and public relations techniques, talk show and electronic town hall appearances, and novel variations on these formats such as Ross Perot's famous infomercials in the 1992 campaign. Reporters, understandably enough, resent being manipulated by image consultants, and they seem to resent being ignored and circumvented by politicians even more. Discouraged by the often-futile search for anything meaningful to write home about, journalists stalk the candidates, looking for the slightest sign of weakness or the hint of a controversial idea.

The result is a vicious cycle in which reporters put politicians under the microscope, and politicians fear every spontaneous encounter with the press. During political campaigns, controlling the press pack thus becomes essential for holding on to the voters targeted by the image-makers and for maintaining the support of financial backers who quickly place their bets on other candidates who appear to be doing better in the election horse race. Enter the technology of media management, with its Orwellian vocabulary of *spin doctors, damage control, sound bites, line of the day,* and *photo opportunities,* all orchestrated by the ever-present *handlers,* whose job is to keep reporters as far removed from spontaneous contact with the candidate as possible.

A NEW AMERICAN ELECTION SYSTEM

Welcome to the new American election system. One of the arguments of this book is that candidate marketing, media control, and the huge sums of money required to engage in these activities have, indeed, created a new electoral system. Since we are not talking about a revolution here, many reminders of the old system still remain. The names of the parties are unchanged; the rules for deciding winners and losers are the same; and there is more than enough of the old hype, hoopla, and negativity to go around. But the heart is missing: the promise of governing is gone.

Political communication in the new American election is a private, emotional affair between individual candidates and individual voters. The aim is getting votes, not developing broad support for governing ideas. Society has become an abstraction of media audiences and voter market segments. Missing almost entirely is any sort of give-and-take exchange through which social groups, parties, and candidates might develop mutual commitments to a broad political agenda. America has arrived at a point of nearly complete separation of elections and government.

Elections, Government, and Everyday Life

The connection between elections and government matters so greatly because the strength of that connection affects the quality of life for everyone in society. In recent years it has become apparent that although the nation's problems grow in size and number, candidates for political office seem ever more obligated to financial backers and less interested in leading. For reasons to be explored in this book, the national marketplace of ideas has broken down. Voting and elections no longer work as demand-side forces shaping the quality of candidates and ideas. It is as though some hidden hand has restrained national debate, reducing the range of choice in one of the world's most important political forums. The search for what moves this hidden hand takes us into the netherworld of political finance, Madison Avenue–style candidate marketing, and the emerging science of media control. These facts of modern political life explain a good deal about the current national scene, from the decline of political parties to the reasons why few politicians seem to be interested in bringing discouraged citizens back into the system.

Opinion polls and declining voting rates (the small, encouraging upswings in 1992 and 1994 notwithstanding) show that faith in politicians, trust in government solutions, confidence in the press, and other important measures of citizen satisfaction have dropped steadily over the last twenty years. During the same time, the list of unsolved national problems has grown longer and more worrisome, including debt and budgetary paralysis, foreign competition, political corruption, declining economic security for workers, and a host of social ills—from crime, drug abuse, and homelessness to a failing educational system. Above all, the governing crisis is about the relationship between the quality of political life and society's ability to define and solve its most pressing problems.

This is not a gloom-and-doom prophecy about how America is on the brink of total collapse. Even worst-case scenarios like economic depressions can be (and have been) overcome. Nonetheless, the nation's social and economic problems have come home in ways that are troublesome and worth thinking about. Whether we are talking about the stress of holding down jobs in economically embattled workplaces, the sensory overload of city streets, the amnesia-producing atmosphere of public schools, or the risks of going out at night in crime-ridden neighborhoods, life in contemporary America is disturbingly out of sync with what one might expect in one of history's richest and most powerful societies. The trials of public life take their toll in the private realm as well. In the words of one observer, Americans have adapted to the long winter of their discontent with a "bunker mentality," zealously protecting private lives from a declining civic culture and rising social ills.[24]

When the governing center does not hold, individuals must fend for themselves. This lesson applies not just to the down-and-out but to the up-and-coming as well, since for everyone the quality of private life depends on the quality of public life. Above all, our personal well-being rides on the strength of the political system and its leaders. This idea is hardly news. Aristotle long ago observed that the "good life" begins (and can end) with the kind of political arrangements and leadership a society accepts. Restoring public interest in government, trust in leadership, and commitment to a livable society for all are essential steps toward effecting real solutions for problems such as crime, homelessness, drug abuse, educational ills, economic stagnation, and other obstacles to the "good life."

The point is simply this: At a minimum, lively political debate is required to engage the creative imagination. Such debate depends on leaders who are willing to articulate new ideas, take risks, and motivate public action. Until the problems with the election system are fixed, these kinds of leaders will not emerge because they will be cut short by the press and devoured by the negative images created by opportunistic opponents.

Tired of waiting for compelling leaders to appear, many people have left the political arena altogether for other, less frustrating pursuits. By the end of the last decade, for example, more New Yorkers were buying lottery tickets than voting, by a ratio of 3 to 2.[25] And the current decade opened with a solid majority (60 percent) of the American public agreeing that "people like me don't have any say about what the government does."[26] As noted earlier in the chapter, by the 1994 election that number had increased to 66 percent who felt that politicians did not care what people like them thought.

This does not mean, of course, that politicians are unaware of what people want them to do. No nation on the face of the earth is polled more often by more politicians than the United States. After the data have been mulled over by pollsters, the media consultants advise their political clients about images that can be marketed to voters who remain in the system. And so, politicians and parties do battle over who appears to care the most about the issues that most concern the voters. Yet the parties and the politicians continue to disappoint. In 1992, for example, the Democrats promised the voters serious campaign finance reform, beginning with curbs on special interest money in elections and carrying through to curb lobbying influence in between. Shortly after the election, however, party leaders began to cool on the idea. After all, they had secured control of both Congress and the White House for the first time in a dozen years, and beating the Republicans in the campaign money game had helped.

Similarly, the Republicans pledged in 1994 to honor their campaign center-piece, a Contract with America that included a pledge to support term limits on Congress and, if necessary, to introduce a constitutional amendment to do so. Within weeks of the election, however, the party leadership began edging away from that position. Even before the new Congress had been sworn in, the prospective House majority leader Dick Armey (R-Texas) opined that Americans might not be so concerned about term limits if the newly elected Republican majority "can straighten out the House."[27] And so it goes.

Failing to see leadership emerge anywhere but on the easy moral high ground of drugs, crime, and other inflammatory social issues, many disillusioned citizens have retreated from voting, which surely ranks among the least demanding forms of political participation. Meanwhile, a steady procession of candidates continues to walk softly into public office carrying the big stick of high-cost, Madison Avenue campaigning. Yet other voters continue to stir, with the 1992 turnout up slightly to nearly 55 percent, and the 1994 midterm figures at about 38.5 percent of eligible voters. What is more encouraging than these modest turnout increases is that those who vote are clearly in a mood to experiment, as reflected in the 19 percent who supported a partyless Perot in 1992 and the majority who handed the Republicans control of Congress in 1994. Term limit initiatives continued to sweep every state that put them on the ballot. Various polls showed support growing for a third party going into 1996. For example, a Times Mirror survey in 1994 found that 53 percent thought that a third party would be a good idea, up from 44 percent in 1982.[28] And a poll conducted by President Clinton's pollster, Stanley Greenberg, for the Democratic Leadership Council showed that people using a 100 point "favorability thermometer" favored an as-yet-unknown third party (57) over either the Republicans (50) or the Democrats (49).[29]

The question is whether any of this restlessness and change will produce useful solutions. The best place to begin thinking about useful solutions, of course, is with useful understandings of the problems, which brings us to the plan for the rest of this book.

THE PLAN OF THE BOOK

The plan of this book is to develop a simple thesis about media, money, and marketing as the roots of the governing crisis, see how this thesis holds up under criticism, explore the consequences for democracy in America, and propose a set of simple political reforms.

The remaining two chapters of Part I trace the emergence of the new

American election through the campaigns of 1988 and 1992. Chapter 2 examines the first clear-cut case of the new American election in the 1988 campaign, a contest that left voters dazed by distasteful extremes of negative campaigning, not to mention a host of other puzzling features, including Michael Dukakis's abandonment of traditional Democratic constituencies while driving around in a tank like a Charles Schulz cartoon character, and George Bush's recitation of lines from Clint Eastwood movies. Beneath the tragicomic surface, we find the convergence of forces that have pushed American government into its current status as a veto system. Among other things, 1988 was that memorable year in which the House of Representatives achieved the pinnacle of a 98 percent reelection rate for incumbent candidates, while a disgusted public complained about the quality of Congress. Understanding these and other puzzles is necessary preparation for analyzing the elections that came after.

Chapter 3 turns to the 1992 election, with a focus on the constant invention and reinvention of Bill Clinton as a thoroughly electronic candidate, and the elements of the new voter psychology that make such media creations possible. Understanding the mass psychology of the new electoral system explains how public figures can experience great highs and lows of popularity of the sort that sent George Bush from the highest recorded levels of popular approval (89 percent) following the Gulf War against Saddam Hussein to an ignominious defeat in an election the next year. In the victorious 1992 campaign, Bill Clinton's strategy team profited from these lessons about unstable voter psychology to get Clinton elected, only to watch him ride the rollercoaster of public approval after he took office.

Part II addresses the origins and workings of our new electoral system. Chapter 4 explains the historical conditions and political reforms that created this system over the last several decades. The new electoral system is not so much a radical break with traditions of the past as a fascinating series of reforms of existing practices. Fueled by historical events, these reforms have produced a communication process that has in recent times elevated the worst tendencies of American politics to the norm. The changes in the ways people and their leaders communicate can be traced to several historical changes in modern American politics, including the shifting and, ultimately, declining loyalties of voters to political parties beginning in the late 1960s and early 1970s and the rise of a new campaign finance system legislated by Congress during the 1970s and early 1980s.

Chapter 5 explores various criticisms that might be raised against the idea that a significant change is taking place at the center of American politics. A brief review of the history of elections shows which of these criticisms have merit and which miss their mark. Chapter 6 returns to the three main elements of money, media, and marketing, showing in greater detail how each affects the quality of campaigning. So ends Part II.

The third part of the book examines what happens to political culture when its central ritual begins to fall apart. Beyond the command of any individual, culture is the memory bank of collective experience and the guidance system for defining problems and thinking about the future. The American guidance system is currently on the blink. Chapter 7 illustrates the difference between election rituals that are devoid of meaning for their participants and those that remain vital sources of social inspiration and renewal. Even though election campaigns are becoming increasingly emptied of social vision and spontaneous expressions of candidate character, they continue to display many familiar ritualistic fragments, including the traditional rallies, flag-waving, and negative campaigning. When candidates continue to go through the motions of the ritual, it becomes more difficult to spot what has gone awry. Comparing several recent elections helps to pinpoint where the changes are occurring and why.

Chapter 8 examines the crucial importance of leadership in American politics. In many ways, our elections are more about choosing the right leaders for the times than about a specific policy or program. Perhaps the most distressing element of the new politics is the reduced chance of seeing the candidates respond intuitively and spontaneously to each other and to the stresses of the year-long campaign ordeal. In this respect, the combined effects of high finance, candidate marketing, and media control have short-circuited the election as a basic test of character and leadership.

Instead of letting voters and candidates work out new political plots through the rough-and-tumble exchanges of an open campaign, media consultants play it safe. So it is that they replay old plot lines that worked the last time around and add a few image twists that market researchers have tried out on test audiences before splicing them onto the candidate's (or the opponent's) character. The result is that American elections are becoming, in the famous words of Yogi Berra, "like déjà vu all over again." The 1992 and 1994 contests contained important exceptions that proved this rule. For example, the entry of Ross Perot into the 1992 presidential race clearly stimulated greater issue debate and enabled Bill Clinton to set himself apart from George Bush on a number of issues that made a difference to voters. Yet the appearance of a third candidate is hardly a stable solution for the underlying problems of the electoral process. In 1994, for example, the "Perotistas" went the other way, reversing the party alignment in Washington in just two short years. It is hard to find stable solutions in this development either.

Far from being the vital centerpiece or nerve center of a thriving political culture, elections have become a fig leaf for a political system in crisis. The result, as noted above, is that we are dangerously close to losing our guidance system, our collective intelligence, if you will. As Republican commentator Kevin Phillips has observed: "From the White House to Capitol Hill, the critical weakness of American politics and governance is becoming woefully apparent: a frightening inability to define and debate emerging problems. For the moment, the political culture appears to be brain-dead."[30]

The crucial question, of course, is, How long will this moribund cultural condition persist? If I thought the prognosis irreversible, I would not have written this book. Part IV looks at politics and national leadership in the 1990s with an eye to reforms. Chapter 9 begins by exploring both the kind of politics and politicians we can expect if nothing is done to derail the current system of financing, marketing, and media control. Celluloid candidates and imaginary issues are just the symptoms of deeper problems within the system. The weakening link between elections and governing is the more fundamental problem. Although it has never been easy to draw straight connections between votes and eventual government policies, the results of the midterm elections of 1990 and 1994 reflect an alarming reversal of the vote–policy connection on a number of important issues. It has become a common charge that Congress will play politics rather than keep promises or search for workable solutions. The budget deadlock of 1990 and the health care fiasco of 1994 are cases in which political party actions were clearly based more on campaign strategies for the next election than on fulfilling the promises of the last. It is significant that the issues people care about are increasingly corrupted by political concerns about undermining the opposition party, reaping large sums of money from interests while avoiding the appearance of corruption, or both. It is no wonder that voters withhold their loyalties from candidates and parties in response to these kinds of political games.

Indeed, the system's dysfunctions have not been lost on the great majority of the people. The current decade opened with a whopping 77 percent agreement on the belief that the government was being run for the benefit of business and a few special interests. This belief has increased steadily with each passing decade since the rosy dawn of the 1960s, when only 25 percent shared that view.[31] Not surprisingly, nearly 80 percent of the voting age population, when asked about the growing subordination of national problems to electoral politics, expressed the opinion that "America is in serious trouble."[32]

How long can this pressure and these contradictions build without exploding? Which election will produce an even greater voter eruption than occurred with the Perot movement of 1992 or the Republican land-slide of 1994? What results, if any, will come of such turbulence?

The scenarios about politics and politicians offered in Chapter 9 are intended to stimulate thinking about the reform proposals outlined in the final chapter. No doubt, politicians in power will continue to resist funda-mental change in the current system. After all, they have learned how to use this system successfully. Why should they want to change the rules that brought them to power? As in the past, the process of fundamental change will have to emerge from the grass roots. Just as the century opened with the Progressives' attack on machine politics and political corruption, so it may close with another "progressive" crusade against political finance and distorting campaign practices. Chapter 10 closes with a set of "Scorecards" that the reader can use to follow the key political forces through the elections and governments of the rest of the decade. The key question, of course, is what reforms should be on the agenda. I invite the reader to be thinking about that question all along the way.

CHAPTER 2

The New American Election: Marketing George Bush in 1988

More and more the candidate was just the front man; more and more he was just the talker. Our Senate and House candidates, even some of our presidential candidates: they are becoming like anchormen. . . .

At the end of the Reagan era all the presidential candidates looked like local TV news guys.

At the end of the Reagan era they had all gone to the same TV coaches, and they all talked the same way. They talked with their voices low and cool . . . moving their hands within the frame for emphasis, moving their hands the same way with the same studied, predictable natural mannerisms. . . .

. . . candidates with prefab epiphanies, inauthentic men for an inauthentic age.

—Peggy Noonan, speech writer for Ronald Reagan and George Bush

The last several elections cap a long process in which the very language of public life has been transformed to the point that most citizens are offended by it, and many can no longer find the sense in it. As writers like Lewis Carroll, George Orwell, Harold Lasswell, and Murray Edelman have warned, the quality of political rhetoric holds the key to the satisfactions of public life and, ultimately, to the security of private life as well. The debasing of language, and, more broadly, communications, in American elections is one of the mysteries that this book seeks to solve. How did it happen? What can be done about it? What are the consequences for the political system as a whole if these trends continue?

The central thesis of this book is that we have entered a political era in which electoral choices are of little consequence because an electoral system in disarray can generate neither the party unity nor the levels of public agreement necessary to forge a winning and effective political coalition. The underlying explanation is that the political and economic forces driving our national politics have created a system in which the worst tendencies of the political culture—the hype, hoopla, and negativity—have been elevated to the norm in elections, gaining a systematic dominance in campaign content as never before. Meanwhile, the best hopes for creative leadership are systematically screened out by political and economic forces that are only dimly understood, when they are recognized at all.

THE POLITICS BEHIND THE IMAGES

The declining quality of the national political dialogue is subtle and, at first glance, hard to define. Neither the amount of verbiage nor the number of position papers has withered away noticeably. But there have been notable deficits in the quality of ideas—the "vision thing" that George Bush confessed to having so much trouble with. In the 1980s, the quality of political rhetoric deteriorated to the point where fewer than 10 percent of those voting in the 1988 presidential election felt the candidates adequately addressed their concerns. At the beginning of that contest, two-thirds of the voters expressed hope that the choices would be meaningful ones. By election day, two-thirds of those still planning to vote wished that two different candidates were running.[1] Despite this lack of runaway enthusiasm, a slim majority felt at least some warmth toward one or the other candidate and made the trek to the polls. For several elections in a row, similar levels of lukewarmness had registered on the "feeling thermometer" measure used by the University of Michigan National Election Studies to survey voter feelings about candidates. Perhaps the growing sense of voter distress in 1988 was due partly to the frustration of going through too many lukewarm elections against the backdrop of so many hot social problems.

It would be too easy to blame voter dissatisfaction on the declining quality of the individuals running for office. The pattern of citizen discomfort and candidate similarity has become so pervasive that it makes more sense to look for its origins in the contemporary system of campaigning itself. Indeed, one does not have to look too deeply into the data to see the signs of a system in distress. The election of 1988 was marked by a collection of warning signs:

- The highest (then) recorded levels of voter dissatisfaction with politics and politicians were coupled with a vote that produced the highest recorded levels of victories by incumbent candidates (98 percent in the House).

- Increasing numbers of independent voters faced increasing numbers of independent candidates in personalized, emotional, negative campaigns that aroused fears and social divisions instead of hopes and common goals.
- Record amounts of money were spent marketing prepackaged candidates to shrinking numbers of voters.
- A strong victory for George Bush was swept away in four short years by the 1992 victory of Democratic challenger Bill Clinton, who then experienced even greater levels of public controversy and press criticism than had Bush.

WELCOME TO THE FIRST NEW ELECTION

"Read my lips."

"Senator, you're no Jack Kennedy."

"Make my twenty-four-hour time period."

Just a few of the high—or low—points of the Campaign '88, depending on one's view of political language and its proper uses. If the rosy electronic theme fashioned for the election of 1984 was "Morning in America," then 1988 was, in the characterization of a noted political scientist, "Brunchtime."[2] Welcome to the first new election: all text and no context; all rhyme and no reason. It is time to meet the candidates:

- George Bush, Republican candidate for president. A patrician New Englander who had such trouble putting a spontaneous speech together that former Texas Governor Ann Richards dubbed him the man born with a silver foot in his mouth. Would be saved by get-tough campaign scripts provided by top media consultants.
- Dan Quayle, Bush's surprise VP pick to court the youth vote. He quickly became the easy target of press criticism. Lost points in VP debate when opponent Lloyd Bentsen pointed out that he was no Jack Kennedy. Would later go on as vice president to misspell "potatoe" while helping a contestant at a school spelling bee, and condemn TV character Murphy Brown for having a baby out of wedlock.
- Michael Dukakis, Democratic presidential candidate. His wife Kitty confessed that his idea of a good vacation was reading political science on the beach. Selected as the candidate least interesting to have over for dinner by the American people. Most serious campaign mistake: not hiring the Bush media team.
- Lloyd Bentsen, Democratic VP candidate. The first candidate who couldn't lose by virtue of holding onto his Texas Senate seat as insurance against what turned out to be a disaster for the Democrats. Later served as secretary of the treasury under Bill Clinton.

For most scholars, commentators, and the majority of the American public, the presidential election of 1988 was the worst in memory. It was no easy last-place finish, considering the stiff competition in recent years. Evidence from polls, editorials, and academic studies suggests that, even by minimal standards, the most expensive contest up to that point in history failed to accomplish what an election campaign should do: to introduce intelligent, well-reasoned, and occasionally inspiring debate into the voter choice process. Yet—and here's the rub—the superficial one-liners and telegenic sound bites that dominated the campaign were just what speech writers, consultants, and willing candidates aspired to achieve in their communications with the electorate.

POLITICS IN THE TELEVISION AGE

The easiest explanation for the decline of political ideas is television. Volumes have been written blaming TV for most of our social ills, from the destruction of family conversation to the senseless violence on our streets, poor school test scores, and widespread public ignorance of even the barest facts of history, geography, and government. Indeed, when the dim electronic glow of the TV screen illuminates the interior of the American home an average of eight hours each day, there is cause for alarm. What can politicians do but fashion their messages to this passive medium, leaving most of the challenging ideas on the cutting room floor? As former New York governor Mario Cuomo put it, taking a stand on political principles these days "requires that you explain your principles, and in this age of electronic advocacy this process can often be tedious and frustrating. This is especially so when you must get your message across in twenty-eight-second celluloid morsels, when images prove often more convincing than ideas. Labels are no longer a tendency in our politics. In this electronic age, they are our politics."[3] While appreciating the problem, Cuomo failed to work out much of a solution. He lost his 1994 governor's race to one of the new breed of politicians, George Pataki, a millionaire who ran against politics, against government, and against liberals like Cuomo. These now-familiar strains of anti-politics burst forth with a vengeance in 1988 and have been reborn in new forms in every election since.

While ex-Governor Cuomo may have perceived correctly the effects of our political transformation, identifying television as the cause of it all is a bit too easy. There is little doubt that television has changed the way we do politics, but it is not the sole, or even the major, source of our political decline; it is merely the most visible sign of it. Behind the television images lies a whole set of political and economic changes that limit what politicians say, how they say it, and to whom they can say it. These hidden limits make television the perfect medium for saying nothing, but doing it with eye-catching and nerve-twitching appeal. Recognizing that we will not exit this analysis by placing the blame solely on television, we can nevertheless look at TV to start understanding how citizens encounter the new political experience.

Crossing the Electronic Divide

For many elections now, television has been the decisive factor in voters' reports about how they make up their minds. For reasons that will soon become clear, political advertising is often the most influential part of the TV picture. Yet the election of 1988 struck many observers as something of a capstone in the TV age—not so much for voters, who had already adapted to televised information, but for campaigns and candidates. After decades of experimentation and flirting with TV as a strategic weapon in election battles, Election '88 suggested that campaign managers had fully and unashamedly accepted the use of TV technology to reconstruct candidates. The subordination of communication between candidates and public to the dictates of "tele-campaigning" was revealed, among other places, in Democratic candidate Michael Dukakis's transformation during the campaign from traditional campaigner to a creature of television (albeit an unsuccessful one).

Many observers agree that something happened in 1988.[4] "Some invisible line has been crossed," said Marvin Kalb, a former network correspondent and, more recently, director of Harvard's Shorenstein Center on the Press, Politics, and Public Policy.[5] That line, according to John Buckley, a media consultant who has worked for both the Republican party and CBS News, is between print and video, the word and the image: "This is the first election of a newly mature style of politics wherein it is accepted as absolute gospel by both sides that what you need to do is create . . . a message . . . that communicates itself on television. . . . There is no longer a value judgment on the need to tailor a message to television. It's now a matter of survival, not a matter of ethics or intellectual honesty."[6]

Like most historical changes, this realignment of our political discourse to fit the medium of television did not occur overnight. The first step over the electronic line probably occurred in 1960, the year Richard Nixon arguably won the presidential debate in print and on the radio but lost it, along with the election, on television. Goodbye *logos,* hello *logo.*

logos: reason as constituting the controlling principle of the universe, as manifested by speech

logo: short for logogram: the word replaced by the sign, or the visual image

Crossing the line from reasoned to unreasoning discourse has altered the ways in which we (are forced to) understand and participate in politics. The most fundamental change, as noted above, is the decline of the traditional political argument itself. A case in point is the now legendary incident in the 1984 campaign involving CBS correspondent Leslie Stahl. In a news report Stahl attempted to point out the logical inconsistencies between candidate Ronald Reagan's campaign appeals and the contradictory positions and policies Mr. Reagan advocated on the same issues as president. To her amazement Stahl received a thank-you call from the White House after the lengthy piece was aired. The reason for the thank-you was that the visual images of Reagan speaking, no matter what the contradictions in his speech, were more powerful than the argument Stahl had fashioned to go along with those images. The moral we can derive from this incident is that political ideas are no longer anchored in reason, logic, or history; political ideas as we may have known them once upon a time don't exist.

A number of shock waves have flowed from this fundamental transformation in our national political communications. Witness, for example, the eclipse of the newspaper as a significant factor for the mass public. It is too easy to blame the decline of the print media on creeping illiteracy or lack of time for reading. To the contrary, we are beginning to learn that printed information is highly valued when it is available in useful form. The key words here are "available" and "useful." For example, research by political scientists Russell Neumann, Marian Just, and Ann Crigler found that people who already have an interest in a subject actually learn more from printed media. However, the majority of people get their information about most political subjects from television.[7] Not surprisingly, the experts who design political communication shape their messages to the fragmentary, visual, emotional medium that reaches people most easily.

Consider the possibility that crossing over to the television side of the communication line has created a political content so disjointed and diminished that it isn't fit to print. Newspapers have become the odd medium out in elections because they are literally starved for content. This judgment on the demise of the newspaper was handed down in the spare postmodern vernacular by ABC correspondent Brit Hume in 1988 when he referred to the newspaper reporters following the candidates as "printheads" (translation: logocentric throwbacks to the age of reason, or, if you will, people of little consequence for the outcome of the new election). Yet Hume later lamented to colleagues in a postelection seminar, "I'd like to tell you anecdotes about what it's like to cover George Bush up close, but I never got close to George Bush."[8] Nobody ever said that being significant in the new political age would be meaningful.

Crossing the rhetorical line to the bullier pulpit of television emboldened ABC News president Roone Arledge (formerly president of ABC Sports) to pronounce the 1988 Democratic National Convention boring. He found it so boring, in fact, that he threatened to cut back coverage of the Republicans the following month.[9] Something must be going on when a threat like that is issued on the heels of a convention that offered its audience no fewer than four or five excellent speeches by prominent members of the party—speeches recalling a bygone era of rousing, thought-provoking, morally challenging rhetoric.

No matter. Speech of any caliber or length greater than a sound bite seems to be the problem. ABC's executive producer for the conventions dismissed the television coverage of these speech fests as a "dinosaur."[10] So, we witness the demise of what has been the most important rhetorical form at least since the time of Aristotle: The Speech. Welcome to the first new election.

Shaping the Message for the Moment

Looking at television gives us a rough picture of how political messages have been transformed over the last few decades but not much of an idea about what transformed them. Though tantalizing, it is ultimately unsatisfying to leave our understanding at Marshall McLuhan's household phrase, "The Medium Is the Message." It is useful, therefore, to look beyond this glassy surface of elections—the transparent screen through which most people experience their political reality. What makes television the overwhelming medium of choice for the new politics is that it suits the needs of what Jarol Manheim calls strategic communication—that is, the continuous shaping of messages to create impressions that lead people to behave as political strategists want them to.[11] Television is suited to continual updates and short-term changes in political scripts because the medium accommodates the failing logic of the new politics through visually communicated emotions that operate independently of words. In the case of elections, the overriding goal of communication strategies is to produce votes against the opponent. In the logic of the new politics, voting against the opponent produces the same result as voting for one's client—namely, winning the election. The only thing lost, of course, is the positive element of understanding what one has voted for.

In Campaign '88, one side understood and accepted the foundation of the new politics, and the other came around to it too grudgingly and too late. Perhaps the outcome would have been different if Michael Dukakis had not clung stubbornly to the old politics until he had lost his early lead. If he had crossed the line separating the new politics from the old earlier in the campaign, perhaps he would have found a campaign management team better schooled in the new politics. Perhaps they even would have employed the lessons of the grand master of the new politics. Mike Dukakis, meet Roger Ailes, the electronic guru who brought us Spiro Agnew, the "new" Richard Nixon, the ever-present Dan Quayle, and, more recently, the Rush Limbaugh experience. Ailes added to his reputation as the wizard of the new political age when he crafted the 1988 media strategy for George Bush and created a candidate who parlayed his "wimp factor" into a "kinder, gentler" guy who "went ballistic" only when he really had to. As Ailes put it, "There are three things that get covered: visuals, attacks and mistakes."[12] As a challenge, try to fit this typology into any of the traditional ways of thinking about argument, debate, or public speech. Yet this is the philosophy of the new politics. And it is the philosophy that separated the Bush campaign from the Dukakis camp and, ultimately, the winner from the loser.

DOING IT RIGHT: MARKETING GEORGE BUSH

And now for a few words about the strategy used to elect George Bush under the masterful planning of "the three marketeers": campaign manager Lee Atwater, chief pollster Robert Teeter, and top media advisor Roger Ailes (with strong assists from pollster Richard Wirthlin and public relations expert Sig Rogich). Saddled with a candidate who had an overwhelming image problem of being "a wimp," the Bush team went to work fashioning tough-guy attacks on the opposition. Bush's attacks on his opponent's alleged failings on crime, abortion, prayer, and the flag salute weren't pretty, but given the diminished confines of what the candidates were willing to talk about, they were effective. The heart of the Bush strategy was to keep the targeted population of blue-collar Reaganites in the Republican fold with a host of shrill attacks summarized by conservative columnist George Will as the "Eeeeek!—a liberal!" campaign.[13] *New York Times* reporter Mark Green dubbed the Bush strategy the *slur du jour* approach.[14]

Pollster Teeter dignified the approach by explaining that "People don't decide based on some great revelation. They form their views based on thousands of little bits of information that shake out from television ads and news stories, from pictures of the candidates' wives, kids, dogs and homes."[15] Knowing how to deliver those bits of information in a range of styles from family pictures to the *slur du jour* is made easier by working up what Teeter calls a perceptual map—that is, a psychological model of how people see the candidates and what happens to that perception when this or that bit of information is added or subtracted.[16]

It turned out that adding slurs about the liberals' stand on crime, the flag, and other such quagmires both solved the Bush wimp problem and exposed Dukakis's greatest weakness with the target audience. The Bush consultants worked with focus groups of Reagan Democrats (blue-collar voters who had suspended their traditional Democratic loyalties to vote for Ronald Reagan in previous elections). At last, they hit on the images that drove these voters away from Dukakis and toward Bush. As noted in Chapter 1, the most effective image of all was the story of a prison fur-lough program in Dukakis's home state that released a black convict named William Horton for a weekend. Horton, a convicted murderer, raped a white woman during his release. The story was rich. Some said it appealed to deeply held racism among the targeted blue-collar groups. Beyond the racial overtones, it was clear that the story, when properly communicated, evoked the image that Dukakis, like all stereotypical liber-als, was soft on crime. After observing the effects of the Horton story on focus groups of targeted voters, Lee Atwater is reported to have said, "If I can make Willie Horton a household name, we'll win the election." He is reported to have followed up that remark at another Republican gathering by saying, "There's a story about a fellow named Willie Horton who, for all I know, may end up being Dukakis's running mate."[17] Willie Horton did become a household name, and Dukakis never recovered. It is worth noting that the Bush campaign did not officially produce or pay for the Horton ad. The sensitivity surrounding the ad required that the campaign have "plausible deniability" if it backfired. However, the "independent committee" that produced this and other attack ads had close ties with the campaign, as Atwater's boasting suggests. (Later stricken with a terminal illness, Atwater is said to have repented of the Willie Horton ad, although his counterpart in the Bush 1992 campaign, Mary Matalin, has disputed that claim.)

To counter the danger that all this negativity would make the Bush image too tough and mean-spirited, the attacks on Dukakis were limited to about 50 percent of the content of the media campaign. The other half of the messages showed Bush exuding sympathy: playing with his grandchildren; promising relief for the poor and the overtaxed alike; and occasionally pointing out that he really liked Dukakis, who was a decent human being underneath that regrettable liberal exterior. In the end, Bush would forgive his poor opponent for being hopelessly out of step with America—that is, with that tiny slice of the American public for whom most of the campaign was staged.

When Bush was not slashing away at Dukakis or issuing campaign promises in Clint Eastwood, "read my lips" rhetoric, he spoke of a "kinder, gentler nation" illuminated by "a thousand points of light." At first, the candidate expressed some discomfort with the new persona fashioned for him by his consultants. Roger Ailes summarized Bush's early reactions to the negative ads and the attack days on the campaign trail by saying, "He hates it, but he knows we'd be getting killed if we didn't go negative."[18] Although expressing a preference for the "kinder, gentler" days, the candidate acknowledged that the sweet and sour personality was having its desired effect on those voters for whom it was created. "I like the mix," Bush told *New York Times* reporter Maureen Dowd in a tone that she described "as though he had just sipped a martini or tasted a pasta sauce and found the ingredients perfectly blended."[19]

In this age of the mass-marketed candidate, it did not matter who the real George Bush was, just as it was beside the point to ask what the real Michael Dukakis stood for. Candidate marketing shapes a candidate's personality and rhetoric. The key to it all is the ironic human capacity that leads voters to make sense of almost any available information. The hardy souls who stay tuned to the contest must strive to make the whole experience credible. As political scientist Marjorie Hershey put it, these "voters respond to the political stimuli they receive"[20]—even, it seems, when those stimuli are offensive, contrived, or devoid of political consequence. Thus, in the words of one analysis, "The public's response to symbols— the flag, tanks, liberals, and criminals—dominated the 1988 campaign."[21]

DOING IT WRONG: THE DUKAKIS CAMPAIGN

Marketing-based communication strategies help us make sense of many peculiarities of contemporary election campaigns. Consider, for example, the great Democratic dilemma of 1988 (and, indeed, the great Democratic dilemma of recent times): How to appeal to traditional party constituencies, such as black voters, when such appeals might drive away other crucial groups, such as the blue-collar workers who have been effectively targeted by Republican marketing strategies? To complicate things, Democratic party loyalists are less likely to vote than their Republican counterparts. If we are to believe political scientists, this is because Democrats do not have the requisite amounts of education, income, and occupational status to inspire higher levels of civic virtue. Alternatively, the Democrats may have been less successful in rewarding their followers with prizes such as better tax benefits, better job training, or more access to education—incentives that might bridge the loyalty and socioeconomic gaps between Democratic and Republican party faithful. Whatever the reasons, people who say they are Democrats are less loyal than their Republican counterparts. Compounding the problem, larger numbers of traditional Democrats than Republicans have slipped into the independent category, and many of them go all the way across the line to vote for the other side. These shifts account for the phenomenon described above as Reagan Democrats or blue-collar Republicans.

The trick, as party strategists saw it in 1988, was to hold the line on those 10 million or so voters and thereby reverse the Republican lock on the presidency. The problem with their analysis was that the party had already lost those voters in the first place because it offered them little in the way of job programs, health care, or other economic incentives to balance the otherwise attractive Republican rhetoric on abortion, welfare, and civil rights—a rhetoric that translated fairly well across religious fundamentalist, lower middle-class, and blue-collar lines.

"But," cried an equally large faction within the highly fragmented party, "what about the black and minority vote?" With a little encouragement, that market segment could also be delivered to the party nominee. The trouble with the black vote, countered the marketing experts, was that it was only one-sixth of the total needed to win, and it was distributed badly over the geography of the electoral map. This meant two things. First, a lot of blacks lived in the North and East, where the Democrats might do fairly well anyway without them. Second, a lot of blacks lived in the South, where appealing to them would surely drive those sensitive conservative Democrats (who had become the key "swing voters") into the arms of the Republicans. After all, blue-collar Democrats all around the country would be listening carefully to what Dukakis said to black voters, creating the possibility of white flight in places as far away as California and Illinois. Such are the dangers of pursuing a marketing strategy in the media age. An appeal to each targeted group must be weighed against its possible effects on other key groups who may be listening.

After much gnashing of teeth and infighting, the marketers won the day by producing poll data showing that two-thirds of the targeted voters strongly opposed Jesse Jackson (who ran strongly in the primaries) and were equally opposed to the kinds of campaign appeals that would be required to win over Jackson's constituency.[22] Even though the social programs and defense cuts on Jackson's agenda might have won the support of large numbers of Americans, the prevailing wisdom in this age of high-finance, mini-market democracy is that large numbers no longer rule. Victory goes to strategic market segments.

It was therefore decided to cut the minorities adrift and go after the blue-collared birds who were in danger of flying into the Bush camp. The trouble was, Dukakis had nothing to offer them. Undaunted by this apparent Catch-22, the marketers followed their own strategic analysis and tried to win them over anyway. As Gerald Pomper observed, "Dukakis presented no striking new programs, nor did he provide any content to his promises of 'the next American frontier,' and 'a new era of greatness.' The values he stressed were uncontroversial: economic opportunity, pride in ethnic traditions, good jobs at good wages, honesty among public officials, community concern."[23]

At the same time that he was offering little to his target audience, Dukakis opened himself up to attacks on his exposed moral flank through his positions on abortion, school prayer, civil rights, and the flag salute. Basking far too long in the fleeting electronic glow of his convention speech, the candidate finally woke up to the fact that he was losing the election and was losing it badly. His midsummer dream lead of seventeen points dwindled to a dead heat following the Republican National Convention, and then plummeted to an eleven-point deficit by late September and a fifteen-point disadvantage in October, following the relentless attacks of the Bush campaign. As Willie Brown, speaker of the California Assembly, put it, "By this stage, people have given up on Dukakis. When you manage to go from a 17-point lead to an 11-point deficit in a matter of 8 short weeks, they're not inclined to buy a lottery ticket from you, never mind electing you president."[24]

Responding to the cries of state and local campaigns and the encouragement of liberal editorialists, the Democrats finally lifted a page from the Republican playbook: think short, talk negative, get mediated. In the closing weeks, the Duke's handlers withdrew their candidate from informal contact (especially question-answer sessions) with the press corps and replaced his basic stump speech emphasizing competence and economic recovery with a positive/negative format emphasizing the profound message, "I'm on your side. He's on theirs."

Meanwhile, the campaign went after Bush's "negatives" (a key word in the new political vocabulary) with a vengeance. So negative was the closing Democratic campaign that its newly appointed advertising director estimated an even higher negative-to-positive ad content (60–40) than the Bush campaign's more "balanced" target ratio of 50–50.[25]

Although Dukakis still lost the election, and lost it convincingly, his rhetorical rebirth near the end of the campaign is significant. It suggests that what I propose to call "tele-rhetoric" has become the absolute gospel that media consultants proclaim it to be. One suspects that Dukakis did not bow easily to the new rhetorical doctrine. Much of his punishment at the polls and on the editorial pages may well have resulted from his stubborn resistance to the dogma of the electronic age. Yet, convert he did, even if too late.

Once the decision was made and a new ad firm was in place, the candidate went before the cameras with exhausting, if not shameless, determination. A *New York Times* "Campaign Trail" piece on his TV blitz began "H-e-e-e-e-r-e's . . . Michael." A splashy front-page article the same week aptly summed up the tone now unifying the two campaigns: "TV's Role in '88: The Medium Is the Election." The author, Michael Oreskes, described the last weeks of the Dukakis campaign as an electronic whistle stop: "This is the electronic age's equivalent of the final whistle stop tour, seeking Nielsen ratings, not crowds at the tracks."[26]

Once all the candidates were on board, that rhetorical train moved rapidly down its electronic track. The average length of a TV sound bite plummeted to 9.2 seconds in 1988, down from a robust 14 seconds in 1984.[27] As the very concept of sound bite indicates, the new American election comes complete with euphemistic and ambiguous jargon to help bridge the uneasy gap with more familiar and, one might add, meaningful, electoral realities past. It is hard to discuss the meaning of any 9.2-second slice of a text, particularly when such slices are constructed to stand alone, rendering the rest of the text something like a serving utensil. But in the new age, it is unnecessary to fret over meaning; meaning is a throwback to an earlier political age—or, to state it in the latest academic mode, a pre-postmodern phenomenon.

THE NEW POLITICAL COMMUNICATION

The new political language is slippery by design. It is as if baseball legalized the spitball as a concession to pitchers and paid no mind to the inevitable declines in batting averages and fan interest in the game. And so, to pursue the analogy, the new political rhetoric comes as a welcome change only to the political pitchmen and the winning candidates. Despite the disapproval of spectators and journalists alike, the place of minimalist, ambiguous language seems secure in the new American politics.

The language of the new politics is preverbal; it is anything but proverbial. It transcends easy distinctions between issues and candidate images, reason and feeling. May the Greeks forgive us, it throws out the classical categories of *logos, pathos,* and *ethos.* Indeed, it was when the Bush message, for all its rhetorical hubris, was universally declared effective, and the Dukakis message, for all its traditional tenacity, was pronounced a blur, that Dukakis entered the new age.

There is both good news and bad news for democracy in the fact that Dukakis played out his "death wish" marketing strategy to the bitter end. First, the good news: there are some things that marketers, no matter how sophisticated their technique or strategy, just can't sell. There was more than a little arrogance in the notion that you could get a working-class and redneck audience to buy a cowering liberal with no substantive promises and the contrived image that, beneath the Boston technocrat exterior, he was really just "an average guy, with a 25-year-old snow blower, a modest duplex, a loving family. He was Joe Suburbia ennobled—worthy of the White House."[28]

But before breathing too deeply in relief that the threat of an Orwellian democracy has been lifted, consider the bad news. So binding is this gospel of candidate marketing that campaigns embrace it all the way through, even in losing causes. Candidates simply don't know what to do without their consultants. Even when Dukakis realized his scripted strategy was failing, he could do no better than fire one set of marketers and hire another who served him no better. This brings us to the worst news about the universal hold of political marketing on the electoral process: even when one side's marketing strategy is inept, the other side's marketing strategy is winning the day. Whether the strategies are good, bad, or indifferent, one of two marketed candidates will always win the election.

The Politics of Spin

The strategic ambiguity of political language has become so important that campaigns these days employ people known in the new vernacular as spin doctors. These specialists come into play when a political pitch is released and heads too far off its intended spot at the plate. The spin doctors rush out ahead of it, trying to influence or deflect the way reporters pass it along to the political audience.

In 1988, the Democratic National Convention boasted a Spin Control Coordination Unit. In October of that year, when Bush's campaign chairman, Lee Atwater, made a rare appearance on the press plane, he was surprised with a chorus of boos and a chant for a "Spin Moratorium." Undaunted, he solemnly explained how Dan Quayle had done a splendid job in the debate. Initially pleased that everyone seemed to be taking him seriously, Atwater looked up to discover a sign being held above his head. It read: "The Joe Isuzu of Spin—He's Lying."[29] (Joe Isuzu was an unpleasant car huckster in the company's ad campaign that year.)

For all their private disgust with the proceedings, the press dutifully reported what the spin doctors, handlers, and distant candidates served up to them each day. For their part, the public expressed their disdain for media coverage that appeared to be driven by the press's morbid, insider fascination with the new politics of communication. Reporters played both sides of the fence, reporting public disgust and then reporting what was most disgusting. By the end of the campaign, journalists were competing with politicians for new records of unpopularity. Perhaps cartoonist Lynda Barry said more with a picture than these words can convey. Her cartoon version of Election '88 was titled "The Election from Hell." The devil was a journalist.[30]

Given the decline of traditional concerns about meaning, reason, debate, and evidence in postmodern rhetoric, it becomes challenging just to talk about it, let alone evaluate it. For the sake of American democracy, one can only hope, as Mark Twain is rumored to have said about the music of Richard Wagner, that "It is really much better than it sounds."

Unfortunately, the best evidence from the consumers suggests that the new tele-rhetoric is really no better than it sounds. As with other aspects of the new political age, from campaign attack ads to thoroughly managed candidates, people consume tele-rhetoric despite (one hopes it is not because of) being actively offended by it.

Meaning Isn't Everything—The Political Results Are What Count

True, the 1988 voter turnout—the lowest since 1924—indicates that many people chose to preserve their sensibilities at the expense of giving up the franchise. But the more remarkable figure is the 50 percent who made a voting choice despite the self-confessed moral and intellectual pain involved. This suggests that we cannot understand the new rhetoric on the traditional grounds that it reflects some sort of positive, responsive communication, however "deep," worked out between candidates and their audiences. There is little that is sympathetic about tele-rhetoric. Even as they made their decisions, voters told pollsters that they disliked their choices and regarded them as negative, uninteresting, and insubstantial.[31] Nevertheless, these same polls, along with other market research studies, showed that the offending political messages "worked."[32]

This perverse dynamic of disaffected voters who tuned in but did not drop out of the election built to a crescendo of sorts on election eve. The NBC/*Wall Street Journal* poll followed levels of voter dissatisfaction throughout the contest. At the time of the conventions—the last memorable moments of traditional speechifying—two-thirds of the voting public were satisfied with their choices. By the last week of the campaign, when Dukakis had made his conversion, two-thirds wished that two different candidates were running.[33]

Perhaps the most telling set of statistics on the disjuncture between the popularity and effectiveness of the new rhetoric came from a *New York Times*/CBS News poll reported on October 30, 1988. Fully 63 percent of the voters said that issues were the most important factor in choosing a president. Next, the respondents cited their most important issue. Health care, homelessness, education, the economy, the deficit, and defense accounted for 64 percent of the responses. Then, a majority (54 percent) revealed that neither candidate was talking enough about their issue. Even more telling, only 5 percent for Bush and 4 percent for Dukakis felt that either candidate addressed their issue adequately.[34]

The New Politics Leaves the Press Spinning

Trying to make sense of why people were planning to vote at all in light of the above information, the *Times*'s analyst argued that the issues must have been out there somewhere but that they just didn't look the way voters expected them to look. The *Times* can be credited for publishing one of the few pieces anywhere claiming that meaningful issue differences had been located in the campaign. However, the analysis quickly dissolved into the suggestion that many deeper, seemingly personality-related appeals were issues in disguise. This was precisely how the Bush campaign introduced its personal attacks on Dukakis (e.g., that he was "naive" and "weak" on foreign policy)—namely, as issues.[35]

No wonder voters were fed up. To their credit, many journalists in postcampaign laments recognized this mass disillusionment. At first, it appeared that the press was as caught up in the negative thrall of the campaign as the public. Yet, as events unfolded, a faint signal came from the press. Actually, there may have been two faint signals from the media—a sort of one-blink, two-blink communication between a paralyzed press and its bedside public.

The first sign of media dis-ease is revealed in a study by Marjorie Hershey. She found that, on average, print media (largely wire service) coverage from September to election day dealt with issues only one-third of the time, while devoting two-thirds of the content space to campaign strategy. Even though the prestigious *New York Times* tried to hold to issue coverage 50 percent of the time in September, it was filling less than 20 percent of its campaign "news hole" with issues by November when it actually topped the wires in percentage of campaign strategy reports.[36] In short, the campaign became its own news. The media reflected on their own role as never before, resulting in redundancy, self-referential logics, and loss of context, which are the hallmarks of postmodern symbolics. The media couldn't get out of their own loop.

The second signal that the media seemed to send to the political audience was an unprecedented number of stories on voter dissatisfaction itself. In the past, reporters generally have been happy to buy the political science dicta that nonvoters would have voted the way voters vote and that voters find their acts meaningful. This time around, however, the press interviewed thousands of disgruntled citizens who challenged both assumptions.

Typical of these stories is one of a series by *New York Times* senior correspondent R. W. Apple, Jr., titled "From Jersey to Missouri, Voters Are Fed Up."[37] In another "fed up" article by another reporter, the wife of a former (read: unemployed or underemployed) steelworker lamented that current voting choices made no sense to people like her who grew up in normal, modern households "with mothers like June Cleaver that stayed home with the children. . . . And now we are in our thirties and forties and, bam! Everything falls apart on you."[38]

When things fall apart (as manifested in industrial decline, an emerging underclass, increased homelessness, rising health care costs, the disappearing dream of home ownership, etc.), people expect the election rhetoric to sharpen the issues, define the problems, and point to the solutions. Yet just the opposite occurred in 1988. An early warning for voters to disabuse themselves of their normal expectations came in June when two publications no less diverse than *The Nation* and *Time* agreed on what the coming contest held in store. In what may well have been a first, a *Nation* editorial cited *Time* as its source: "As *Time* aptly put it last week, 'The contest . . . will be less about ideas and ideologies than about clashing temperaments and styles.' "[39]

Perhaps we need greater distance to appreciate the irony here. As Lynda Barry's cartoon cuts to the quick of it, so, too, did French television's response to the first debate (arguably the more "exciting" of the two). After no more than a few words had been exchanged, French viewers were whisked back to the newsroom where a deadpan newscaster pronounced judgment: "This debate is not too exciting. Let's go to the Olympics."[40]

Back to Television: The View from the Academy

It would be surprising if crossing this thin communication line had been lost on the academy. It is the job of academics, after all, to keep track of the various thin lines within which our realities are contained. To be sure, the importance of television has been a favorite subject of communication scholars since its advent. However, as Bruce E. Gronbeck explains, only recently have the transforming effects of television on political rhetoric been recognized.[41] Approaching the "rhetorical presidency" from different angles, scholars Jeffrey Tulis,[42] Roderick Hart,[43] and Kathleen Jamieson[44] all concluded that the contemporary presidency has become essentially a rhetorical office increasingly oriented to the medium of television. Political psychologists Shanto Iyengar and Donald Kinder demonstrated through a series of laboratory experiments that television may not be able to tell us what to think, but it is amazingly successful at telling us what to think about.[45] In a more recent account, Roderick Hart proposes that television is inherently corrupting of communication and that its simplistic images "seduce" citizens into equally simplistic understandings of society and its problems.[46]

Of all these analyses, Jamieson's explores most fully the transforming effects of television on political (mainly presidential) communications. Drawing on the traditions of classical rhetoric and modern mass communication research, she concludes that the electronic medium rewards a "feminine" style. (I prefer the concept of an "intimate" political style suggested by Swedish professor of rhetoric Kurt Johannesson.) This style is warm and personal, and it emphasizes narrative over reason and logical argument. The intimate style accounts for part of the "Great Communicator" in Ronald Reagan. It also helps explain why the unpopular, offending rhetoric of Campaign '88 still had a powerful effect on its audience. Since tele-rhetoric works at a preverbal, prelogical, affective level, it permits voters to reject its content on logical, rational terms while still being moved at deeper levels that determine attention, commitment, and behavior.

The intimate style thus transcends positive and negative. Ronald Reagan was positive. The "kinder, gentler" George Bush had a negative streak that came out on cue 50 percent of the time. Both moved large audiences who disavowed much of what both men said at the level of truth, logic, and reason. For example, polls repeatedly showed that majorities of Americans disagreed with nearly all of Ronald Reagan's specific policy initiatives both as candidate and president.[47] And, as noted above, in 1988 George Bush's specific issue appeals played to the full satisfaction of a tiny 5 percent of the voters prior to election day. Yet both men captured the presidency.

Jamieson's view of tele-rhetoric contains the seeds of an even more important insight into the contemporary electoral and political scene. During her tour of duty as one of the most cited academic experts on the 1988 election, she told a *New York Times* reporter that there was, in effect, nothing about television itself that determined the vacuity of the new rhetoric. There was, she said, a glimmer of hope that television might lead the way back to an age of reasonable rhetoric. To put it simply, there is no reason why television couldn't extricate itself from the candidates' loop and create an independent context for viewer evaluation of everything said during a campaign. With the achievable technology of a computerized tape retrieval system, TV could play for its viewers everything a candidate has ever said and done about any given subject, and let the audience judge whether the rhetoric of the moment has any historical or other contextual significance. When the networks made brief use of this potential in Campaign '88, Jamieson seized on it as a ray of hope, saying that "what you're seeing is the very beginning of an attempt to hold candidates accountable for inconsistency without placing the reporter as an intruder."[48]

To some extent, some improvements (as reflected in the "adwatch" and other campaign analysis features) were developed by the media following 1988 in response to some of the most troubling aspects of the new political communication. However, as the Leslie Stahl incident suggests, it is not always possible to dissect or logically criticize the disparate messages and free-floating images of video collages and subliminal advertising. The direct solution would be, as most other nations do, to regard political communication as too important to be left solely to market researchers, advertising hacks, and their willing candidate clients to fabricate as they see fit. If the government regulates auto safety, alcohol advertising on television, and public access to pornography, why can it not also set standards for how much candidates can lie, bamboozle, and misrepresent themselves before the American public? Or, failing that, why not change the formats for political communication so that ideas are presented in different, fuller form? Yet the journalistic profession lines up with the majority of the American people against such regulation of "free speech." Perhaps the crusading journalists would appear less noble if we examined the billions of dollars in profits that the media would lose if they had to change from an advertising-based communication process to one of several alternative models for the more serious presentation of ideas. We will come back to these concerns about reform in Chapter 10 of the book.

For now, let us return to Jamieson's hint that television may be neither the sole nor the basic cause of the national political breakdown. Taking off from this idea just might help us reach a new understanding of the problem—one that may offer a better explanation for the current state of affairs than pointing the finger of blame (or, in the language of social science, the causal arrow) at television alone.

EXPLAINING THE NEW POLITICAL COMMUNICATION

Consider the possibility that tele-rhetoric is an epiphenomenon, or, in everyday parlance, a symptom of something deeper. Television, after all, is a passive medium, having the capacity to show us everything from talking heads, the public affairs people, to Talking Heads, the former rock band. What this means for elections is that television could bring us an entirely different political reality. Debates could become true forensic exchanges. Conventions could be conferred special status rather than threatened with cancellation. Candidates could be grilled one at a time by journalists for extended periods under the television lights, as they are in Sweden, for example.[49] Again as in Sweden and most other democracies, networks could be required to provide free air time to candidates, and restrictions could be imposed on the length and format of political commercials (encouraged, of course, by appropriate legislation).

The list of "coulds" and "what ifs" is too long to continue. The point is that TV isn't an explanation; it is merely a medium. Who uses TV? Why do people use it? How do they employ its mediating potentialities? These are the underlying elements of an explanation of tele-rhetoric. As for television itself, it may be a worthy object of blame and a useful window on an important problem, but it is not a valid cause in an explanation of the nation's political breakdown.

As a first step toward identifying larger forces in the electoral arena, consider the curious role of the political audience. Murray Edelman has argued that this is the age of the political spectator.[50] Citizen-spectators confronted with mass media spectacles may feel entertained, dazzled, confused, or bored—the normal range of audience emotions. There is even a role for the audience to play: voting. However, Edelman argues that meaning for voters tends to be a shallow affair produced by symbol-waving and flimflamming by candidates. Would-be leaders create enemies, announce crises, and generally push symbolic buttons in ways that make political audiences see red—or red-white-and-blue. The most substantial result of voting is that people get meaningfully involved in the battle of symbols and the seal of public approval is stamped on the government that goes into office. At the very least, then, elections have traditionally served the role of legitimizing governments.[51] But do they continue to serve even this function in the new political order?

The decline of voter interest and satisfaction suggests that even the symbolic meanings of electoral choices have been undermined in recent elections. This explains the instability of public support for elected governments and the anger toward everything from government and politics to politicians and the press. The main reason for the building anger and volatility of the electorate witnessed from 1988 onward has to do with a common psychological response to being trapped in dysfunctional communication processes in which the recipients of mixed and distressing messages are unable to respond in ways that straighten out the communication again. Unlike audiences of other spectator media, the audience for the new politics is captive of a political system with no competition. Political marketers have finally figured out the beauty of the captive political audience: voters are unable to command new programming, even when their lack of interest sends the ratings plummeting. To expand this point a bit, there are at least two important differences between political spectators and the audiences who respond to theatrical performances and other entertainment in various ways from buying tickets to laughing at the funny lines. First, spectator displeasure with the quality of the electoral performance, even to the extremes of not voting, does not shut down or otherwise "condition" the spectacle itself—as lack of patronage conditions the content of both the fine arts and popular culture media. Second, and even more ironic, many of those who continue to participate in the political audience are not necessarily enjoying or finding clear meaning in the experience—as one expects audiences for music, theater, or film to connect with their chosen medium. Recall here that full satisfaction with electoral choices was expressed by a tiny 9 percent of those planning to vote for the two candidates.

The immunity of elections from the most important market forces of consumer dissatisfaction and outright withdrawal from the marketplace helps us recast traditional thinking about candidate–audience communication. The easy assumption is that the effectiveness of electoral rhetoric turns on some sort of meaningful, positive, responsive exchange between communicator and audience. Throwing out this assumption raises the question of what does shape the content of electoral language and, more broadly, political communication these days. For some preliminary answers, we return now to our framework.

Begin with Money . . .

Instead of competing with each other for audience approval, candidates increasingly compete for the support of a much more select and seldom recognized group: political campaign contributors. Presidential candidates spent more than $300 million in 1988 (and nearly double that amount by some estimates if we include the "soft money"— explained in Chapter 6—that parties can pour into presidential contests "off the books"). These figures roughly doubled by 1992. Although federal funding covers part of a candidate's immediate costs, campaigns must raise vast amounts from private backers. Competition for these staggering sums of money is stiff, and the nature of this offstage maneuvering does not reward those who expand the domain of issues and policy proposals. Simply put, a restricted range of political ideas makes backing a candidate a safer bet for big money interests. In fact, restricting the range of ideas enables backers to hedge their bets and support both candidates. This is, of course, a bad thing for the health of democracy but a very good thing for those who invest their money in elections.

This flood of money in politics was unleashed by a series of campaign finance reforms dating to the early 1970s (for more detail, see Chapter 4). Not only does money drive the political process of the nation today, but also there are routine methods for cranking the money machine to higher revolutions each time the cost of campaigning goes up. And despite predictions that it cannot go any higher, the cost of selling candidates to skeptical voters has escalated each year. In California, candidates for public office spent more than $60 million in 1988, with the legislature costing more than two-thirds of that amount. In 1990, California's gubernatorial candidates alone spent about $40 million. To put these statistics in perspective, the campaigns for a British general election during that same period cost a bit more than $10 million—this for a national contest in a country with more than twice the population of California.

The total cost of running for public office in the United States in a presidential year has topped $2 billion. The average winner in a U.S. Senate campaign spends close to $4 million. The typical cost of a House seat in 1988 was nearly $400,000, while incumbents in 1992 upped the average spent to over $570,000.[52] Unless serious reforms limit campaign spending, restrict television advertising, and change the financing procedures, these staggering figures will continue to drive out any serious, grass-roots competition in the American democracy. Occasional third candidates who are wealthy enough to fund vanity races (e.g., Ross Perot in 1992) may come along and stir debate on selected issues, but even in such cases, it is money that decides the issues and the terms of debate. For the most part, the things people care about and the political resolve to actually do something about them are undermined by the issue and action agendas of those who pay the political bills. We will develop these ideas more fully throughout the book.

Next, Add Marketing . . .

This brings us to the second major constraint on campaign discourse: the wholesale use of marketing techniques and strategies to generate campaign content. Enter marketing experts into elections in a big way. Their task is to transform a product of diminished or dubious market value into one that wins the largest market share. The result is an emphasis on communication that short-circuits logic, reason, and linguistic richness in favor of image-making techniques. This means that candidates are not sold to a broad general public but to narrow slices or "market segments" of that public. These market segments need not understand the candidates; they need only vote for them. Thus, people are induced to vote for Candidate A over Candidate B much as soap buyers may favor Brand X over Brand Y without feeling they have established a meaningful relationship with their laundry detergent in the process. This further diminishes the importance of language, logic, and reason in the articulation of campaign issues.

Since at least 1980, the Democrats have encountered a difficult problem, one that paralyzed the early Goldwater Republicans until the Republican party solved it with the successful marketing of the "new" Richard Nixon, the even newer Ronald Reagan, and the tougher, less wimpy George Bush. The problem is simple: a narrow, unpalatable issue agenda that is hard to sell to the general public. The Republican secret was to turn the liability of voter avoidance into an asset by targeting key segments of the shrinking audience that continued to vote. Since votes aren't dollars, profitability isn't an issue. Only victory counts, no matter how many voters boycott the electoral process altogether.

In a classic commentary on the new political age, Paul Weyrich, a Republican strategist whose fundraising and marketing techniques have made the party an election powerhouse, ushered in the election of 1980 with these words: "I don't want everyone to vote. Our leverage in the election quite candidly goes up as the voting population goes down."[53] Borrowing this page from the Republican playbook, the Democrats in the 1980s went after the narrow market segment of blue-collar Republicans with a vengeance. Perhaps the most blatant example involved the Dukakis campaign's avoidance of anything resembling an overt appeal to Jesse Jackson's constituency. This market analysis, even though flawed, was followed to the end: the liberal Jackson wing of the party was not viewed as essential to victory, while the Reagan Democrats were. The constraints on campaign rhetoric and issue definition were equally clear: it was feared that anything said to liberal segments of the fragile voter market would send more conservative segments into the Republican camp. As it turned out, this feared pattern of conservative defection occurred anyway, owing in part to Dukakis's withering at the charge of being a "liberal" (the dreaded "L-word"), and in larger part to the inability of strategically hamstrung Democrats to compete rhetorically on remaining issues like prayer, patriotism, civil rights, and abortion. Such is political life without a credible political vision.

Despite the election of Bill Clinton in 1992 (as discussed in Chapter 3), this Democratic dilemma has grown worse. The resolve of party leaders after the 1994 disaster was to market themselves more zealously as New Democrats. Yet, Bill Clinton was in many ways the first New Democrat on the scene. Putting more substance into this squishy category only seems to raise voter questions about the difference between New Democrats and Old Republicans. As the marketers drive both parties and their candidates, the political process excludes more and more voters and leaves even those who do participate skeptical about the leaders they have elected.

Now, Try to Control the News Media . . .

In the three-factor model proposed here, the marketing and money constraints necessarily engage a third limiting condition operating on electoral communication: the highly controlled use of the news media. The press, like the voting public, generally regards issues and ideas as the most important grounds for electoral choice. (At least that is what most journalists say.) Idea-less elections antagonize reporters searching for meaningful differences between the candidates. An aroused press can be expected to assume an adversarial role, leaping on inconsistencies, making much of candidate slips and blunders, seizing on anything inflammatory in the absence of much to say about policy positions. As a result, campaigns tend to isolate their candidates from the press corps and stick to a tightly controlled, carefully scripted daily schedule. At the same time, politicians retreat behind an electronic wall of advertising and staged media events designed to shape their images in ways that win short-term public acceptance. Thus, the media become part of a two-pronged communication strategy based on news control and message shaping through advertising. This means, in Roger Ailes's words, that reporters are handed a lot of visuals and attacks, while mistakes (and ideas) are held to a minimum. In

the new American election, the news becomes at best a pale reinforcement for the messages delivered through advertising.

It is by now well accepted that good media strategy entails three
requirements: keeping the candidate away from the press; feeding the
press a simple, telegenic political line of the day; and making sure the
daily news line echoes ("magnifies" may be the better word) the images
from campaign ads, thus blurring the distinction between commercials and
"reality."[54] Candidates and their "handlers" vary in their ability to keep
the press at bay, but when they succeed, reporters are left with little but an
impoverished set of campaign slogans to report. As ABC reporter Sam
Donaldson said on an election-week news analysis program in a tone that
resembled that of the coroner disclosing an autopsy result: "When we
cover the candidates, we cover their campaigns as they outline them."[55]
Thus, a willing, if unhappy, press becomes a channel for much of the same
meaningless tele-rhetoric that emerges from the interplay of advertising
strategy and the concessions made to campaign contributors.

In recent years, the media have shown signs of becoming more critical
of campaigns. Encouraged by a public that is angry at candidates and
politicians, the news contains increased coverage of the celluloid world of
marketed candidates and media manipulation. This increase in media
coverage of media campaigns, however, has not brought candidates out of
hiding or appreciably affected the way campaigns are run. The ironic
result of media attempts to "deconstruct" candidate images and expose
the techniques of news control may be to reinforce public cynicism about
the whole process. Taking the public behind the political illusions has not
succeeded in bringing the candidates out of hiding behind those illusions.
The net result is still an election system dominated by mass-marketed,
Madison Avenue messages that deliver quick emotional punches instead
of lasting visions and governing ideas to voters. In other words, the way in
which news organizations have exercised their critical skills may result less
in changing the system than in reinforcing (albeit inadvertently) the public
cynicism that helps keep it going.

One might think the press would do something bold to elevate election
news content above the intellectual level of political commercials. For
example, the various news organizations could separate themselves from
the pack mentality and develop a thoughtful agenda of important issues
(based, if need be, on opinion polls) and score the candidates on how well
they address these issues. But that is not very likely. A news executive
vetoed out of hand a very modest version of this suggestion. When asked
why the media did not make more of George Bush's well-documented
connections to the CIA hiring of Panamanian dictator Manuel Noriega—
an issue that was bubbling around the 1988 campaign—the producer of

one of the three network evening newscasts explained simply, "We don't want to look like we're going after George Bush."[56]

Despite this reluctance to tackle candidates on the issues, it is apparently appropriate to go after them on grounds of health (Thomas Eagleton in 1972), character (Edmund Muskie, 1972), gaffes and malapropisms (Gerald Ford, 1976), family finances (Geraldine Ferraro, 1984), extramarital sex (Gary Hart, 1988), or hypocrisy and bumbling (Dan Quayle, 1988). However, the press draws the line when it comes to pursuing issues beyond where the candidates are willing to take them. Indeed, as political scientist Thomas Patterson's research shows, the levels of news negativity and personal attack journalism have risen steadily throughout the recent era. No doubt, this situation has reinforced the conviction of those who run campaigns that the press must be managed at all costs.[57]

Never mind the resulting decline in the quality of campaign discourse and citizen interest in politics (not to mention public faith in the press), the media seem determined to steer a safe course of "objectivity." Elaborating the doctrine behind Sam Donaldson's earlier words, the ABC vice president in charge of campaign coverage in 1984 and 1988 said: "It's my job to take the news as they choose to give it to us and then, in the amount of time that's available, put it into the context of the day or that particular story. . . . The evening newscast is not supposed to be the watchdog on the Government."[58]

This self-styled impression of what the media are "supposed to be" marks a nearly 180 degree change from the hallowed role of the press as defined by the likes of Peter Zenger and Thomas Jefferson. The new norm of press passivity enables increasingly profit-oriented and decreasingly critical media to chase political candidates in dizzying circles like cats after their own tails. To wit, two-thirds of the coverage in 1988 was coverage of coverage: articles on the role of television, news about campaign strategy, and updates on voter fatigue in response to meaningless media fare. As the irrepressible French social critic Jacques Ellul said about the contemporary mass communications industry: "The media refer only to themselves."[59] Meanwhile, politicians have learned how to get their messages across in ways that bypass the press, ranging from the lethally effective Bush ads of 1988 to the Clinton bus trips, talk show appearances, and electronic town halls described in the next chapter.

COMMUNICATION AND THE NEW POLITICS, REVISITED

Each of the related constraints on political communication imposes a substantial limit on what candidates say to voters, creating, in turn, important limits on the quality of our most important democratic experience. Taken together, these limiting conditions go a long way toward explaining the alarming absence of meaningful choices and satisfied voters in recent elections. These restrictions on political speech also explain the mysterious elevation of tele-rhetoric to gospel standing in contemporary campaigns. With ideas safely out of the way and the press neutralized, television has little use other than as a medium for turning a seemingly endless election process into the world's longest running political commercial without programmatic interruption.

Other puzzles about the contemporary election scene also become less baffling. Take the rise of negative campaigning, for example. Because of the severe content restrictions imposed by money, marketing, and media, candidates suffer the problem of appearing unattractive (i.e., negative). In this strange world, victory goes to the candidate who manages to appear the least unattractive or negative. The easiest strategy is to play up the opponent's negatives in an effort to look less negative by comparison. (One can hardly hope to look positive in this context.) Hence, the obsession with the opponent's negatives, as emphasized in commercials and played up in news sound bites spoon-fed to the press.

The rhetoric without vision, the telegenic sound bites, and commercialized advertising and news production—all happen to play best (or, in keeping with the new spirit, least offensively) on television. In the words of a leading campaign consultant commenting on a race in California, "A political rally in California consists of three people around a television set."[60]

Considering the magnitude of these forces working against the traditional forms and contents of political communication, it is not surprising that candidates say so little these days. One marvels that they are able to say anything at all.

CHAPTER   3

The Angry Electorate: Reinventing Bill Clinton in 1992

They call him the terminator. The robo-candidate. A torpedoed battleship that is still afloat. A Civil War soldier leaning against a tree, bleeding from a stomach wound. Of all the issues raised in this scalding political season, one of the most interesting is this: How did Bill Clinton take so many shots and keep on coming? *—Maureen Dowd, reporting on the 1992 election*

Few rodeo events can match the ups, downs, and spins of public attitudes toward politicians these days. Just a year before the 1992 election, the pundits agreed that George Bush could not lose his bid for a second term. Yet the election was not even close, and the hero of the Gulf War slipped quietly from the political scene with questions about what his earlier record levels of public approval really meant. Then Bill Clinton rode the wild beast of public opinion through a rough and tumble political campaign and into a presidency marked by the absence of a honeymoon period.

Both of these presidents discovered one of the sharp lessons of the new politics: the political campaign never ends. Governing in these times of low trust and little solid support from one's party or fellow politicians requires much the same daily attention to maintaining image and public approval that goes into campaigning. Whether the candidates deserved their fates or suffered unduly at the hands of the press is subject to debate. However, their political responses were much the same: both Bush and Clinton came to regard the press with suspicion and hostility. (Though no president could ever say so in public, they probably developed a healthy mistrust of the public as well.) Both brought key campaign and media advisors with them into the White House, despite vowing that they would not need such contrivances after receiving election mandates from the people to carry out their governing agendas. Perhaps the most intriguing comparison between these two unlikely politicians is that both ignored the advice of their image masters at key political moments and suffered grave losses of public approval as a result.

THE PSYCHOLOGY OF THE NEW POLITICS

In their own ways, both presidents Bush and Clinton seemed to resist the idea that they had built up little credit with the people who elected them. Indeed, the quick anger of the citizenry is one of the most dominant symptoms of the new politics, as well as one of the most difficult to understand or to resolve politically. In this chapter we consider the possibility that the citizen anger setting the tone of our everyday politics, and peaking at two-year and four-year intervals, is not some caged emotion of a people on the outside of the system looking in. Rather, the turbulence of the public is part of the new politics in action.

People are adrift psychologically in a system that offers few stable guideposts or orientations. Washington, the national symbolic center, has become a negative. Politicians, the hope for government action, have also become negatives. Parties, the great guideposts for people seeking direction, are strange amalgams of independent-minded representatives proclaiming themselves new and different from the old models. In such an environment, it is not surprising that people often change their minds or lash out in frustration at the most commonly available symbols and targets for emotion: government, Washington, Congress, politicians, the press, and passing presidents.

It is also understandable that people take in the images and tidbits of meaning that are fed them, from campaign commercials to political finger pointing to the latest news story about corruption in the capital. There is an addictive quality to these daily bits of meaning, no matter how negative they may be. People cannot help trying to make sense of their lives, and so they watch the commercials, listen to the politicians, and tune into the news. Yet when the day's symbolic offerings are sorted and processed, often a hollowness is left behind—that widely reported feeling of not knowing what to believe. People who are exposed to this daily flow of political messages (dare we call it propaganda?) are in some important respects like addicts who become dependent on physical substances: unsatisfied in their cravings, yet unable to resist more, and generally unpleasant to be around when the supply disappears. And so, politicians oblige them by promising tax cuts along with balanced budgets, smaller government while maintaining most services, more prisons without sacrificing education, and more—all without bothering to explain how these things will realistically come to pass.

Such promises may provide quick fixes for daily emotional dependencies, but the long-term substance and the satisfactions of politics are lost in these exchanges. People may vote for the politician with the most emotionally appealing promise, or the one whose ads most effectively demonize the opposition, but what kind of bond is built between the citizen and the representative in the process? What kind of expectations are created that government could possibly fulfill?

Traditional ways of thinking about publics in the political process have missed an important change in the status of citizens: their need for continual psychological reassurance and emotional maintenance. At the core of the new politics is a dominant chain of communication logic:

- political independence breeds isolation,
- isolation creates emotional vulnerability,
- and vulnerability opens individuals to the methods of strategic communication (marketing, image-shaping through focus groups, advertising, and the continual renewal of images that have become ineffective).

The vulnerability of individuals and the volatility of public opinion also reflect the breakdown of older, more enduring identifications with parties, leaders, and political programs—the stable references or psychological cues that once encouraged citizens to trust government and tolerate politicians.

In the next section, we review traditional ways of thinking about voters in the political system. At issue is how these traditional views of publics must be modified if we are to grasp the psychology of the new politics, and explain, among other things, how Bill Clinton was elected president despite the attacks of press and opponents and the doubts of many voters. As we will see, this is more than just a story about Bill Clinton; it is a story about profound changes in the electoral process that have shaken the very foundations of voter psychology.

TRADITIONAL VIEWS OF
THE AMERICAN VOTER

Political scientists have long puzzled over a whole collection of strange American voting habits, ranging from one of the lowest turnout rates among the advanced democracies to high reelection rates for incumbents despite a long-standing skepticism of professional politicians that predates the current crisis. Are these and other curious features of voter mentality signs of gross negligence and ignorance, or are they the results of people trying to respond sensibly to a system that requires voters to make a large number of decisions (compared to voters in most other political systems) based on a high volume of often ambiguous information? This question, it turns out, is one of the oldest, yet still unresolved, debates about the American voter. There is evidence for both sides, suggesting that we are not dealing with an "either/or" type of choice, but a more complex relationship between individual voters and the political system in which they operate.

On the "voters are fools" side of the argument, there is considerable evidence that Americans possess little knowledge about the "who, what, when, where, and how" of government.[1] Moreover, voters historically have not tended to think in big-picture, ideological terms; instead they have relied on party and group identifications, along with an occasional big issue to guide their choices.[2] Given this portrait of the voter, it is tempting to conclude that candidates have never had much incentive to elevate the level of national debate. Even if they did, there is little chance that such ignorant voters would approve of sophisticated political debates. Two leading students of American elections have described voters in the following terms:

> Most of them are not interested in most public issues most of the time. In a society like ours, it apparently is quite possible to live comfortably without being politically concerned. Political activity is costly and eats up time and energy at an astounding rate. . . . One must attend meetings, listen to or participate in discussions, write letters, attempt to persuade or be persuaded by others, and engage in other time-consuming labor. This means foregoing other activities, like devoting extra time to the job, playing with the children, and watching TV.[3]

"Wait a minute!" say proponents of the opposing "voters are *not* fools" school. If voters sometimes act like fools, it is because politicians treat them that way, offering few meaningful choices and seldom inviting the public inside the decision-making process. Supporting this claim is a long research tradition that attributes the failings inside voters' heads to the choices they are offered in the elections taking place outside.[4] Viewed this way, voters make the best sense out of what little candidates may offer them. When few issues are solid enough to use for thinking about the future, voters look back and vote "retrospectively," based on their judgments about who did the best overall job in the past.[5] When there are no issues or ideas (whether forward- or backward-looking), voters tend to screen candidate personalities for information about leadership and emotional qualities.[6] As noted in the analysis of the 1988 election in the last chapter, when reliable information of any sort becomes scarce, voters continue to do the best they can, trying to decode political advertisements and well-staged public appearances for clues about what the candidates represent. This flexibility in voter strategies for handling political information may help to explain why voters who say they are unhappy with their choices often remain willing and able to make them. It also may explain why those choices these days are subject to change shortly after they are made.

RETHINKING VOTER PSYCHOLOGY

Are voters a cause or a casualty in an electoral system that offers few meaningful choices? Probably both. The dual dangers of unsophisticated voters and shallow candidates have been with us for some time. What has changed in recent years, however, is that these weaknesses in the electoral process have been magnified, increasingly moved to the center, and institutionalized, if you will. As a result, candidates with ideas and voters who might want to think about them are less and less likely to find each other—at least (and this is the key) in the numbers required to create stable governing coalitions. In order to understand how some of the worst tendencies of American politics have become elevated or institutionalized in the electoral process, it is important to expand the eternal debate about "ignorant voters versus shallow elections" to include several more recent underpinnings of citizen psychology:

- First of all, consider the decline in party loyalty, particularly the drop in voter identification with the Democrats, and the above-mentioned rise of the "independent" voter over the past two decades. (All of these phenomena are explained more fully in Chapter 4.) Among other things, this change has reinforced the importance of candidate marketing strategies aimed at these elusive swing voters. In short, people have opened themselves to hearing quick political pitches, and the marketers are working full time to meet the psychological demand.
- Now, include the overall decline in voter turnout over the same twenty-five-year period (the small upswings in 1992 and 1994 notwithstanding), which has reinforced the temptation of campaigns to pour more marketing dollars into the chase for fewer voters. As a result, targeted citizens are bombarded with dizzying volumes of competing messages. This does not make for stable relations between voters and politicians.
- Finally, to this portrait of fewer—and more independent—voters who receive more personalized communication than ever before, add the fact that most Americans draw the "political participation line" at voting and, in some cases, giving money to interest groups. If neither voting

nor ordinary lobbying activities are likely to fix the problems with the current election process, levels of frustration understandably rise from election to election. One result is retrospective anger at candidates who promised voters that they could vote their way out of the problem. People can, of course, be faulted for failing to learn that solutions are not that simple. Yet the contemporary aversion to social movements, party-building, or other, more serious forms of participation, leaves many voters vulnerable to the next candidate who promises that, this time, things really will change.

Each of these features of contemporary American politics contributes to the rise and fall of politicians and to the failure to implement popular governing programs. The 1992 election illustrates these underpinnings of voter psychology at work, particularly in the communication strategies used to overcome voter doubts about Bill Clinton. Let's meet the candidates.

MEET THE CANDIDATES

"He wore cheap sunglasses. He blew the saxophone. He explained that he really wanted to inhale; he just didn't know how."[7] Is this the description of a fallen Hollywood star trying to stage a TV comeback after a scandal? No, it is the opening of a news story on the 1992 election campaign. The actor, of course, is Bill Clinton, who appeared on the Arsenio Hall show as part of an elaborate, direct-to-the-people media campaign to reconstruct his ailing character before the voting public. It turned out that a plurality of that public suspended their usual levels of disbelief to follow the "Comeback Kid," as his media strategists promoted him, through scores of talk shows, electronic town halls, and madcap bus trips across the heartland. In the end, the prize of victory was his.

While Clinton was building his tenuous electronic relationship with the mass public, another improbable candidate by the name of Ross Perot was managing to sell himself as a billionaire populist to another 19 percent of a clearly destabilized electorate. Pursuing a different strategy within the same electronic media, Perot's string of talk show appearances and info-mercials may not have won him the presidency, but the $35 million that Perot spent on television appeals was regarded as so successful at getting public attention that *Advertising Age* magazine crowned Mr. Perot the "Adman of the Year" for 1992.[8] (The Perot persuasion style became a model for commercial advertisers, who immediately cloned Perot scenarios for dozens of product ad campaigns.)

It was George Bush who felt the sting of the new voter psychology most painfully, if only because he engaged with it most ineptly. By all accounts, the incumbent president took it for granted that the effects of his masterful psychological campaign of 1988 (recall the discussion from the last chapter) were still in place, and he resisted a replay in 1992. It was widely known that the patrician Bush had found the construction of his '88 campaign persona distasteful, from his focus group makeover as a tough-guy character whose attacks helped pin the "wimp" label on hapless liberal opponent Michael Dukakis, to the droning negative backdrop of Willie Horton and revolving door prison ads. It is easy to imagine how Bush was tempted to think this tawdry business could be avoided in 1992. First, he may have succumbed to the euphoric assumption that the people truly loved him when his public approval ratings hit record highs of nearly 90 percent following the United States and allied victory in the Gulf War of 1991. The temptation to run a traditional campaign "on his record" must have been even greater after the pundits pronounced him unbeatable just a year before the election.

As it turned out, however, George Bush experienced the greatest recorded public approval free-fall in history. He lost the election with a campaign that missed the great lesson of his own victory in 1988: the psychology of the American public had changed in fundamental ways. When he "went negative" with a vengeance in the closing weeks of the 1992 election, he seemed perplexed that the attacks were not having the effect that they had in 1988. And it was not until the last desperate days of the campaign that he finally agreed to an appearance on MTV, an electronic venue he had dismissed earlier as "a teenybopper network." Not surprisingly, Bush finished a poor third in the youth vote. In fact, his ragged campaign organization failed in its attempts to reach so many groups that the candidate finally canceled his daily poll briefings in the last week of the campaign.

The campaign that clearly learned the lessons of 1988 was the Clinton team. They saw that there was a new psychology forming in the electorate and that simplistic formulas such as "going negative" did not fully grasp it. Negative appeals and personal attacks did not produce stable opinions, nor were they the only way to reach voters. To the contrary, majorities in the polls in 1988 reported that they hated the negative psychology. The effectiveness of that strategy had to do almost entirely with the failure of the Dukakis campaign to alleviate the doubts that those attacks planted in the minds of voters.

The 1992 campaign demonstrated that responsiveness, intimacy (no matter how contrived), and continual reassurance were the keys that unlocked the hold of negativity (as well as the keys to understanding the underlying public psychology). There is much evidence for this proposition in the Clinton campaign. It is doubtful that any modern candidate suffered more negative press than Clinton did in 1992. He overcame so many seemingly fatal media blows that, as noted in the opening of this chapter, he earned the nicknames "Robocop" and "Terminator" from the same press pack that inflicted many of those wounds. Among those who put the mystique of negativity to rest was Pat Buchanan's media consultant, Ian Weinschel, who said of Clinton's comebacks from repeated character attacks: "I've never seen anybody come back from being attacked in that fashion. It's like going through a car crash with no seat belts and then going through the window and hitting a wall and walking away. It's absolutely astounding."[9] How did Clinton deflect so much negativity and go on to win the election? What was the basis of his appeal to a cynical public?

THE SECRETS OF THE ELECTRONIC POLITICIAN

The destabilization of voter psychology means that it is not an easy time to be a politician. The rules of the political game are changing. Public wrath against government can turn today's hero into tomorrow's fool. We have entered what might be called the "Age of Political Independents": increasingly independent voters who seem to prefer independent politicians who make their own ways without emphasizing party allegiance or the virtues of government. In this climate of anger, suspicion, and restlessness, politicians must continually work up new strategies to keep themselves on the good side of the public, as the Clinton campaign illustrates so vividly.

Above all, successful candidates must manufacture short-term images and feed them back continually to skeptical voters in as intimate a style as electronic media permit. What matters most is that isolated individuals sense that a candidate understands their questions of the moment and is making an ongoing effort to answer them. In the end, the relevance of the questions or the quality of the answers may be less important than the psychological experience of fragmented individuals feeling somehow connected on a daily basis to a highly personalized (if distant) political figure.

The key to the new electoral communication is continuous polling, focus group research, and the production of short-term marketing strategies to maintain this extremely tenuous psychological bond. This new imperative for candidates (and once elected, for leaders) to continually reinvent themselves is the result of a widespread loss of faith in the holy trinity of psychological cues that drove the old voter choice process: party, issues, and character.

THE BIG LESSON:
THE OLD VOTER CUES DO NOT WORK

In the microcosm of Bill Clinton's election, we find signs of an institutional breakdown in the psychological ties that once bound citizens to parties, candidates, and, in turn, to each other in the American polity. Elections still go on, and voters still vote, but the psychology of the public political experience has suffered a decline in the stable cues and identifications that once allowed individual citizens to feel they were part of solid political groups, such as parties, and to have confidence in their leaders. In other words, we are witnessing the deterioration of the psychological ties that once gave private citizens stable public identities.

The core of this analysis is that changes in the electoral process over the last two decades have undermined the psychological cue system of *party, issues,* and *candidate character* that have long provided the foundation of voter choice and, therefore, have set the strategic guidelines for traditional campaigning.[10] As with most historic changes, substantial ghosts from the old order persist as vague and familiar outlines in the new historical context. This has led some conservative analysts to proclaim that the American voter is, in fact, "unchanging."[11] Indeed, there is evidence that voters continue to use party identification above all other psychological linkages with the electoral environment in making their choices. However, this evidence must be evaluated in the context of severely diminished levels of party identification that highlight the chaos, not the continuity, of contemporary elections.

In other words, party, issues, and candidate character may remain as the voters' leading information categories, but the salience of all three categories has been substantially diminished as voters increasingly shun party affiliation, regard election issues with greater suspicion, and find that contrived, marketing-driven campaigning offers few satisfying insights into the character of candidates. A brief overview of these changes illustrates how they have affected both the conduct of elections and the kinds of political problems that elected leaders face after they take office.

Party

Party identification has declined in the electorate from the peak levels recorded in the 1950s and 1960s while something resembling a culture of political independence has emerged to turn shifting voter loyalties into a virtue. Even if there was some clear meaning to the idea of a "radical middle" in American politics, the inability of parties to win and hold the loyalties of stable voter blocs at different levels of government leaves little incentive for elected members of those parties to worry about a governing agenda beyond the narrow promises required for personal reelection. The resulting personalization of politics (both the decline of candidate loyalty to party and the increasingly individualized appeals to voters) has de-stabilized both elections and governing.

Issues

Perhaps the breakdown of parties and party voting would not be a bad development if it corresponded to a higher level of issue voting and seri-ous policy debate in elections. However, the long-term view suggests that much of what passed for issue discourse in past American elections was tied to traditional party stands on social and economic policy matters. The issue discourse in recent elections has been constructed largely through marketing research aimed at winning the short-term support of key voter blocs. As a result, there continue to be discussions about matters that candidates represent as issues, but neither the media nor voters take most of those issues very seriously. As opinion expert Everett Ladd noted in his analysis of these trends, the candidates increasingly talk about "problems" that marketing research reveals to be on voters' minds. However, Ladd concluded that these "problems aren't necessarily issues. A problem be-comes an issue only when voters see the parties differing in their approach to it or their capacity to solve it."[12] Although the 1992 election produced higher levels of voter issue satisfaction than other recent contests, the reason must be attributed to the third candidacy of Ross Perot. Indeed, given Bush's ill-fated decision to run largely on his record, and the Clinton campaign's droning insistence on "The Economy, Stupid," a Perot-less 1992 race would probably have satisfied few voters on the issue dimension.

Character

The increasing construction of candidate images through marketing techniques has produced an increasingly wary electorate. Character still matters, of course, and it may matter more than ever to voters who are preoccupied with concerns about honesty and trust. The problem is that *credible cues* about character are being driven out of elections. Preferring to go with pre-packaged character displays, campaign strategies generally avoid the kinds of risky stands on principle through which candidates might display genuine leadership. Thus, the resulting character cues that voters have available to them are likely to become heavily discounted in the choice process.

A NEW KIND OF POLITICAL POWER?

In short, the traditional foundations of voter psychology are crumbling. While fragments of the old order remain, they are unable to support satisfying or stable political choices in the modern electorate. Voters still receive cues, of course—and they probably receive them in greater sheer volume than ever before. However, the psychological cue system underlying contemporary voting choice involves appeals that are manufactured for short-term effects: aimed at the voter psychology of the moment, addressing diffuse problems rather than substantial issues, and targeted at the ongoing manufacture and renewal of short-term identification with untrustworthy politicians. The result of substituting these short-term individual appeals for more enduring, socially integrative political references is that the nature of both campaigning and governing is changing.

In the view of CNN pollster and political analyst William Schneider, Washington is increasingly a town of individual political entrepreneurs who rely less on parties for their political support than on their own media images, along with the popularity of visible politicians such as the president. When the president appears to be a loser, nobody wants to be associated with him or his programs, and the real power of the presidency goes down. When the president appears to be winning in the news, everyone wants a piece of the media action, and the real power of everyone who jumped into the television spotlight—most of all the president—goes up. And so, when Bill Clinton was heralded in the media for engineering a victory in Congress on the controversial North American Free Trade Agreement (NAFTA), even his archenemies, such as Georgia Republican Newt Gingrich, jumped into the media power circle, complimenting the president on his leadership. Later, when Gingrich engineered a Republican landslide in the 1994 congressional elections, Clinton vowed that he had heard the message and began talking about middle-class tax cuts, budget slashing, welfare reform, and other ideas promoted by Gingrich, the toast of the media and the new Speaker of the House.

Thus, the changing reference system on which mass psychology rests may be changing the nature of political power in American politics. The reverse is surely true as well, with contemporary public psychology not emerging from mere whims in the electorate (although it may often seem that way), but from origins in structural changes in the electoral process itself. These changes span more than two decades and are explained in more detail in Chapter 4.

With the increasing personalization of politics and the growing role of the media and public approval in determining who has political clout, it is not surprising that the very core of campaigning has become centered on destroying the opponent's personal image and designing defenses against personal attacks from that opponent. These defenses amount to continual shaping and repositioning of one's image in the so-called cognitive map of individuals who are targeted by the steady attacks of the opposition. In other words, the very thing that people report as most offensive about contemporary American politics—the personal battling among politicians—has become built into the struggle for political power itself. Whether this sort of political power translates into much in the way of good government is another question, but it certainly shapes election campaign strategies.

In light of this new voter psychology, as noted earlier, the great mistake of the Dukakis campaign in 1988 was the candidate's palpable failure to respond to the questions that the Bush attacks raised in voters' minds. By contrast, Clinton was at the ready to answer the steady flow of personal attacks, both from Bush and, more generally, from the press pack, on an almost daily basis throughout the 1992 campaign. Even as polls showed that voters were not interested in the character issue in 1992 and longed for more discussion of the policy issues, the Clinton campaign was continually preoccupied with how to address the nagging voter doubts about Clinton that continued to surface in the tracking polls conducted by the campaign management team.

It no doubt helped that the Bush team grabbed a tired replay of 1988 off the shelf and had no attack that packed the punch of the Willie Horton commercials from the previous election. The Clinton team, for its part, never forgot the motto on the wall of campaign headquarters: THE ECONOMY, STUPID. Perhaps most damaging for the Bush camp was its failure to respond with the necessary flow of psychological reassurances to the voter doubts raised by the Clinton campaign's steady emphasis on the economy. It is an open question as to how much of the damage might have been reversed had the Bush team remembered the first maxim of the new voter psychology: "A reassurance a day keeps doubts away."

The Clinton campaign illustrates this necessary process of short-term image construction, maintenance, and defense with a generally fickle public. Clinton's viability as a candidate hinged on responding to a huge volume of press attacks on his character by going over the heads of the press to convince voters that he was willing to submit his character to direct scrutiny—or, in the electronic age, what passes for direct scrutiny.

Welcome to the Clinton campaign of 1992, with its electronic town halls; true confessions on *60 Minutes;* appearances on Arsenio Hall, Phil Donahue, and Larry King; MTV; madcap bus trips; and more—all of it aimed at the continuing reinvention of Bill Clinton. He was not called the Comeback Kid for nothing.

REINVENTING BILL CLINTON ON THE CAMPAIGN TRAIL

As Clinton learned during the campaign and after the election, the mass psychology of contemporary American politics requires constant attention from pollsters, marketers, and communications advisors. Initially, this fact may have been lost on the candidate. Following the disastrous allegation of a twelve-year extramarital affair with former TV news personality and aspiring singer Gennifer Flowers, Clinton spent a three-hour drive through the snows of New Hampshire brooding and reading Lincoln on leadership.[13] Finally realizing that the Gennifer Flowers incident was not to be solved by Lincoln's advice on leading a nation through civil war, Clinton turned to the campaign team of pollster Stan Greenberg, media consultant Mandy Grunwald, and political strategist James Carville for insight. What emerged was a broad media strategy of continual personal renewal and reinvention that carried the candidate through the primaries and all the way to victory in November.

The first TV appearance in the emerging strategy of "electronic intimacy" was a January 26 interview on *60 Minutes* immediately following the Super Bowl. Although Clinton was outraged by the program's editing, the campaign spin doctors (most notably Carville) went forth on other talk shows to attack both Flowers and the media, while applauding Clinton's willingness to bare his soul before the voters in direct TV appearances. An ABC News poll that week showed that only 11 percent of the voters had been swayed by the Flowers episode. More important for the "reinvention strategy," 79 percent said that the press had no business dramatizing such personal matters, and 82 percent said that they had heard enough about Clinton's personal life.[14] The campaign escaped New Hampshire with a respectable second place finish, to which Grunwald added the right psychological spin by categorizing Clinton as the "Comeback Kid."

Grunwald's symbolic move fits Murray Edelman's definition of a "category mistake": a label that leads people to ignore important features of a situation as they form their opinions about it.[15] Not only was it unclear what Clinton had come back from (the political undead, one guesses), but also the same categorization continued to be offered throughout the primary campaign, the convention, and the general election. (As explained below, an embattled Comeback Kid was symbolically rescued by The Man from Hope after the convention, setting the stage for the greatest comeback of all—winning the election.) Never mind the contradiction of a candidate recumbent in a perpetual state of comeback; if voters could be induced to think of the endless flow of character problems less as problems and more as occasions for continuing comebacks, negative judgment could be suspended. The psychological margin created by this oxymoronic suggestion of an eternal comeback fit nicely with "reinventing Bill" as the underlying psychological strategy of the entire campaign. Thus, by invoking a simple category mistake, voters were invited to continually suspend negative judgment in the face of information that would have finished off candidates with lesser political strategies.

This strategy also fed nicely into polls showing high levels of public disgust with the personal preoccupations of the press. Similar levels of public discontent over "the character issue" were recorded in 1988, but the Dukakis campaign developed no psychological strategy for playing into that opinion. To the contrary, Dukakis's indignant and offended posturing, along with his awkward denials, may have undermined the kind of intimacy needed to reassure undecided voters that a vulnerable and open character was on continual electronic display.

The Beat Goes On: Character and Comeback

The continuing media drumbeat proclaiming Clinton's character flaws offered the campaign an opportunity to remind voters that they did not like the press's preoccupation with candidates' personal lives. Like it or not, of course, that preoccupation created doubts in many voters' minds. Thus, the reminder that such information was distasteful was not, in and of itself, enough to dispel those doubts. The important next step was the ironic but effective move of countering every new negative input by putting an increasing amount of Clinton's personal life on public display. The campaign therefore took on a strange dynamic: As more negative personal images emerged in the press and from the Bush camp (and, to a lesser extent, from Perot), the Clinton team found new ways to expose Clinton's private side on morning breakfast programs and through paid "minidocumentary" ads. Even the bus trips displayed a casual, relaxed, "just folks" side of Clinton, who with vice presidential sidekick Al Gore turned the campaign into a kind of lighthearted buddy movie: *Al and Bill's Excellent Adventure.*

All of these personal campaign episodes were drawn together around a steady schedule of TV town halls in which the serious, issue-oriented Bill

Clinton effectively winked to the studio audiences (with a nod to the viewers at home) and communicated the punch line, "We know that the press doesn't care about the issues in this election, but we can beat them by having our own face-to-face conversation about them right here." When election day rolled around, exit polls indicated that voters found the issue content of the 1992 campaign far superior to that of 1988 and that Clinton owned the issue positions that mattered to the largest number of voters.[16] It is unlikely that the higher levels of self-reported issue voting were due just to the carefully designed relationship between "personal Bill" and "policy Bill." As noted earlier, much of the elevation in issue voting in 1992 must be attributed simply to the entry of a third candidate in the race, which disrupts the typical two-candidate strategy of minimizing issue differences.

While the reasons for a resurgence of issue voting may be debated, the personalized campaign strategy (of continual reassurance through staged moments of intimacy) was clearly the context in which the various elements of the Clinton appeal fit together. Thus, the public was continually reminded that the media were the culprits responsible for failing to shift the focus from Clinton's character to more important issues. To make the best of the intrusive press, everyone was invited to hit the electronic road with Bill and Al following the convention (courtesy of the same press pack that kept the character problems flowing). The bus trips, the talk shows, and the town halls all provided the daily intimacy required to answer the character question. At the same time, people looking for an alternative to Bush and Perot were invited into a fantasy of renewal and hope. Indeed, the subliminal message that held this campaign fantasy tour together was *hope,* as in "A Man from Hope" and "A Place Called Hope."

However, the Man from Hope was not an easy invention. He was born of necessity in the midst of a crisis of voter confidence that nearly killed the Comeback Kid. The following analysis follows the story from the primary trail to the convention and on through the campaign, showing how and why the Comeback Kid was reinvented as the Man from Hope.

Slick Willie Meets the Comeback Kid

In the months after New Hampshire, the Flowers scandal was joined with charges of draft evasion, unpatriotic antiwar activities in England during the Vietnam era, and the marijuana incident that made Clinton the butt of comedians' jokes following his ill-advised "didn't inhale" disclaimer. Opponents soon collected the multiple character blows into the summary slur "Slick Willie." This name took on a life of its own in the media, making the top ten list of most-mentioned terms in newspaper and broadcast coverage of the campaign. Character flaws were never out of public view. During the extended primary period, measured from September of 1991 through June of 1992, "Gennifer Flowers" and "draft dodging" were among the top ten most-mentioned terms in campaign coverage of all candidates from both parties. The campaign top ten list from all print and broadcast coverage was: Desert Storm, Middle-Class Tax Cut, *Roe vs. Wade*, Family Values, Rodney King, Gennifer Flowers, America First, *Murphy Brown* and Dan Quayle, Draft Dodger/Draft Dodging, and Larry King and Ross Perot.[17]

During the final campaign period from July through election day in November, Clinton faced even more heat from the press and opponents. He had the dubious distinction of scoring four personal character categories ("character issue," "draft dodging," "Gennifer Flowers," and "Slick Willie") among the most-mentioned topics in newspaper and TV coverage of all three candidates combined. The top ten list in the media coverage of the final phase of the campaign was enough to cast grave doubts on the viability of the Comeback Kid:[18]

- Family Values
- Tax and Spend
- Larry King and Ross Perot
- Trickle Down
- Desert Storm
- Character Issue
- Draft Dodger/Draft Dodging
- *Murphy Brown* and Dan Quayle
- Gennifer Flowers
- Slick Willie

Through it all, the pundits routinely pronounced Clinton politically dead. In February, for example, Evans and Novak cited the conventional wisdom among "mainline Democratic politicians" that Clinton was "one of the walking dead who will sooner or later keel over."[19] Not only did Clinton fail to keel over, but he also went on to win primaries in the South and continued to collect enough delegates to secure the nomination. The remarkable fact amidst all the negative press is that Clinton's poll ratings against Bush held fairly steady in the high 30s and low 40s during a primary season in which Bush maintained a stable 50-percent-plus rating against the embattled Democrat.

However, a steady 40 percent rating would not be enough to win in November. To make matters worse, the Comeback Kid had begun to wear thin in the polls toward the end of the primary season. The crucial segments of swing and undecided voters were not sure why Clinton wanted to be president. They did not know why they should care about him. Worst of all, he was rated as just another politician—the kiss of death in an anti-political age. Thus, with the nomination in the bag, the campaign was in a crisis in June.

The candidate had to be reinvented again. Within the next six weeks, the Comeback Kid was given a new and psychologically more resilient persona as the Man from Hope. From the convention on, Clinton added the famous bus trips to his already steady schedule of talk show appearances. There was a stunning reversal in the poll standings, as Clinton jumped into the 50 percent range and Bush slipped steadily through the 40s and into the 30s.[20] What happened? Let's take a closer look at how the campaign went to the marketing department and searched for an image that was stronger than Slick Willie, who was giving the Comeback Kid a daily beating in the polls.

The Comeback Kid Fights a Talk Show Holding Action

The Comeback Kid was Clinton's direct-to-the-public emotional loss leader throughout the campaign, but by June he was clearly losing ground to Slick Willie. As Slick Willie began to take root in the public imagination, The Kid was able to do little more than fight a psychological holding action on the talk shows. Each time his poll ratings began to slip, the Clinton campaign launched another barrage of direct talk show appearances, making their candidate the undisputed talk show king of the 1992 election with 47 national appearances (and many more local forums) to Perot's 33 and Bush's puny 16.[21] Clinton's talk show appearances were divided fairly evenly between the primary season (23) and the months leading to the general election (24). Clinton far outstripped his eventual general election opponents in the crucial character test period of the primaries, during which Perot scored only 14 TV talk show appearances and Bush appeared just twice.[22]

The Clinton TV barrage became heaviest when poll ratings began to slip; at the very least, displays of electronic intimacy were calculated responses to moments when new character blows from Slick Willie began to erode Clinton's position in the polls.[23] The direct media strategy that evolved during the primaries was clearly a crisis management effort to save the ever-embattled campaign. In a postelection interview with *TV Guide* (appropriately enough), Clinton explained how he and his campaign managers decided to bypass the news in an effort to regain control of the media content of the campaign:

TV Guide: It's been an incredible year for both TV and politics. When did *you* decide you needed to run a radically different kind of campaign?

Bill Clinton: New Hampshire. During the first primary, in February. I started getting bad press [about alleged infidelities and the draft] and nobody wanted to talk about the issues anymore. I wondered if the voters felt the same. So I started having town hall meetings. . . . I noticed there were large crowds at our meetings. So I just took that idea to television.

TVG: [There was] quite a jump—from TV town halls to Arsenio Hall. Was there a particular moment when you and your advisers said "OK, nobody's listening—time for the sax, time for the shades?"

Clinton: Yes, during the New York primary. Again . . . what I was saying was still not being reported. The media were more interested in the horse race. That's when we decided to go full steam ahead in the new way. When people look back at this year and ask, "What really happened?" I think the two-way communication on TV between the candidate and the people will be the story.[24]

Loosely translated, "two-way communication" in this context implies the candidate's ability to respond directly to damaging information. As previously noted, that strategy became little more than a public opinion holding action as polling and focus group research revealed new vulnerabilities in the Clinton character. Put simply, the Comeback Kid was not strong enough as a language category to contain the repeated revelations that came after the Flowers episode. As layer upon layer of doubt-inducing character attacks surfaced, Slick Willie became all the more damaging, particularly when the image was popularized as much by Democratic opponents such as Jerry Brown as by the Republicans. To make matters worse, as indicated in the "top ten" list above, Slick Willie eventually took on a life of his own in the media during the final months of the campaign.

Although the Comeback Kid eventually drove leading challenger Paul Tsongas out of the race, Jerry Brown continued to drill Clinton with the Slick Willie charge. Brown would eventually self-destruct over a poorly developed "flat tax" proposal, losing New York and Pennsylvania, and thereby his presidential hopes, to Clinton. However, Stanley Greenberg's polls showed continued vulnerability to the Slick Willie label, particularly when voters were asked to think ahead to an eventual contest between Bush and Clinton. Greenberg's polls showed Clinton trailing Bush by 24 points on honesty and trustworthiness.[25] It was clear that Slick Willie was much too strong a character for the Comeback Kid to combat alone.

The Man from Hope Rescues the Comeback Kid

In June the campaign team launched "a top secret project of research and [character] recasting" that Mandy Grunwald dubbed the "Manhattan Project," both for its secrecy and for its reliance on science to develop an unbeatable strategic weapon.[26] Focus group research revealed that the Clinton character had eroded to such an extent on the eve of the convention that the project team reportedly circulated copies of Nixon's Checkers speech for inspiration.[27] As noted earlier, what eventually emerged was the psychological insight that voters did not know why Clinton wanted to be president. This fact was compounded by the impression that he was a typical politician, a problem that was magnified further by the devastating trust issue. The campaign was in turmoil following a string of frustrating failures to discover anything that would move focus groups of undecided voters to identify personally with the candidate or his proposals.

The solution reportedly proposed by pollster Greenberg was to act quickly to "depoliticize" Clinton and replace his tarnished political image with a human persona that was vulnerable, humble, and accessible to ordinary people. The search began for an image that at once alleviated doubts and answered the key questions "Who is Bill Clinton?" and "What makes him run?" The public holding action escalated during this period with the campaign's largest number of talk show appearances to date. While the Comeback Kid gamely made the TV rounds, focus group results began to show that much of the checkered details of Clinton's childhood (alcoholic stepfather, poverty, small-town upbringing) actually evoked sympathetic responses. Elements from Clinton's background in Hope, Arkansas, that had been kept hidden from public view seemed to answer those nagging voter questions.

And so "A Man from Hope" was invented, with his allegorical invitation to imagine America as "A Place Called Hope." The new character was launched with a convention video biography and Hillary Rodham Clinton's suggestion of closing the acceptance speech with the Comeback Kid's transition line to the Man from Hope: "I end tonight where it all began: I still believe in a place called Hope."[28]

The new character provided an image of Bill Clinton with which millions of undecided voters looking for hope in the election could identify. More important, the Man from Hope appeared to be at least the psychological equal of Slick Willie. The rest, as they say, is history. History in this case was also aided by a collapse of the Bush campaign, a breakdown that ironically rivaled the Dukakis fiasco of 1988.

MEANWHILE, BACK AT THE BUSH CAMPAIGN

While the Clinton campaign found a symbolic defense against its candidate's greatest weakness, the Bush camp never recovered from its disarray. Roger Ailes never joined the team. James Baker was recalled too late from his duties as secretary of state. And there was little time to reconstruct the Bush character in midsummer when public relations expert Sig Rogich was brought in from Iceland, where he was serving as ambassador as a reward for his work crafting attack ads in 1988.

Without a market-tested political communications strategy to go on, the Bush campaign became a wooden recast of 1988. Both the speeches and the ads became more negative as election day drew closer.[29] On the campaign trail, Mr. Bush's personal attacks turned into ineffectual name-calling. He referred to Clinton and Gore with these taunts, among others:

"The Waffle Man."

"Governor Taxes and the Ozone Man."

"He smokes but he doesn't inhale. Sure."

"A couple of yuppies dressed as moderates. Watch your wallet."

"Those deadly talking heads."

"Bozos."

As noted earlier, when Bush's daily tracking polls reported that all this unguided negativity appeared to be backfiring, he simply canceled his poll briefings.

By contrast, Bill Clinton never lost his "convention bounce" in the polls, suggesting that the new character unveiled before the nation that week in July did the trick. Greenberg's polls not only confirmed a strong Clinton lead, but also revealed that he was steadily overtaking Bush on the leadership dimension.[30] That was the final indication that the character problem had been solved—at least long enough to get Clinton elected.

If something as complex as an election can be reduced to campaign strategies, and, in particular, to the organizations that create the communication that goes out to the voters, the Bush and Clinton camps in 1992 provided as dramatic a contrast as did the Bush and Dukakis campaigns of 1988. Here is how communication scholar Joanne Morreale summed it all up:

In 1992, Bill Clinton was the first Democratic candidate in years to learn from the mistakes of his predecessors. . . . His Communication Director George Stephanopoulos had worked on Dukakis' 1988 presidential campaign. The advertising team was headed by Frank Greer who had worked for Walter Mondale in 1984. . . . In addition, Squier, Eskew, Knapp, and Ochs, the top Pennsylvania Avenue Democratic consulting firm, came on board. . . . The campaign hired a Madison Avenue advertising agency, Deutsch, Inc., known for producing controversial, innovative advertisements. Clinton's longtime friends, producers Harry Thomason and Linda Bloodworth . . . were responsible for creating television campaign materials, in particular the biographical campaign film, *The Man from Hope.* The film . . . demonstrated a keen awareness of the requirements of emotional televisual communication that appeared "authentic." The visual techniques—soft lighting, dissolves, integrated on-camera interviews, slow, sentimental music—supported the film's message that Bill Clinton was an earnest, sincere candidate who aimed to "re-unify" the country under his leadership.

But the Republicans' tight organization fell apart in 1992. The incumbent candidate George Bush suffered from the loss of the key political operatives who had been active in Republican presidential politics in the past. Bush's former campaign manager, James Baker, was serving as Secretary of State and had no desire to rejoin a political campaign, media consultant Roger Ailes declined to formally participate . . . and master strategist Lee Atwater had died the year before from a brain tumor. . . . Unlike the people behind the past three Republican presidential elections, the inexperienced media team received little direction and their campaign materials, including the campaign film, were not widely heralded. Republican political consultant and presidential campaign veteran Ed Rollins referred to the 1992 Bush effort as "the worst campaign I have ever seen."[31]

THE ELECTRONIC POLITICIAN COMES OF AGE

The electronic intimacy at the heart of the Clinton campaign—from the Comeback Kid to the Man from Hope—suffered the defects of all such illusions. In the end, the public is brought no closer to candidates on talk shows or bus trips than on conventional newscasts or meet the press programs; just the opposite may well be true. However, it is the short-term, continually reinforced illusion of intimacy and responsiveness that counts—all of which raises doubts about the kinds of forums that "talk show democracy" and "electronic town halls" actually create. This curious feature of the 1992 election appears to be an unsettling coming of age of Roger Ailes's original use of audience forums to create the "New Nixon" in 1968.[32] In many ways, the continuing evolution of this electronic intimacy echoes Daniel Boorstin's early warning about the threat to social and political credibility posed by media-based pseudo-events.[33]

Perhaps the greatest irony of the 1992 campaign is that at the same time that the Man from Hope was being introduced to the voting public with great success, the candidate was found brooding and burdened with doubts about his personal ability to engage effectively with that public. According to one report, Clinton considered his childhood in Hope to be the source of his greatest political weakness because, as one close associate put it, "the trauma of having an alcoholic stepfather who abused his family had made him shy away from face-to-face conflict."[34] It seems that the very image that helped get him elected ended up masking the basis for his own and, more important, the public's sincere doubts.

As Bill Clinton soon discovered, his fragile support (carefully cultivated on a daily basis during the campaign) would soon crumble. Like his predecessor, Clinton felt the sting of public disapproval. Where Bush fell from grace following what appeared to be a career-making victory in the Gulf War, Clinton suffered the loss of the traditional presidential honeymoon period with the press. Clinton's response appeared to involve turning the presidency into a continuing campaign. First he broke his vow not to bring his image-makers into the White House (as James Carville quietly moved into the White House basement), and then he hired David Gergen, one of the people who had learned the secrets of day-to-day communications psychology required to make Ronald Reagan the Great Communicator.

It may be asking too much to turn Bill Clinton into a Great Communicator. However, if Clinton thought he had overcome voter misgivings by winning the election, he failed to understand the fragile public psychology of the times. Indeed, the turbulent fortunes of the campaign trail must have appeared mild compared to the ups and downs of his first year in office. Even Mr. Clinton's budget plan in 1993, one of his more successful policy initiatives, was greeted with mixed reactions, as noted in this news account:

> The ratings for Mr. Clinton's August 3 budget speech are not in. But a CNN-USA Today opinion poll after the address suggested it was tuned in by about half of adults, but that only about 21 percent persevered to the end. That would seem to place the president perilously close to Bill Cosby's movie *Ghost Dad*, which attracted 16 percent of viewers in a network outing some months ago . . .
> . . . the presidency these days is less a bully pulpit than a telephone solicitor, interrupting the dinner hour or "Roseanne" for a pitch that the folks at home either deeply mistrust or simply don't want to hear. Make it

quick; we just got home and it's only two hours till bed. And no, you can't have our credit card number.[35]

The Clinton image and communication problems did not become any easier as the next election approached. Gergen quietly left the scene, unable to seize control of the president's daily communication with the public as he had done on the Reagan team. Clinton suffered a falling out with the old campaign team of Greenberg and Grunwald, who continued to point out the need for marketing and image management to a president who apparently hoped for some relief from such hype while he was governing.

One can understand the weariness of politicians such as George Bush and Bill Clinton who become uncomfortably trapped in the daily business of image management and the emotional maintenance of their publics. Yet they are caught in a system of their own making. It is a system from which there may be no escape without serious reforms.

The ultimate problem with the constant reinforcement psychology required to sell politicians to ever-wary citizens is that it permits little room for public dialogue about the issues and programs that politicians are elected to deal with. As the ties between leaders and citizens become ever more illusory, the reality of serious issues seems ever more harsh. It is small wonder that most modern politicians prove better at getting elected than at governing.

PART II

The Roots of the Crisis

CHAPTER　　4

Origins of the
New American Politics

There are no necessary evils in government. Its evils exist only in its abuses. —*Andrew Jackson*

Money, media, and marketing have been factors in American politics for some time. The corruption of big money goes back at least to the Gilded Age of Robber Barons and the rise of the industrial giants following the Civil War. Precise measures of power are elusive, but a reliable observer of that era credited the captains of industry with so much financial clout that they "declared war, negotiated peace, reduced courts, legislatures, and sovereign states to an unqualified obedience to their will, disturbed trade, agitated the currency, imposed taxes and boldly setting both law and public opinion at defiance, have freely exercised many other attributes of sovereignty."[1] No less an authority than President Grover Cleveland warned in his 1888 State of the Union Message to Congress: "We discover the existence of trusts, combinations, and monopolies, while the citizen is struggling far in the rear or is trampled to death beneath an iron heel. Corporations, which should be carefully restrained creatures of law and servants of the people, are fast becoming the people's masters."[2]

The Robber Barons purchased much of their political protection by financing electoral politics, an arrangement that culminated in the Republican party funding system under the direction of Mark Hanna. The election of William McKinley in 1896, for example, was funded by something akin to a tax on big business, whereby corporations and "fat cat" entrepreneurs were "assessed" contributions according to their wealth and prominence.[3]

The infancy of modern media manipulation can also be traced back to at least 1896 when Hanna staged McKinley's campaign largely from the front porch of the candidate's house in Canton, Ohio. Complete with marching bands, parades, and pilgrimages by loyal supporters, the campaign from beginning to end was what we would today call a media event.[4] It even had a sound bite. "McKinley and a Full Dinner Pail" was the slogan aimed at tens of thousands of urban workers who had been uprooted from the farms and were suffering the hunger produced by the nation's first major industrial-era depression in the cities.

The differences between then and now, however, are considerable. Swirling around McKinley's gilded campaign and its fledgling attempts at media manipulation were fierce national debates. McKinley's opponent William Jennings Bryan toured the country in 1896 calling for nothing less than a national referendum on the American future: small-town agrarian society versus urban industrial wasteland. In the process, Bryan delivered some 600 speeches to crowds that totaled 5 million people (almost the number who voted for him that year). Meanwhile, the Populist party, which allied with the Democrats in support of Bryan's candidacy, was divided intellectually over populism's failure to mount an effective national appeal to the workingman to counter McKinley's tempting "full dinner pail" imagery. In the end, enough voters rallied around the idea that both labor and business shared a common interest in industrial development to forge a governing Republican coalition.[5]

The moral of this story involves "governing ideas." Ideas that guide the process of governing are the central concern of this book. The genius of a political system lies in its capacity to innovate and articulate broad visions and ideas for citizens and politicians to follow. A governing idea or a governing vision, put simply, is a broad set of national goals supported by enough citizens and powerholders within institutions to sustain new courses of action aimed at changing basic social and economic conditions. Throughout this argument, the concern is not so much with whether governing ideas are good or bad, right or wrong, but whether they are likely to develop and be sustained given the limits of the contemporary political system.

GOVERNING IDEAS: AN EXPANDED DEFINITION

A governing vision emerged from the money-tainted contest of 1896, and in the decades before and after, society was alive with grand political debates and galvanizing conflicts. Indeed, campaign finance problems go back over a century, but the effects of money are different today. Currently, money acts more as a centrifugal force pulling political coalitions and governing visions apart rather than as a centripetal force pushing them together.[6] Voting turnouts in the late 1800s rose above 80 percent of the eligible electorate. Even if inflated by some degree of corruption, as in the infamous "voting graveyards" of Chicago, political participation was not dampened by the uses of money as it is today. Nor was corruption left solely to government to correct. After the turn of the century, the Progressive movement actively pushed for reforms in corrupt party politics at state and local levels. The fight even broke out within the Republican party itself, when Theodore Roosevelt became president after McKinley's death and moved against a few of the worst industrial offenders, quarreling with his own party over corporate campaign contributions.

In the decades between 1900 and 1930, alternative political visions were presented and debated in a muckraking press, in novels, especially those of John Dos Passos, Theodore Dreiser, and Sinclair Lewis, and in a militant labor movement. All contributed to the intellectual ferment of the times. After the economic bubble finally burst in 1929, a new governing coalition came to power and drew from that legacy of political debate. Under Franklin Roosevelt, the Democrats promoted a new governing vision (the New Deal) and built a forty-year foundation of voters and party government in support of that vision.

Governing ideas need not be complex. At the core of the New Deal was a very simple principle: the idea of a more activist government that would help people who could not solve their own problems. It is easy to see how this idea caught on in the midst of a great depression that rocked nearly everyone in society with problems that were neither of their own making nor within their individual powers to solve. From this simple idea came several decades of social and economic programs that protected people from sinking into poverty when their working years were over, that provided health care for the poor and the elderly, and that offered opportunities for education and job training for those who had been kept out of mainstream society because of poverty, race, or gender.

Like most ideas, the vision of an activist government leveling the social playing field eventually ran its course. By the early 1970s, many people objected to the size of the bureaucracies and the inefficiency of many of the programs created out of the legacy of the New Deal. Many argued that the best course was to return to the tried and true path of the conservative tradition that can be traced to a vision of government, society, and the individual that dominated American politics through much of the nineteenth century. Traditional conservatism espouses a cluster of three related ideas: small and restricted government, unregulated economic enterprise, and freedom for individuals to compete in the marketplace and live their private lives as they choose (within moral guidelines established by the government). In 1995, when he was asked how he planned to generate consensus in an often divided Republican party that he would help lead as Speaker of the House, Newt Gingrich articulated these governing ideas as clearly as Herbert Hoover, Dwight Eisenhower, Richard Nixon, Ronald Reagan, and George Bush had before him: "less government, reduced intrusion into our private lives, less regulation."[7]

Since the 1970s, there has been considerable debate about whether either the old liberalism or the old conservatism is capable of setting the government course for a society that has become one of the most complex and diverse on earth. Recent generations of Republicans and Democrats have added the prefix "new" to their names, but large numbers of voters remain skeptical about the claims of the "new" Democrats or the "new" Republicans that they, in fact, have new ideas. In this chapter we examine the reasons why those in power in recent decades have failed to convince large numbers of voters for long periods of time that they really have new political directions for the nation. In this discussion, the terms *governing ideas* and *governing visions* refer to broad definitions of the relations among government, society, and the individual that appeal to enough citizens to give government clear electoral mandates to make economic and social policies. When these policies appear to fulfill their guiding visions, politicians maintain enough (i.e., majority) support to return their government to power. Having the people's trust, elected representatives can continue making policies and laws as new social issues arise, until social changes create demands for new governing ideas.

Today's politics evidences little display of public trust, little enduring mandate to govern, and, at the heart of it all, remarkably little consensus on what the relationship between government, society, and the individual should be. When governments make policies and laws, as they continue to do, voters often register their disapproval by installing different players in the White House or Congress, as has been the pattern in recent elections. Today, citizens seem to be asking "Where is the national leadership, the principled opposition, or the credible exchange of competing ideas that ought to be swirling around government?" The roots of these concerns can be traced to fundamental changes in the political system. Exploring these changes makes it clear that, while money, media, and marketing have been around for many years, historically they have not undermined the capacity to govern in the same way they do today.

HOW THE NEW POLITICS CAME TO BE

As with most broad historical changes, the merging of money, media, and marketing into a new system of electoral politics cannot be attributed to a single event, a sinister conspiracy, or a dominant individual. Rather, a convergence of historical forces during the 1960s, 1970s, and 1980s created the conditions for forming this system. In what will necessarily be a brief review of this history, the main developments discussed in this chapter are these:

- The decline of the old Democratic vision and the rise of the independent voter (late 1960s–1970s).
- Campaign finance reform and the power of PACs (1970s–1980s).
- The rise of a national veto system (1980s–1990s).

The Decline of the Democrats and the Rise of the Independent Voter

The Democratic heyday of the 1960s came to a screeching halt in 1968 and went into reverse in 1972. After the New Deal of the 1930s was refashioned into the New Frontier and the Great Society visions of the 1960s, things fell apart. The Vietnam War began to appear both corrupt and unwinnable, creating huge divisions at home. At the same time, white southern voters started to express anger at the Democrats' imposition of civil rights on their communities. "Middle America" joined the reaction against the civil rights movement as urban riots and protests created turmoil across the land. The rebirth of religious fundamentalism took on a political dimension in reaction to the loose morals of the "liberals." And the welfare system created by the Democratic War on Poverty came under fire from all sides for creating dependency, being overly bureaucratic, and generally not producing the desired results.

The Democratic party itself was split into three factions: traditional New Deal liberals; the rising radical flank from the antiwar and civil rights movements; and the conservative southern ranks who threatened to bolt the party altogether at the national level if the radicals became more dominant. The election of 1968 was the turning point. After a season of violence, protest, and the assassinations of civil rights leader Martin Luther King, Jr., and Democratic antiwar candidate Robert Kennedy, an embattled Democratic party convention nominated Hubert Humphrey, a candidate who was offensive to two of the party's three wings. An old New Dealer, Humphrey angered the antiwar movement by his association as vice president with government policies in Vietnam; at the same time, he alienated conservative southern Democrats with his support for civil rights. Meanwhile, one of the most successful third-party candidacies in history was launched by the conservative Alabama Democrat George Wallace. When the chaos finally settled on election day, Richard Nixon eked out a narrow Republican victory but pointed to a growing block of southern support, despite Wallace's candidacy, as the basis for a grand Republican renaissance. This election and the turbulent era that produced it ushered in a period of great decisions and setbacks for both parties.

Party Reform for the Democrats: Was It a Mistake?

Following the 1968 defeat, the Democrats went back to the drawing board and began reforming the party structure itself. Blaming the old party's backroom politics for nominating an outdated candidate in Humphrey, the radical wing of the party (grass-roots organizers, civil rights leaders, antiwar factions, and women's groups) reformed the nomination process drastically to open more seats at nominating conventions to delegates who were directly elected by voters in state primaries. Unfortunately, the party reached little consensus about a new unifying vision or program. As a result, in 1972, the national television audience watched a Democratic convention that appeared to be out of control, with groups of all sorts fighting to get their issues into the party platform. In the end, antiwar candidate George McGovern discovered how little sympathy middle America had for his grass-roots Democratic agenda, and suffered one of the most decisive electoral defeats in history. This time, Richard Nixon's claims about a new Republican majority and a solid Republican South appeared to be convincing.

Political scientists have debated the wisdom of the Democratic party's decision to permit more direct democracy in the nominating process—perhaps more than any other major party in the world. Some argue that the party now suffers a lack of organization and leadership through the ranks.[8] Others retort that the Democrats were in trouble before the reforms and that the decentralization of a dying organization is actually a sign of vitality and life.[9] For our purposes, this debate misses the rush of later events. To appreciate the larger reasons for the decline of the Democrats, we must also look at changes in the voter market and the campaign finance system before we can put the whole picture together. For now, it is enough to remember that the changes inside the party produced a grass-roots takeover of the party platform process in the early 1970s that frightened many Americans. Why was there not a wholesale run to the Republicans as a result? Here we must introduce the equally large problems suffered by the GOP during this same period.

Corruption in the Republican Camp: The Legacy of Watergate

A simple "snapshot" of the lost party opportunities at the dawn of our current political age might show the Democrats busily shooting themselves in the left foot while the Republicans under Richard Nixon were shooting themselves in the right. Although Nixon survived four more years of the Vietnam War to win handily in 1972, he did not survive his own venom against his political critics. Using a system of campaign finance (and here we get to the next chapter of our story) that resembled the old tithing or assessment scheme from the Mark Hanna days, the Republicans amassed a political fortune that it socked away in foreign bank accounts and often delivered to party "bag men" in cash. In what has been described as a shakedown racket, wealthy individuals were pressured to give 1 percent of their net worth and corporations 1 percent of annual sales.[10] Much of this money was used to fund illegal activities that included spying on the Democrats and a host of other political opponents. By the time the ensuing scandal was over, dozens of companies, top executives, White House officials, party employees, and Nixon campaign workers were found guilty of illegal activities. As for the commander-in-chief, Mr. Nixon resigned and rode out of town ahead of an impeachment posse. But the legacy left behind still haunts the Republicans.

To an extent we will never know precisely, the spectacle of power and corruption seen on television daily during the Watergate hearings halted independent voters in their tracks, at least temporarily heading off any grand migration to the Republican side. Even a temporary halt in a possible Republican conversion was important for the formation of a new election system. Millions who had just voted for Nixon learned the seamy details of how the Committee to Re-Elect the President—or CREEP as it not so affectionately became known—channeled millions of dollars in unmarked bills into White House spying efforts against the president's political enemies. Those activities involved break-ins, burglaries, buggings, and political sabotage against people whom White House officials believed to oppose their political goals. One of those presumed enemies turned out to be the Democratic party and its candidate, George McGovern. When a team of burglars was caught at Democratic party headquarters in the Watergate office and condominium complex in Washington in 1972, the whole scheme began to unravel, and the nation was transfixed by what came to be known as the "Watergate scandal." For nearly two years the public followed the media spectacle of spying, wiretapping, political extortion, laundering of campaign funds, and flagrant disregard for (if not intentional subversion of) the principles of democratic politics. In the wake of Vietnam and the demise of the Democrats, a weary public now watched what looked to be the self-destruction of the Republicans. Again, it is impossible to know how many independents were halted in the middle of the road by those distressing events, but rising levels of general distrust of parties and politicians following Watergate suggest that many probably were.

The Result: An Independent Middle and Two Minority Parties

As the Democrats' old vision failed them and Republican scandals discouraged many voters from crossing to the other side of the party line, the first sign of a major voter change in several decades began to emerge: the rise of the independent voter. Increasing numbers of citizens declared no allegiance (or only weak allegiance) to either party. This trend continues to the present day. In the earliest voter studies conducted by the University of Michigan in the 1950s, slightly over 20 percent of the electorate declared themselves independents. In recent years, anywhere from one-third to 40 percent report themselves as independents. In the current era, in which massive marketing efforts will be launched to win the votes of just 10 or 15 percent of the voters in the middle, this change becomes significant.

Even the meaning of voter identification seems to have changed. In the past, as noted in the last chapter, party allegiance was a fairly stable psychological foundation and predictor of what people would do in future elections. Now, party identification is often offered as a summary of what someone did in the last election, holding neither the same personal significance nor the predictive accuracy about future behavior.

Our political plot thickens when we add the fact that the greatest shift has been away from the Democratic party, which registered as much as 47 percent of the electorate in the early 1950s. And it gets downright interesting with the discovery that, although the Republicans picked up some of these shifting voters, most have remained in the independent ranks. They are showing a continuing willingness to split their tickets, often voting Republican for president and Democratic for Congress. The Republican landslide of 1994, which defied all the normal bases for predicting midterm election shifts, indicates that there are no safe bets about what voters in this stubborn political middle will do with their votes.

Such an electorate presents a continuing marketing challenge for candidates who increasingly reject the old party trademarks in making their appeals to voters. This is particularly true of the Democrats who still have not come up with either a vision to replace the idea of activist government or a party program to replace the New Deal/New Frontier/Great Society era programs from 1932 to 1968. In the midterm elections of 1994, for example, large numbers of Democratic candidates removed any mention of their party affiliation from campaign advertising, position statements, and other printed materials. Many of these candidates actively campaigned against their own president and declared their primary allegiance to the voters of their districts in the fight against the big government monster in Washington. Following the election, both parties began a campaign to line up middle-class support in 1996 by promising tax cuts. In a postelection speech that shocked many members of the already beleaguered Democratic party, House minority leader Richard Gephardt promised an economic agenda that "will come from America's houses, not the White House."[11] Some in the White House suspected that the speech was the opening of Gephardt's own presidential campaign for 1996. This concentration of candidate and party competition on the voters in the middle of the political spectrum further weakened the abilities of both parties (particularly the Democrats) to develop distinctive governing ideas.

Thus, the first major change in the contemporary American political system was in the voter market itself. Today's voter alignment is roughly as follows. (Since these figures tend to shift from election to election and poll to poll more than in the past, ranges are given here.)[12]

Democratic voters (who vote less often than their Republican counterparts): 27–33 percent.

Independent voters (including those with weak "leanings" toward one party or the other): 33–40 percent.

Republican voters (who vote more often than their Democratic counterparts): 30–33 percent.

The growth in the ranks of independent voters created a new electoral dynamic that could have taken the system in any number of directions, some of them very positive. However, the political developments that came next in our story turned independent voters into the objects of what might be called the *great marketing chase*. In recent years, both the Democrats and the Republicans have discovered the limits of the marketing chase (without being able to stop it). Although both parties have won their fair shares of elections in the short run, they have not been able to hold on to government in the long run. However, in earlier days, both took up marketing as a quick means of recovering from their respective disasters of the 1970s. Turning to marketing with a vengeance, the Republicans began with the impressive rise of Ronald Reagan, and the Democrats followed with a successful effort to maintain control of Congress during most of the Reagan years by reselling themselves to their own former voters. This wholesale marketing of politicians created an unprecedented demand for money in the political process. The dilemma of parties caught between the limits of their own ideas and the need to win elections set the stage for the next historic development: the *money game*.

Campaign Finance Reform and the Power of PACs

First, a very brief history of political finance reform. Seeking to distance himself from the scandals of the Mark Hanna era, Teddy Roosevelt made a show of giving some corporate donations back in 1904 and promised to reform the system. The Tillman Act finally appeared in 1907, setting limits on corporate contributions but merely winking at enforcement. Companies blithely gave "raises" to their executives, who passed them along as personal contributions to politicians. The scandals returned with a vengeance in the 1920s when the Harding administration made a practice of selling government posts and favors to the highest bidder. (Harding's motley crew of cabinet officers and their underlings then turned government to their private plunder, selling properties at bargain prices and cutting enforcement protection deals to liquor interests during prohibition. In the most famous offense of all, they depleted the nation's oil reserves with bargain leases to private individuals in what became known as the Teapot Dome scandal.)

The Federal Corrupt Practices Act of 1925 made vague gestures at establishing spending limits and recordkeeping, but contained little in the way of serious reporting, accounting, or enforcement procedures. As a result, not much changed in the hazy world of political high finance. However, the 1929 shakeup in the economy itself brought a serious round of political reforms aimed at curbing the worst abuses of big business through direct government regulation. In the process, considerable amounts of political money were redistributed between the two parties.[13]

After the Second World War and continuing into the 1960s, a growing list of problems plagued the political system as a result of a haphazard campaign funding process. Among the troubles that finally moved Congress to take another stab at reform were the huge personal fortunes spent by wealthy individuals and families (e.g., the Kennedys and Rockefellers) to establish political dynasties. The dynasties magnified the misfortunes of candidates who had neither personal wealth nor the backing of party fat cats. Several presidential campaigns of this era lived hand-to-mouth, incurring large debts for candidates like Harry Truman in 1948 and Barry Goldwater in 1964. Last but not least, the shakedown tactics of the Nixon regime struck many Democrats in Congress as scandalous, not to mention politically threatening. Over the objections of Nixon and many other Republicans, work began in the late 1960s on the Federal Election Campaign Act. After securing agreements not to put its provisions into effect until 1976 (when his allowable time in public office would be over), Richard Nixon signed the bill into law in 1971.

In the meantime, the CREEP abuses of 1972 made the 1971 legislation calling for modest federal election subsidies and better reporting procedures look like another cosmetics job. With an election scandal too large for cosmetic treatment and the Democrats smarting under the double blast of the Nixon attack and the voter retreat, Congress settled down to more serious reform business and passed a series of amendments to the 1971 law. The Federal Election Campaign Act of 1974 (FECA) created the basic campaign finance structure that we know today. It required: (1) detailed public reporting of contributions, (2) limits on individual contributions, (3) federal matching funds for presidential candidates, (4) limits on how much personal money candidates can spend (amended in 1976), and (5) the creation of a Federal Election Commission to watch over the system, along with criminal and civil penalties for violations. This system was adjusted several more times, beginning in 1976, after the Supreme Court ruled in the case of (U.S. Senator James) *Buckley* v. *Valeo* that it was unconstitutional on First Amendment/free speech grounds to limit the total amount of personal candidate spending in a campaign.[14] As a result, Congress passed a 1976 amendment to FECA that established the principle of voluntary spending limits. This means that presidential candidates who voluntarily accept federal funding for their campaigns must also accept the campaign spending limits attached to that funding. A second major amendment came in 1979 when the parties realized that all the emphasis on giving money to individual candidates further threatened the viability of parties. The 1979 amendments to FECA permitted broader roles for state and local party branches in national elections, and authorized unlimited political action committee (PAC) and individual soft money donations to parties. ("Soft money" refers to a loophole in campaign finance law that permits unlimited donations for party activities "unrelated" to specific candidate races, as discussed further below.)

On paper, the reforms looked pretty tough. Indeed, compared to the freewheeling money madness of the past, they were very strict. In addition, the FECA reforms spared weak national presidential candidates the occasional indignity of begging for money to keep campaigns going. The combination of finance reforms and the party nomination reforms that preceded them even enabled relative outsiders like Jimmy Carter to have a shot at the highest national office. Debates have arisen about whether this sort of opening up of the top political office without a disciplining party structure around the lucky winner is desirable.[15] Nonetheless, the larger point is that underneath all the positive aspects of the reforms was a loophole big enough to push a Trojan horse through. This loophole— PACs—interacted with other political conditions of the times to create a new electoral system.

How the PAC System Works

Political action committees had been in existence on a small scale since the 1940s with the development of labor union PACs to channel funds and other assistance to Democratic candidates. However, they now became recognized as the vehicle for moving from a "fat cat" finance system to a system based on corporate and interest groups. The Federal Election Campaign Act of 1974 outlined the formal procedures through which business, labor, and other groups could form political action committees for the express purpose of channeling money to candidates, parties, and campaigns. On the face of it, the PAC provisions looked innocent enough. For example, no PAC could contribute more than $5,000 to a single candidate, and in practice most PACs do not give even that much to many candidates. Many saw it as only a drop in the bucket at the presidential level, and not much more than that at the congressional level. American politics is still reeling from the millions of drops that turned into a downpour of political pressure.

As we will see, even the $5,000 PAC contribution has its effect, but it is important to realize that these limited contributions to individual candidates are just one part of the larger system. As politicians, interest organizations, corporations, and lawyers began to understand the possibilities contained in the fine print, several creative developments occurred with PACs. The first creative innovation was the discovery that individual candidates could allow PACs to be created for them, thus amassing huge personal war chests, collecting political favors by giving large sums to other candidates, and, until 1992, saving the balances as fat retirement funds when their days in public office were over. But that is another story. The model of the candidate PAC in our story was Ronald Reagan's Citizens for the Republic. Years in advance, this committee raised millions to launch Reagan's 1980 candidacy. In addition, the Reagan PAC gave millions to other Republican candidates, personalizing the Republican party financially and, it seemed, ideologically. It was a model that nearly all major national politicians were soon to emulate. The list of personalities in both parties who have since formed their own so-called "leadership" PACs to promote their political fortunes reads like a "Who's Who" of American politics.[16] In the 1990s, for example, Newt Gingrich engineered his remarkable rise to power, along with the 1994 Republican congressional victory, with the help of his personal PAC, called GOPAC. Using gray areas in the reporting requirements, Gingrich refused requests through this period for the list of donors and the amounts they delivered to his cause.

The second creative innovation was the discovery that it was legal for independent PACs to form and to pour unlimited amounts of money into campaigning for (or against) candidates as long as the PAC was not directly or legally connected with the candidate's campaign committee. ("Direct" links are, of course, easy enough to avoid.) The model for independent PACs was the National Conservative Political Action Committee (NCPAC), which emerged as a force in the late 1970s and has since spent millions for and against candidates in pursuit of its agenda of moral issues. Following the success of NCPAC, other "independents" popped up around agendas as diverse as guns, medicine, conservation, and abortion.

The third creative innovation was the 1979 amendment to the law that opened the door for state and national parties to raise (and PACs to give) unlimited amounts of what has become known as *soft money* to the political parties for help with voter registration and organization-building activities. Again, the donations cannot be earmarked for a particular campaign or candidate, but such fine lines are often hard to draw in practice. The model for soft support by PACs was pioneered years ahead of the 1970s reforms with labor union support for the Democrats through the AFL-CIO Committee on Political Education (COPE). COPE also mounted independent efforts for the Democratic cause in the form of voter registration and get-out-the-vote drives. However, FECA opened the door to a flood of soft support from newly formed PACs to state and national party organizations.

The ultimate irony is that these laws, though aimed at curbing personal and corporate (direct) contributions to campaigns, in the end created a "money engine" capable of pumping previously unimagined amounts of money into the political system. But the final plot twist in our story is the way all that money has undermined any broad political consensus in the system. Special interest money is indispensable to political success, yet any base of special interest support for a broad political vision is inherently unstable. It would require the use of media management techniques to disguise, and marketing methods to repair, continual fissures and defections in such support.

Consider just one of the many ways in which PAC pressures undermine institutional support for governing ideas. In Congress, even small contributions add up. A few thousand dollars may not seem like much, but the average incumbent's political career depends on his or her ability to keep hundreds of PACs making their small contribution each year. Suppose, for example, that Senator Truegood needs to raise $6 million for the next election. That translates into $1 million a year over the six-year term, or around $3,000 that must be raised every day of each of those six years, weekends and holidays included. Suddenly those small PAC donations start to make sense. Just as suddenly, it becomes clear that even if U.S. representatives cannot promise their votes in advance, neither can they afford to turn PAC representatives away from their office doors very often.

Next, factor in the power of big PACs that have the resources to shower funds on dozens or even hundreds of representatives each year. Just to cite one example, the American Telephone and Telegraph PAC gave over $1 million, distributed to nearly every member of both parties in Congress in 1988.[17] With all the key votes "wired," so to speak, it becomes easier to secure passage of legislation and influence the regulatory statutes affecting an industry. Most PAC strategies involve concentrating large sums on the politicians responsible for writing the laws in particular interest areas. A large industry or a group of related industries can create PACs representing differing companies (and subsidiaries), and these "overlapping" PACs can concentrate their collective contributions. In the defense industry, for example, individual companies may be competitive when bidding on specific contracts, but there is no better way to ease the pain of competition than joining together to protect the overall budget for defense spending. During the heyday of military spending in the 1980s, Congress and the president turned on the afterburners on defense spending, and the defense PACs generously subsidized both political parties. One study showed that 82 percent of all military contracts in 1987 went to one-third of the states with the 11 percent of key legislators who served on the Senate and House Armed Services and Defense Appropriations committees. Those lucky legislators received millions in defense-PAC campaign contributions for the billions they awarded in defense contracts.[18]

In the 1990s, the PAC spotlight was given over to health care interests. They battled fiercely to make sure that national health care reform would not alter profitable aspects of the nation's soaring health care bill, such as the capacity of insurance companies to set their own rates, doctors to set their own fees, medical schools to turn out more high-priced specialists than the average person ever needs to see, or hospitals to determine the fees charged for rooms and services. When the final defeat of the Clinton health care plan was conceded on the eve of the 1994 election, the Center for Public Integrity (a policy watchdog group) estimated the total PAC contributions to Congress during the 1993–1994 election cycle at $100 million. The Center's report concluded with a sobering assessment: "There is no issue of public policy in which the sheer strength of those special interests have so overwhelmed the process as in the health care reform debate."[19] We will return in Chapter 6 to examine some of these finance patterns in more detail, and in Chapter 9 to look at how such important political issues have increasingly become pre-election battlegrounds.

What PACs Buy

Any direct exchange of campaign dollars for national priorities is, of course, scandalous, not to mention illegal. But many members of Congress are coming to precisely such conclusions.[20]

> "The only reason it isn't considered bribery is that Congress gets to define bribery."
>
> "If you give a dog a bone, he'll be loyal forever. And if you give a congressman some money, he may not fetch your slippers for you, but he'll always be there when you need him."
>
> "I fear we could become a coin-operated Congress. Instead of two bits, you put in $2,500 and pull out a vote."
>
> "I take money from labor, and I have to think twice in voting against their interest. I shouldn't have to do that."
>
> "More and more on the floor I hear people say, 'I can't help you. I've gotten $5,000 from this group.' "

The point of this discussion is not to debate whether defense spending is a boondoggle, tobacco subsidies are silly, or junk food legislation is junk. The question, rather, is whether any semblance of governing is possible when the governors are being pulled from so many sides at once, by so many narrowly defined and often utterly unrelated interests. Perhaps Senator Robert Dole (R-Kansas) has made the point best: "When these political action committees give money, they expect something in return other than good government. It is making it difficult to legislate. We may reach a point where everybody is buying something with PAC money. We cannot get anything done."[21] And yet Senator Dole has been one of the most successful of all in playing the PAC game.[22] Therein lies the essence of the system.

The Bottom Line: Structural Limits on Party Appeal

In 1980, when Ronald Reagan was elected, the pundits talked about a coming Republican realignment. In 1992, when Bill Clinton gave the Democrats control of the two institutions necessary for laws to be made, the pundits talked about an end to gridlock. In 1994, when the Republicans took control of Congress, the pundits talked about a return to the unfinished Republican agenda. Yet what is most notable about these flip-flops of party power seems hard for pundits to address from their journalistic preoccupation with who's in and who's out in the highly personalized Washington power game:

- Neither party has cultivated the leadership or the discipline to govern effectively over the long haul.
- Neither party has figured out how to develop governing ideas that appeal over the long run to more than the roughly 30 percent of voters who seem to be the ceiling of stable support that can be generated under the new election system.

On the first point, consider this often-overlooked result of the PAC system, with its leadership PACs: it is nearly impossible to maintain institutional support for broad policy initiatives, much less for new governing ideas. Why? The president and the members of Congress are all leaders, not followers. There is a double whammy in this system that compounds the divisive legislative lobbying forces with the system of personal PACs in which individual politicians allow funds to be gathered for their own political ambitions. In Congress, this means that dozens of powerful leaders accumulate huge financial bases independent of the political parties. Those with presidential aspirations may even rival or try to capture party organizations so that they can control the financial rewards given to supportive colleagues as well as the punishments meted out to competitors. If we factor in the capacity of independent PACs to work alongside politicians who support their pet issues, we see the rise of feuding political fiefdoms within Congress, the executive branch, and the parties themselves. It is no wonder that any individual or any party that emerges from this system claiming to have broad political ideas generally ends up resorting to marketing and media management techniques.

Consider in this light the interesting cases of both Ronald Reagan and Bill Clinton. Reagan was the "New Republican" whose innovations in fundraising, marketing, and press management presaged the new politics, and Clinton was the "New Democrat" who demonstrated most convincingly (to the voters, at least) that the government's failures had little to do with parties being denied control of both the branches needed to make laws. Let's begin with the Republicans, who celebrated the Nixon landslide of 1972 only to be crushed almost immediately by the Watergate fiasco. Under Ronald Reagan, the Republicans would rebound from the Watergate scandal, but despite some early heady success they would discover the difficulties of cornering the voter market in a new era of campaign finance reform.

Even if the "Reagan Revolution" had succeeded in winning control of the Congress, the GOP would have faced the dilemma of how to sustain that governing power based on a policy agenda voted in by less than 30 percent of the eligible electorate. The new system carries the overriding dilemma of large numbers who do not vote in any given election. This means that governments are installed by minority blocs of the eligible electorate and replaced by new minority blocs who rise to express their discontent the next time around.

It thus becomes extremely challenging to imagine that either party could capture the government for any extended period of time through success at the money game and the marketing chase rather than through the traditional methods of attracting broad voter support and party loyalty. At the very least, such extended government control would require considerable *media management* skill to suppress questions about the extent of popular support for the resulting governing program. Despite their media management abilities, the Reagan Republicans were spared the challenge of sustaining long-term control of government through media imagery alone. The voters never awarded the GOP control of Congress during the Reagan–Bush era.

Yet the Democratic foothold on power proved to be as unstable as that of the Republicans, and for much the same reasons. To put it simply, the Democrats finally learned how to play the money game. They then figured out how to play the marketing chase well enough to capture Congress by the mid-1980s and the White House in 1992, only to lose Congress abruptly in 1994 and scramble to retain some grip on power in 1996.

All of this turbulence is the result of what might be called a national veto system, grinding away at what was left of the Republican vision in the 1980s, and then with the flip-flop of congressional power in 1994, grinding away at what was left of the Democratic vision after that. The Democrats under Bill Clinton must have misread the strength of their popular support as surely as did the Reagan Republicans and as surely as did the Bush campaign of 1992. What the Clinton camp had succeeded in winning was the media, money, and marketing game on a short-term basis. As it is almost impossible to win these tricky games on anything but a short-term basis, the Democrats, like the Republicans before them, discovered the governing crisis the hard way. In limiting the Democrats to just two years in power, some voters declared that they were simply not receptive to what appeared to be old Democratic policies parading under new Democratic advertising. (The health care failure exemplified this.) Others pointed to the Democrats' inability to use their control of government to get major legislation passed at all, raising questions about what party power even means these days (as also exemplified by the health care fiasco). As long as the money game dominates national politics, questions about what the parties stand for, and what they will be capable of doing in government, remain valid.

As the latest political casualties disappear over the horizon, it seems most clear that the veto system that arose toward the late 1980s is rolling on through the 1990s. And so we introduce the final historical change that brought about a new electoral system. With the Republicans poised to make another run at the White House in 1996, the question for both parties was whether they could rise above this final development that has characterized the governing crisis: the rise of a national veto system.

The Rise of a National Veto System

It is common for parties and their supporters to declare each victory the beginning of a new era. Ever on the lookout for a dramatic news story, news organizations and their pundits quickly contribute to the political buzz. Yet observers of this system should recognize that the media are not disciplined by much reporting of history, and they are disciplined even less by political analysis (save for color commentary on the game of musical political chairs inside the Beltway). In this section we examine what happened at key moments when both politicians and the press wrongly interpreted shifts in party positions in government. At each of these moments in the modern era, one party has been blocked by the other, with the grudging help of an electorate that seems to recognize the programs of both parties as representing minority views. Consider how each party has adjusted to this veto system without figuring out a strategy for breaking out of it.

Why the Reagan Revolution Stopped Short

Disorganized and clearly outmaneuvered electorally in the early Reagan years, the Democrats offered little legislative resistance to the Reagan agenda. It appeared that Reagan's promise of a New Federalism (restoring power to the states) and a return to an old morality was on an unstoppable political roll. Indeed, when Reagan later made appointments that tilted the Supreme Court in his ideological direction, even some experts on American politics began to wonder if a political realignment was taking place. In edging toward this declaration, Walter Dean Burnham, for example, reasoned that

> What happens in these realignments is often not success in disposing of the crisis source that gave birth to them [referring to the earlier Democratic New Deal failure to "solve" the depression and the Republican abolitionist failure to peacefully solve the slavery crisis] *but success in capturing the intellectual high ground, in authoritatively defining the agenda of politics, and in organizationally building a revolution by institu-*

tionalizing it. To a very striking extent, this is just what Reagan and a now thoroughly Reaganized Republican party have been able to do at decisively important levels of presidential and, increasingly, judicial politics.[23] [Emphasis added]

Yet as we will see in the next chapter, Burnham was uneasy about pushing his own analysis too far. And for good reason. His and other interpretations of the Republican realignment were based largely (and understandably so) on assumptions that the old American political system— the one with voters, parties, and institutions capable of becoming committed to visions—still existed. However, coexisting with the familiar signs pointing to Republican realignment was another set of rather confusing and unfamiliar signs that did not point that way. The trouble was that in order to make sense of those warning signs, it was necessary to see that the political system itself was changing in fundamental ways. Indeed, even the Republicans appeared to be unable to figure out the warning signs until it was too late. The Reagan crusade marched ahead as though the new system of money, media, and marketing could be played for the same results as the old system of at least somewhat disciplined parties, loyal voters, and ideologically organizable institutions.

Thomas Ferguson and Joel Rogers were among the first analysts to recognize the existence of unsettling signs all along.[24] However, they also tended to interpret those signs in the context of the old system, claiming that the Democrats paved the way for the Republican renaissance by moving to the right in pursuit of campaign money and thereby abandoning many liberal constituents who continued to share the old Democratic vision. This conclusion overlooks the first big step toward the new system—namely, the many voters who had long since abandoned the old Democratic vision to declare their independence from political parties. Moreover, the idea of a Democratic right turn fails to explain why the party began turning back to its old liberal agenda by the beginning of the 1990s—passing civil rights legislation and jobs programs, and talking about health care reform—despite even deeper commitments to the same money sources. A better explanation of what happened is that the Democratic entry into the money chase turned the party into a veto bloc, a loose-knit organization that came to wield political power without much unifying vision. This veto bloc first disrupted the Republican agenda and then, when given the chance, vetoed much of its own agenda between 1993 and 1994.

To return to the Republican story, it is important, first, to see that very early on cracks and fissures appeared in the Republican vision, and, second, to understand how they grew into major faults. To their credit,

Ferguson and Rogers provide a good analysis on the first score. They show that from the beginning public opinion ran moderately to strongly against almost every item on the Reagan legislative agenda in those early years. (This reflects the "30 percent ceiling" of support under which both parties seem to operate in the new system.) Moreover, during those same years of greatest legislative success, Reagan's personal popularity was strikingly low—certainly not high enough to justify the heroic labels that vocal supporters pinned on him and that a well-managed press passed along.[25] In addition, the Reagan landslides of 1980 and 1984, along with the victories of party candidates in campaigns centering on the moral agenda of prayer, patriotism, and abortion, were tempered by exceedingly low and declining voter turnouts. Similarly, claims of a Republican mandate were contradicted by only modest gains (around 5 percent) in voter declarations of Republican loyalty during the 1980s, while the solid independent middle held firm.[26]

To this already impressive set of mixed signals, we may add yet another confusing sign: some key items on the Reagan political agenda were defeated by opposition from groups that were otherwise supportive of Reagan and his visionary rhetoric. For example, senior citizens successfully resisted administration efforts to cut social security and medical benefits. Although many conservative seniors might have been counted among an emerging governing coalition, they resented attacks on programs they regarded as sacred entitlements. In another area, otherwise supportive members of the middle class became less enthusiastic about tax cuts that gave them a few hundred dollars when it became clear that corporations were being given hundreds of millions. By the end of the Reagan era, not even an out-and-out media campaign could drum up middle-class support for a tax reform that, according to polls, seemed driven more by interest pressures on both parties than by the much heralded middle-class economic vision.[27]

A correct reading of these signs as they began to emerge was difficult, in part, because the new election system that would give them meaning was being born at the same time. Sign-reading in the early years was all the more difficult because what emerged in the mass media over the same period was a picture of an invincible leader striding ahead of a national political reformation. To some extent, the prevailing media image surely resulted from the now-legendary White House management efforts to put a favorable administration "spin" on the daily news. But this was far from the whole story. In addition, members of the administration simply ignored or avoided early press efforts to question the administration policy agenda, leaving the media looking like a pack of howling but ineffectual wolves. Perhaps most important of all, however, the Democrats were on the run and were unable to mount much of a vocal (much less legislative) opposition to the administration's agenda.[28]

The illusion of Republican invincibility continued to grow following the economic recovery that boosted Reagan's personal popularity after 1983. A tax cut that same year put money in middle-class pockets, offering short-lived but timely tangible evidence that the Reagan revolution was at last beginning to pay economic dividends. Ironically, at this point between 1983 and 1984, when things looked unstoppable for the Republican vision, the fissures that had been there all along turned into deep cracks in the political foundation itself. Thus, the Democratic veto bloc was born.

The Democrats Regain Their Strength and Create Their Own Weakness

The turning point came when the Democrats learned to play the money game and then turned their newfound fortunes into successful marketing efforts for congressional candidates. This turnaround surely would not have been possible if large numbers of independent voters had sided with the Republican vision, declared party loyalty, and begun voting against Democrats as a matter of principle. As it happened, the Republican "landslide" victories of the 1980s occurred within the rather confined limits of a declining, independent-minded electorate. As a result, all these sophisticated marketing efforts produced about as many Republican votes as possible within those limits. The bottom line is that some combination of Reaganomics, the New Federalism, and the conservative moral agenda gained popularity among a minority of the eligible electorate. However, it never achieved enough popularity to boost turnouts or convert large numbers of independent voters into Republicans. As a result, the Republican vision was vulnerable in precisely the same terms on which it was built: money and marketing.

At this juncture, the Democratic money game came into play. After losing its grip in the Senate, the party realized that only one institution—the House of Representatives—stood in the way of Reagan's achieving an institutional monopoly to secure passage of his agenda. (The Supreme Court was already going Reagan's way.) Beginning in 1982, the Democrats under the leadership of since-disgraced Tony Coelho began approaching the PACs and suggesting that an organized Democratic resistance in the House could create a lot of trouble for PACs that did not support party candidates. The PACs responded much like a business community buying into a protection racket—which, in a sense, is just what they were. By 1984, the Democrats were in a financial position to regroup. Although they still lost the congressional election game that year, they won the PAC game, with a healthy advantage of 57 to 43 percent of PAC contributions going to Democratic candidates. Even corporate America was coming around, with 38 percent of its donations going to Democrats by 1984, despite the more obvious ideological alliance between the corporate sector and the Reagan economic agenda. By 1988, the trend was crystal clear: for the first time in the history of the new PAC system, a majority of corporate PAC money and an even heftier majority of nonbusiness PAC financing were going to the Democrats.[29]

As a result of this sudden balancing of financial power in the new system, the Democrats were for the first time able to enter the marketing chase on an equal footing with the Republicans, and they did it successfully enough to win back their majority in the Senate. In the process, Congress was effectively turned into a veto institution. It became capable of blocking not just the rest of the Republican vision (culminating with George Bush finally being forced to retreat from his Clint Eastwood pledge, "Read my lips. No new taxes," and move his lips on taxes in the budget battle of 1990), but virtually any broad vision for any party or group that threatened the hundreds of special interest commitments on which the Democratic power base depended.

With the financial foundations of their own political agenda thus exposed, it would not take long for the Republicans in Congress to begin going back on their commitments to different aspects of the party vision. George Bush was even deserted by his own party whip in the House after the president changed his stand on taxes. Talk quickly surfaced about challenges in 1992 from within the party against the president who had looked so invincible after his victory in 1988. With the addition of the veto system to the existing configuration of PACs and independent voters, the George Bush story, like all stories in the new political era, has three morals: Live by the money game, die by the money game; live by the marketing chase, die by the marketing chase; live. . . . Well, you get the idea.

Only his victory in the war against Iraq restored Mr. Bush's illusory and elusive political fortunes. After the president went off on his own foreign policy course (which ended up meaning little to voters in 1992), those still loyal to the dying Republican vision remained behind, shaking their heads and sometimes their fists at the party's misfortunes. Perhaps some sincerely misread the warning signs all along, thinking wishfully that the new combination of money, media, and marketing could sustain a governing vision as well as the old combination of voters, parties, and principled leaders. Republican dismay was summed up most bluntly by one of the House conservatives who helped create the original corporate PAC base for the Republicans. Representative Guy Vander Jagt of Michigan once traveled the country persuading corporations to form PACs with the provocative claim that a company without a PAC was un-American. Now that he began to read the political signs more clearly, Vander Jagt declared that "The PACs are whores."[30]

Why should this discovery have come as a surprise? With very few exceptions, PACs are formed not in pursuit of principle, but out of concern to protect the narrowest of special interests. Why should PACs give money if they do not get results? Thus, after it really got up and running, the PAC system created a veto system capable of blocking the implementation of most principled visions that conflict with the narrowly defined interests that keep the system going. There was no better example of this than the spectacle of the Democratic party self-destructing over the health care issue in 1993 and 1994. All that the Republicans needed to point out to the people was that the Democrats had the power now, and they did not need the Republicans in order to govern. If the Clinton-led party could not pass health care, the fault was with them, and no one else. Of course, the Republicans did their share to defeat health care reform, but their basic point was valid, and it draws our attention to the full coming of age of the veto system. By the time of the great health care battle on the eve of the 1994 midterm elections, the veto system had evolved to a point of such severe internal divisions within the Democratic party that it could not pass legislation on an issue that mattered to fully 70 percent of the public. It turned out that the party had booted an issue on which the very maintenance of its own power depended. One wonders what the outcome on health care might have been if the Democrats had been less sure that they could preserve their hold on Congress through outspending and out-marketing their opponents. As it turned out, for the first time in over a decade, the Republicans outspent the Democrats in a congressional election, and the results showed.

The Veto System Comes of Age

What are we to make of all this? First, we see that the electorate, too, has become part of the veto system, deeply suspicious of candidate promises during elections and of government policy failures in between. A prickly, disloyal, hard-to-convince electorate means that the politics of the 1990s (barring reform or system-changing upheaval) will continue to rely increasingly on marketing—both for candidates and for policies. Thus, the system will continue to burn interest money, and both elections and the everyday affairs of government will continue to depend on the short-term political communication strategies that serve as daily reminders to citizens of the shortcomings of it all. And so, the cycle continues.

In short, the veto system has institutionalized the multisided, crosswise pull of interests that we talked about at the opening of the book. A skeptic might argue that it is just good old Madisonian democracy carried to its logical extreme. The original system, after all, was designed to hold factions in check. Perhaps at this ripe old age as a Republic, the United States has simply succeeded in completing the Madisonian vision to the point of governmental near-paralysis. Perhaps. But while Madison's Constitution was designed to hold warring social groups at bay, a principled national leadership was envisioned forging economic and foreign policy while strong state governments were busy managing the domestic life of a much simpler society. Today, half the states are facing financial receivership, and we are living in a society more complex than even the visionary Madison could have imagined. Instead of a principled national leadership with the power to govern by keeping the factions at bay, the leadership has been captured by the factions themselves. Therefore, instead of leading and governing, elected officials cannot do much beyond getting themselves reelected. In order to do that, they must fashion the most delicate kind of political promises: the kind they cannot possibly hope to keep.

MADISONIAN DEMOCRACY MEETS MADISON AVENUE

It is not surprising that people still try to interpret a transformed present as a natural extension of an old Madisonian past. Consider one view of the origins of the old system. Madison and most of the other Federalists used the term *faction* as a euphemism for that most threatening single group in society: the masses of people with no property who might use democratic power to take over the wealth of society. In designing a system to limit this possibility, thanks to the twists and turns of history, the Founders ended up creating a system that checked all the other factions as well. Advocates of this interpretation of Madisonian democracy might argue that even a paralyzed system could be regarded as protecting the interests of the rich over the poor. The status quo favors the rich, and in a veto system the most highly organized special interests are the wealthy propertied and commercial factions who can promote their interests better than the poorly organized, impoverished factions. Indeed, the income distribution figures over the last decade offer some crude support for this thesis. According to Congressional Budget Office analyses of the 1980s, the top 10 percent of American families gained more than 25 percent in real income (adjusted for inflation), while the bottom 10 percent lost more than 10 percent of their real income over the same period.[31]

For the sake of argument, suppose that the new system accomplishes at least this one goal of Madisonian democracy: protecting private property and the related economic prerogatives of the state from the vicissitudes of faction. Yet the new system also undermines the possibility of legitimate national leadership and governing visions in ways that Madison surely would have feared. Madison, though clever enough to design a system that kept factions in check, was not so cynical as to design one that cast its own leadership in doubt among its own people.

And so the paradoxes of the new system sit uneasily with the understandings we carry forward about the old. In one interesting analysis, political scientists Benjamin Ginsberg and Martin Shefter puzzle over the decline of parties and the disappearance of voters, and offer the hopeful possibility that government may be going on "by other means."[32] For example, people who leave the electoral system may be entering the interest group/PAC system. By spending money or working for organizations, people may have decided that if they can't beat the system, they'll join it. Indeed, there is evidence that support for interest organizations and PACs (including citizens' groups like Common Cause) stands at an all-time high.

Yet there is something distressing about a system in which citizens have become just another interest and must lobby in competition with thousands of others to promote something called the "public interest." In such a system, neither governing nor the public interest is likely to be served very well or very often. Instead, the more likely picture of government is that of a mad political scramble for short-term voter support. There remains just enough party organization to deliver the legislative votes (interest protection) needed to raise the money needed to keep up the marketing. Those politicians who play the media, money, and marketing games skillfully will survive, while those who don't will disappear. Meanwhile, the tendency of the system requires that more energy be devoted to the communication strategies necessary, as Jarol Manheim put it in the title of his book, to fool *All of the People, All the Time*.[33] What this boils down to, in Manheim's terms, is the continual polling, focus grouping, and message shaping required to turn individuals' frustrations into anger at opponents, and their emotional concerns into the targets of short-term appeals to win votes and boost approval ratings.

This, in a sense, is the key. Whereas in the past, grand campaign promises were broken, they were often kept, too. Some elaborate rhetorical visions fizzled when put to the test of public policy, but others succeeded in governing the nation. While American politics and elections seldom offered more than simple rhetoric, those simple ideas often turned out to mean a great deal to people. In the political system that has emerged to dominate today's America, the common quality in most political communication is an eerie emptiness.

Yet the emerging system of American politics contains within it so many ghosts of the old that critics can still be heard saying that elections like 1988, or 1990, or 1992, or 1994 do not represent a qualitative departure from the past. Promises are always broken, they say; rhetoric is always simplistic, voters are always lazy and apathetic. However, surrounding the ghostly reminders of elections and politics from the past is a new system that effectively makes the worst of the old about the best we can expect from the new. In the next chapter, we respond to those critics who say that nothing important has changed.

CHAPTER 5

Wait! Hasn't It Always Been Like This?

What Americans see as they watch their candidates do battle for high office is a raging battle between the "oughts" of good government, oughts they have been taught since grade school days, and the "is's" of electric rhetoric—the high-profile, high-priced, shiny-picture messages. . . . filling the air with smoke and mirrors capable of showing nothing of political importance to the citizenry. —*Bruce E. Gronbeck*

Complaining about the quality of elections is as American as apple pie and as old as colonial times. No less a figure than George Washington was condemned for sleazy campaign practices in his pre-Revolutionary races for the House of Burgesses in Virginia. James Madison bemoaned the ways in which Washington and the other candidates "recommend themselves to the voters . . . by personal solicitation."[1] Among the most popular endorsements was that of John Barleycorn. On the use of alcohol to separate the voter from his vote, Madison observed: "On election day the flow of liquor reached high tide. . . . [D]uring a July election day in Frederick County in the year 1758, George Washington's agent supplied 160 gallons to 391 voters and 'unnumbered' hangers on. This amounted to more than a quart and a half a voter."[2] Madison's verdict on that political scene has been echoed through the ages, even as the nature of offending practices has changed from one era to the next: "[T]he corrupting influence of spiritous liquors and other treats [is] inconsistent with the purity of moral and republican principles."[3] The same might be said today about the corrupting influence of slick political advertising that appeals to unthinking passions, and about "other treats" like the promise of tax cuts when government is bending under the weight of huge budget deficits.

If questionable campaign practices can be traced all the way back to the father of the country, it is reasonable to ask what all the fuss is about.

A critic might argue that our elections, if no better, are at least no worse than they ever were. By the end of this book, of course, I plan to demonstrate the errors of such thinking. However, much is to be gained from seeing how the decline-of-elections argument holds up against the strongest objections that might be lodged against it. In the process, we will take a look at some of America's fascinating electoral history and see if the complaints about recent elections truly stand the test of time.

AND NOW, A WORD FROM THOSE WHO SEE NO CHANGE

At least three objections could be raised against characterizing present-day campaign content as unusually nasty, brutish, and short on ideas. In ascending order of importance, these criticisms can be stated as follows:

Objection No. 1: The Good Times Theory. The elections of the last decade are just what we would expect them to be during a prolonged period of peace and prosperity. Far from culminating a trend of impoverished political ideas and unresponsiveness to public problems, the elections of the late 1980s and (thus far) the 1990s were mere blips on the TV screen. They were perfectly predictable responses to a period of domestic prosperity and superpower harmony. The cold war was over, and the economy was relatively sound. What was there, after all, for the candidates to talk about?

Objection No. 2: The Hidden Issue Theory. There are always plenty of ideas, issues, and signs of candidate character to be found if only one bothers to look. In every election year, sizable tracts of national forest land are sacrificed to print voluminous position papers and issue statements. The real problem is that the people just don't pay attention to them.

Objection No. 3: The "What You See Is All You Get" Thesis. American elections have always been shallow and issueless affairs, which means that the hype, the hoopla, and the horse race are what an election is all about. Eloquence and vision would be lost on the American voter.

RESPONDING TO THE GOOD TIMES THESIS

Election choices are bad when the times are good. It is tempting to believe that the quality of American elections rises to the occasion of social crisis, so that we tend to get great leaders just when we need them. In this view, decisive contests, clear issues, and big voter turnouts emerge only in response to big national problems. This version of history is too neat and far too complacent. It makes little sense, in any event, to think of the recent era as one of untroubled complacency. To the contrary, we get a different picture of the times by looking beyond the optimism of a few national cheerleaders and taking the worries of the public seriously. As noted earlier, opinion polls throughout the recent period show majorities seriously concerned about a long list of national problems, not the least of which was a government captured by special interests. On the world front, lurking beneath the surface of reduced superpower tensions were worries about regional civil wars that threatened both political stability and the growth of capitalism in the former Soviet empire. Elsewhere, the rise of unfriendly regimes in the oil zones contributed to continuing U.S. military entanglements of the sort witnessed in the Gulf War of 1991. Such threats to a "new world order" augured for a perpetually oversized defense budget at home, draining hopes for social and economic renewal. Add to these concerns the jitters of world economic restructuring that made American labor less competitive and jobs less secure than even a generation earlier. And to these pressures on government add the social decay in the nation's cities, where gang warfare, poverty, homelessness, and bulging prisons spoke angrily of the need for a restorative vision to replace the increasingly vengeful politics of everyday life.

In light of these and other signs of social and economic stress, it would be hard to conclude that the recent era has been trouble-free. A better assessment is that the times were as troubled as many in the past and more strained than a number of earlier eras. The difference this time around is that for all the communicating on the talk shows and electronic town halls, there is no obvious mechanism through which the personalized politics between lone candidates and independent voters can find a governmental meeting point.

The Retreat from Public Life and
the Rise of the Personal in Politics

The traditional mechanisms for building consensus, sifting ideas, and recruiting converts to new causes are the political party and the social movement. In the last chapter we learned some of what happened to the parties in the modern era. Social movements appear to be the best hope for reviving the political process (and perhaps a new party system in the bargain). Through social movements, people who are concerned about common problems publicize those concerns in face-to-face settings backed up by literature, speakers, and even parties and candidates to bring their ideas to government. In today's political scene, the most effective national social movements have come from those who seek to return to traditions of the past. The religious right, for example, has used a common base of church attendance, direct mail marketing, and televangelism to mobilize a core of partisans who seek to reinvent government in their image. As noted in the last chapter, this movement seems to have reached its peak political capacity without having converted the great political middle to its moral causes of abortion, prayer in school, and various lesser issues.

More populist movements such as the Perot phenomenon of 1992 have discovered a core of middle-class nationalism and economic conservatism, but struggle over the means for sustaining participation in the absence of regular social (or even electronic) contact among members. The point is not to criticize these movements that have revived more traditional, conservative visions of government, society, and the individual. To the contrary, one can only acknowledge the political initiative of those who have mobilized the communication and fundraising technologies of the new politics to their cause.

Unfortunately, elections have not become arenas for broadening the appeal of these visions or developing clear and appealing counter-ideas. The communication methods of campaigns simply do not encourage illuminating debate and citizen deliberation. Guided by their media advisors, today's candidates must have all the answers boiled down to ten-second slogans. Equally troubling is that the new election process has given individuals the mixed blessing of never having to explain their views to others or having to confront others' ideas in face-to-face settings that might lend elections an important edge of social accountability and responsibility. With the occasional exception of local elections, the old-style campaigning is disappearing: gone are the masses of volunteers posting yard signs and canvassing neighborhoods to explain what candidates stand for. Human contact in today's campaign reflects the strangely impersonal yet highly personalized communication of the electronic age, from computer-generated direct mailings to commercial breaks on favorite TV programs. For all the talk-show frenzy and the advertising blitz, there is little tolerance for others' ideas. There is little time or patience for the careful presentation or hearing of proposals. For all the money spent on communication, there is little attention paid to what it all adds up to beyond pushing voters' emotional hot buttons. Indeed, the preoccupation with hot buttons undermines the chances that elections will build enduring political consensus. The churning communication of contemporary politics takes place in private, from the home communication center, over the fax machine, or on the cellular phone during a freeway commute. For all the personalized communication, the majority can still barely manage to get out and vote.

Certainly, this political scene of the 1990s is a far cry from the American public scene described by the French observer Alexis de Tocqueville a century and a half ago.

The political activity that pervades the United States must be seen in order to be understood. No sooner do you set foot upon American ground than you are stunned by a kind of tumult. . . . To take a hand in the regulation of society, and to discuss it, is his biggest concern, and, so to speak, the only pleasure an American knows.[4]

Until recently, conflicting governing visions have dominated nearly every era of American politics, beginning with the first struggles of the Federalists and Jeffersonians over political rights and the limits of government power in the early years of the Republic. In fact, a sweeping look at American electoral history by a distinguished group of historians and social scientists suggests that struggles over governing visions have characterized most periods in our history, including many with arguably greater claims to social harmony than our own times.[5] Consider just a few of the major governing debates of years past.

Political Ideas in Other Times

With the exception of the brief Era of Good Feelings, the first three decades of the Republic witnessed the rise of the first political parties; struggles over various institutional powers; the nullification crisis and states' rights controversies; conflicts over a national banking and currency system; the rapid settlement of the frontier; struggles against property requirements for voting; and the strains of armed conflicts both abroad and at home. All these crises reverberated through political institutions in the form of great electoral debates and party alignments.

In the next era, a society ready to burst under the pressures of an expanding agrarian frontier and chafing under the dictates of a rapacious Eastern banking establishment elected Andrew Jackson in 1828. That contest marked the rise of the Democratic party, along with the emergence of grass-roots power in a fledgling American democracy. Jackson's reelection in 1832 became a national referendum on his veto of a congressional charter for banking czar Nicholas Biddle's Bank of the United States. The resulting (temporary) setback for paper or "rag" money favored the growth of frontier society with a hard currency or specie economy. These elections addressed some of the most important issues to confront the young Republic in its first half century.

The decades before the Civil War saw the importance of governing ideas grow to the point that parties began holding conventions and hammering out platforms. In 1840, for example, the Democrats forged the first recognizable platform around southern demands for limiting federal government powers. Platforms advocating the ideas that would eventually result in the Civil War were proposed in 1844, 1848, and 1852. The Whigs began responding with formal answers to the Democrats in 1844 and 1852.[6] Meanwhile, national debates on issues as fundamental as slavery, territorial expansion, and economic values drew the attention of the nation. Great rhetorical matches like the Lincoln–Douglas exchanges in the Illinois Senate race of 1858 drew national interest. Voting turnouts were high, and the electoral struggles were intense.

Next came the critical election of 1860, which served as a tortured forum on the problem of slavery. The North–South conflict proved too big for an election to contain, as indicated by the fact that four candidates ran for president in that contest. In effect, there was one race between Lincoln and Douglas in the North and another between Bell and Breckinridge in the South. Lincoln was roundly vilified by the others and by much of the national press as well, being called hatchet-faced, a scoundrel, a "horse swapper," a "nutmeg dealer," and a man fit for petty treason who would spoil the great office for all decent white men to follow.[7] Although he carried the electoral college easily, Lincoln won only 40 percent of the popular vote and had little legitimacy anywhere in the South. Shortly after the electoral college results were announced, South Carolina seceded from the Union, and other states soon followed, whereupon Lincoln made his fateful decision to lead the nation into war. Thus, a new direction was charted for the course of history.

During years of painful reconstruction, the North–South conflict became inscribed in the party system. To complicate matters further, the East–West struggle, long simmering since the Jackson years, came to a head again in 1896. A nation suffering under its first great industrial depression agonized over the nature of complex and wrenching new problems. Was it to be workers against capitalists? Or an agrarian society with a free money economy versus the Eastern establishment led by J. P. Morgan and his cozy banking deals guaranteeing the gold standard? Or was it tariffs against free trade? The Republicans readily settled on tariffs as a quick pitch to industrialists and workers alike. As mentioned in Chapter 4, the slogan "McKinley and a Full Dinner Pail" drew many workers into the Republican camp, particularly in response to the agonizing of the Democrats. After a long and divided convention that failed to agree on the problem that needed to be solved in order to pull the country from the pit of economic stagnation, the words of a young orator from Nebraska captured the moment.

William Jennings Bryan galvanized the Democratic convention with his impassioned speech favoring the free coinage of silver money. He proposed free silver as a platform plank aimed at protecting local economies from the tentacles of big banks. His stirring Cross of Gold speech, as it came to be called, sent the convention into pandemonium. His final words produced a thunderous outburst: "You shall not press down upon the brow of labor this crown of thorns, you shall not crucify mankind upon a cross of gold." Bryan was hoisted on the shoulders of the crowd and paraded around the hall, creating a spectacle that led one eastern delegate to remark, "For the first time, I can understand the scenes of the French revolution."[8]

Bryan was nominated by the Democrats and endorsed by the Populists, even though they feared (correctly, as it turned out) that his nostalgic vision of a rural farm society would drive many rootless urban workers into the arms of the Republicans. At thirty-six, Bryan became the youngest candidate ever to run for president. As tireless as he was eloquent, he whistle-stopped around the country delivering more than 600 campaign speeches (as noted in Chapter 4), but to little avail. His defeat left both the Democrats and the Populists in disorder, paving the way for a Republican-led era of unprecedented industrial expansion. Let us take a brief break to introduce a concept—critical elections—that helps identify what was notable in earlier times and what is strikingly absent in the present era.

Critical Elections and the New Politics

The great political scientist V. O. Key, Jr., coined the term *critical elections* to refer to contests in which national referenda on governing ideas actually changed the course of the governments that followed. Walter Dean Burnham has developed this concept into a framework that makes it easier to see what the new politics is missing.[9] Like the two *critical elections* that came before it, 1896 created the new political conditions necessary to change the course of history and to address growing social strains. The conditions determining critical elections usually include some combination of

- *strong new leadership* (Jackson in 1828, Lincoln in 1860, McKinley in 1896, Roosevelt in 1932),
- *a single party rising to dominate national institutions* (the Republicans in 1860 and 1896, the Democrats after 1828 and 1932),
- and *voter loyalties* lining up behind the leading party for a generation or more (this happened following all of the above elections).

This combination of political forces creates the potential for a system that is all too easily paralyzed by its own checks and balances to take decisive actions.

These solutions are not always heaven-sent, as the Civil War and the later excesses of laissez-faire capitalism suggest, but the point is that they move an unwieldy and conflicted political system beyond a sticking point. A new set of problems often emerges from the solutions to the old. Witness, for example, the legacy of civil rights problems since the Civil War, or the frightening loss of control over big business in the 1920s that ultimately resulted in the Great Depression beginning in 1929. It was in response to that last great social crisis that the holy trinity of political forces (leadership, single-party dominance of government, and realignment of voter loyalties) shifted again, shuffled the political cards, as it were, and issued a "New Deal." The political conditions necessary to move the nation in new directions emerged in the election of 1932. That contest produced the proper mix of leadership (Roosevelt), party dominance (Democrats), and lasting voter loyalties required to forge new policies (the New Deal). The result was an era of decisive government actions to relieve profound social conflicts. As a result, the country managed to emerge from the economic darkness, by way of entry into a second great war, and at the time of Roosevelt's death stepped into the dawn of its preeminence as a world power.

As noted in the last chapter, the shock waves of civil rights and white backlash, the loss in Vietnam, corruption in Washington, and prolonged economic recession all set the stage for Ronald Reagan's vision of social renewal. However, for all the reasons pointed out earlier, the vision failed to generate majority support and ultimately fell apart politically. Although the first condition of governing was satisfied in the presence of strong leadership (Reagan), the other two conditions failed to materialize. First, the required party and ideological dominance of national institutions (particularly Congress) failed to happen. Second, and perhaps more importantly, the shift of voter loyalty and enthusiasm to the Republican camp also failed to take place.

The result was that the 1980s became a transition period to a new brand of politics that had not been seen before in America. With the decline of voter loyalties and the rise of new finance and communication methods, a society with tremendous social strains witnessed the defeat of one governing vision. The society has since endured a string of elections in which no visions or potential governing ideas emerged to arouse—much less capture—the popular imagination. An awkward avoidance of great issues fell upon the land in place of a much needed exchange of ideas. For example, as workers discovered that their new jobs turned out to be lower-paying and less secure than the old ones, candidates for both parties could offer no more than promises of tax cuts in place of discussions about the government's role in a period of radical economic transformation.[10]

The Veto System and the Rise of Minority Rule

To put an even finer point on the recent period, we can say that what has evolved is a succession of governmental flip-flops in which minorities assemble in the electronic public space and defeat the governments installed by the last electronic minority. A number of anomalies surround the post–1980 period. The Reagan mandate of 1980 was delivered by roughly 28 percent of those eligible to vote. The Bush victory of 1988 came on the wings of the smallest electoral turnout in sixty years—a figure that jumps to 164 years, as Burnham notes, when we look at voting patterns in the nonsouthern states where the majority of the people live. All these factors led Burnham to withhold 1980 from the pantheon of great American elections including 1828, 1860, 1896, and 1932.[11] And when we examine the three-way race of 1992, we see that Bill Clinton received the support of just 43 percent of the 54 percent of the eligible voters who turned out to vote. In the voting calculus of the new politics, this makes Clinton not a 43 percent president, but a $.54 \times .43$ or a 23.2 percent president! It is no wonder that Clinton had such trouble drumming up popular pressure behind passage of his agenda. (Or in the language of the new politics, no wonder he had so much trouble defeating the churn of negative opinion that was so easily drummed up by various opponents of his agenda.) And the much-heralded Republican "landslide" of 1994 was produced by a whopping 21 percent of the eligible electorate.

In this era of the 21-percent landslide, elections have become political holding actions until someone with more convincing ideas comes along. Part of the trouble, of course, rests with the extreme personalization of the political process. It is easy in this climate of highly emotional, high-pressure appeals to forget that individuals—even those with good ideas—do not govern. The image of Ross Perot going to Washington and "holding their hands" until the members of Congress could agree on what was best for the country may have been comforting to the psyches of the individuals who voted for him, but it is unlikely to have produced spectacular results from the 535 egos on Capitol Hill, many of whom held Perot in considerable contempt.

We may not be far from a multicandidate presidential free-for-all in which the election of a president is decided not by popular ballot (meaning the electoral college methods of translating popular votes into victories), but by the vote of individual state delegations in the House of Representatives (which is the method prescribed by the Constitution when a majority in the electoral college is not produced). Such a spectacle might well send majorities of Americans in search of a great political reform movement to join!

A Simpler Good Times Argument:
It's the Economy, Stupid!

There is a second, much simpler good times argument to which many political scientists subscribe. This narrow view is backed by an undeniably popular myth. All that voters really care about, according to this myth, is the short-term state of the economy, so there's no point in candidates sticking their necks out about anything else. This is a fascinating proposition because, if true, it means that the money, media, and marketing forces are not so much the causes of our political disarray as the side effects of a sort of political dementia that rests almost entirely with the people themselves. In other words, even though the outcome of an election can be predicted by economic indicators that have nothing to do with the campaign, the American culture puts on the world's most protracted and lavish election spectacle just for the sheer hell of it. While this would make for interesting anthropology, it doesn't do a very good job of explaining recent elections. (Nor does it make political scientists among the most regularly called experts to advise candidates on how to put on campaigns.)

This blunt version of the good times thesis states that all the public wants is a regular paycheck and a stable dollar. Devil take the hindmost and the other issues as well. A typical economic good times analysis of 1988, for example, was delivered in August of that year by a political analyst who looked at short-term economic indicators like unemployment (at 5.3 percent, it was the lowest in fourteen years) and inflation (a respectable 4 percent rise over the preceding year) and pronounced Bush unbeatable on those grounds alone: "If you cranked all this into a computer, it would tell you the Republicans can't lose."[12]

The only problem with this analysis is that it predicted much the same results for 1992, a year in which Mr. Bush lost rather convincingly.[13] One could argue that the Perot "wild card" entry in 1992 threw the beauty of a simple equation into disarray. However, it is also the case that the premise on which the economic theory of voting rests was challenged by the Perot candidacy: knowing that Perot had no chance to win the presidency, the rational voter should have read the economic signs and voted for Bush. Indeed, this is much as George Bush tried to explain it to voters throughout the campaign. Instead, the Clinton campaign used its driving motto "The Economy, Stupid!" to create voter doubts about Bush's much acclaimed recovery, while opening up issue debate on a number of other fronts at the same time. As political scientist Arthur H. Miller and communication scholar Bruce E. Gronbeck put it:

> It has become fashionable among some political scientists to argue that presidential campaigns are irrelevant to election outcomes. . . . These authors suggest that elections are won and lost because of conditions (generally economic) that are in place long before the campaign ever begins. According to these writers economic conditions accurately predict the outcome of elections, and thus candidate images, policy stands, negative ads, campaign strategies, and media coverage of events all have minimal if any effect on the eventual outcome of elections.
>
> Let us assume for the moment that these writers are correct and that macroeconomic factors such as unemployment, inflation, and change in income do determine election outcomes. On the surface this would suggest that Bill Clinton won in 1992 because he followed the dictates of James Carville's campaign sign "The Economy—Stupid!" and focused his campaign message on the economy. But that is not what the mathematical models predicted. On the contrary, the models generally predicted a Bush reelection victory.
>
> After all, George Bush was right: economic conditions, objectively speaking, were not as bad in 1992 as Clinton argued.[14]

New Voters, New Politics, New Economics

This is not to discount the importance of economics over perhaps all other issues to voters. Over the long run, incumbent parties seldom lose the White House when the short-term indicators are up and often lose when they are down. But the unanswered question is "Why?" Is it because that's all the voters care about? Or is it because voters are held hostage by politicians who threaten and promise them with little else than talk of economic well-being? Moreover, in most elections, economic indicators may be among the few issues that people can take seriously. Employment and inflation rates are hard to disguise. People tend to notice the presence or absence of a paycheck, along with its purchasing power. As for promises of balancing the budget or winning the war on crime, these things are, after all, only promises. Why should people put any store in them, particularly when it is widely known that politicians are only saying these things to win votes in the first place? The idea here is that people vote on crude measures of personal well-being because much of the time, they aren't given anything better. Period. Recall here the earlier distinction between *issues* and the more vague category of *problems*. The trouble is that *problems* do not automatically translate into *issues* on which people can make voting decisions. The words of opinion expert Everett Carl Ladd bear repeating here: "But problems aren't necessarily issues. A problem becomes an issue only when voters see the parties differing in their approach to it or their capacity to solve it."[15]

There it is. Since candidates and parties seldom address problems in ways that convince voters they really can or even want to do something to solve them, elections often become vague referendums on "How well are we doing?" Or as Reagan put it in 1980 and again in 1984, "Ask yourself 'Are you better or worse off than you were four years ago?' " This, as noted in Chapter 3, was one voting principle on which Ronald Reagan and most political scientists could agree: lacking other information, people tend to vote retrospectively, that is, by asking whether or not the incumbent president or party has left them better or worse off than they were when they last voted.[16] The important qualification here is that people vote retrospectively not because they prefer it, but because they often have no other choice. Thus, many U.S. elections find the nation of 100 million voters backing cautiously ahead with their eyes fixed squarely behind them.

Yet 1992 was different. And 1994 was a year in which Clinton pronounced the economy in better shape than it had been in a decade, only to suffer massive congressional losses in his party. With three candidates in the race, voters expressed more satisfaction in 1992 than they had in years with the ways in which candidates addressed the issues that mattered to them. For example, of the 43 percent of the voters who said the economy was the most important issue to them, 52 percent voted for Clinton (compared to less than 25 percent for either Bush or Perot). Of the 19 percent who cited health care as the most important issue, fully 67 percent voted for Clinton. And fully 65 percent of those who found family values most important in 1992 voted for Bush. The trouble for Bush was that only 15 percent of the electorate regarded family values as their most important issue.[17]

When people find candidates differing in credible ways, they are prepared to stake voting choices on issues, including the economy, that are defined in campaigns. It also appears, however, that elected governments seem unable to convert those credible promises into policies that convince voters to stay with their choices. Hence we find the repudiation of the Clinton administration just two years later and the swing to a radically different government.

There is a turbulence to the new politics that must be brought into account for these outcomes. Underneath the usual concern for their pocketbooks, Americans seem to be saying that the very ways in which they calculate their economic security have changed with the restructuring of the economy. They seem to be saying that other issues, from health care to violence in the streets, must be factored into the quality of life. Above all, they have been saying that they think the nation is on the wrong course politically, and they are not going to vote on the basis of the old formulas until it appears to be straightening out. Unfortunately, the new style of campaigning makes it hard to hear these messages above the din of propaganda, much less respond to them in credible ways. It remains easier to bribe voters with promises of tax cuts than to engage them in thoughtful discussions of economic restructuring.

THE ISSUES ARE THERE, LAZY VOTERS JUST DON'T SEE THEM

There are really plenty of issues. People just don't pay attention to them. We already know what some in the good times crowd would say: All voters care about in peacetime is whether inflation is down and employment is up. To this the "issues are abundant" school would simply add: Besides, people are busy, and the issues are complex and confusing. Who has time to keep track of them all?

Like the good times thesis, the hidden issues view of elections has its advocates all across the political spectrum, finding support from left, right, and center alike. An entertaining version was put forward by no less a liberal than Nicholas von Hoffman in no less a liberal publication than the *New York Times.* In response to the loud chorus of complaints about Election '88, von Hoffman dismissed the call for good (or at least better) elections as nothing more than the tired hymn of good government idealists, or goo-goos as they have been labeled disdainfully:

> Goo-gooism is Calvinism in politics. The operative word is duty as in civic duty. And duty, to win Brownie points in the great Electoral College in the sky, must be onerous, there being no easy road to salvation. The rubrics of goo-gooism prescribe that no man or woman may vote without having given over many hours of thoughtful study to the issues. In a culture like that of ancient Athens, where politics was a central preoccupation of the minority entitled to vote, this hard standard made sense.

So what happens in a mass culture like ours? Von Hoffman goes on to say that

For the majority, it is red, white and blue balloons and the 30 second sound bites so deprecated by goo-gooists the nation over. The majority must be the generalists, the ones who give a few of the issues a quick study before they check their intuitions, consult their prejudices, cross their fingers and vote.[18]

In a strict sense, there are always statements, platform planks, and position papers that candidates point to as issues. Thus, for example, 1988 saw respectable papers like the *Christian Science Monitor* devoting election-eve overleaf spreads to blow-by-blow candidate comparisons on the issues. In this impressive bit of journalism, identifiable candidate differences were spelled out on no fewer than nineteen issues, and few of the positions were shallow enough to be stated in twenty-five words or less.[19] During the primaries that year, the *New York Times* ran a similar issues scorecard, comparing thirteen candidates on seven key issues, totaling more than ninety issue positions.[20] Moreover, the issue voting patterns reported above for 1992 even suggest that people can be moved to take those candidate positions into account if the conditions are right.

Placing the Blame: The Press?
The Politicians? The Voters?

Perhaps part of the problem with issues in elections is explained by Thomas Patterson, who notes that the number and length of candidate position statements have not diminished in the modern period, but press coverage of issues has. While the press may publish a few of these in issue focus pieces of the sort described above, the overall balance of campaign coverage has shifted. The media have gradually dropped coverage of issues and policies in favor of the personalism and the attacks exchanged by candidates in the media campaign horse race.[21] To properly assess this trend, we need—but do not have—an independent measure of the degree to which campaigns may have increasingly promoted personal attacks and image appeals over the same period. Nor is there an independent measure of the degree to which voters have taken issue coverage less seriously over this same time span. Trends in these two other directions would leave journalists wondering—as many today do wonder—about the point of wasting time covering issues in campaigns if neither candidates nor voters are taking them very seriously.

We are left then with deeper questions about the role of issues and ideas in elections. In a broad sense, the press coverage patterns of issues have clearly changed, as Patterson's impressive data suggest. However, has the growing marginalization of issues in news coverage occurred because the press has decided unilaterally to step into the gutter, or because both the candidates and, however reluctantly, the voters have joined them? Understanding these changes in elections is not a simple either/or proposition but requires taking a combination of factors into account.

Understanding Issues in the New American Election

Recall that the press strategy of the Clinton campaign in 1992 effectively bypassed the news media in favor of staged events and image-shaping through advertising. The reasons why the campaign had to take these strategic turns may have involved the personalization of Clinton's negatives in news accounts, as described in Chapter 3. On the other hand, it is also clear that it was the personalization of Clinton in positive terms through events and ads that made his underlying issue appeals credible for voters. Ross Perot also bypassed the news and managed to explain his views on the budget through lengthy infomercials and chart talks on talk shows. More of those who thought that the budget was the most important issue in 1992 voted for Perot than for either of his two opponents.

At the very least, then, the news may not have helped the communication process in elections, but it is possible for candidates to communicate in other ways with voters about issues. However issue-rich or idea-poor this communication may be, the still larger trouble in both 1988 and 1992 remained simply this: the failure of the elected representatives to complete the circuit with voters by producing credible government actions consistent with whatever images voters used in making their election choices.

The case for acknowledging larger changes in the election process is also strengthened by other notable patterns in the 1988 campaign. As long as the two candidates were debating the issues through a combination of news and advertising, the voters favored Michael Dukakis over George Bush by a wide margin. It was the Bush campaign, driven by the advertising and marketing experts, that made a unilateral decision to "go negative." The decision to pursue the Willie Horton (and prison furlough ad) attacks on Dukakis emerged from the darkest hours of the campaign when the experts, backed up by Bush's dismal showing in the opinion polls, were saying that he couldn't win the election by simply debating Dukakis on the issues.

Thus, it may be too simple to adopt a fixed model of candidates who would prefer to debate issues if the news would only cover them, or of voters who would rather hear a solid policy discussion than a mudslinging episode, or of news media that are chronically averse to covering issues when they are present. Rather, what is more true of the new politics is that campaigns have become distilled into communication strategies aimed at getting individual candidates elected, no matter what the voters want to hear, or how the press want to cover it, or what other members of the candidate's party may be telling their own target audiences.

In the New Politics, Communication Strategy Comes First, Ideas Come Later

Sometimes the communication in these campaigns looks like more serious issue discussion, as it did in 1992, and sometimes it does not, as in 1988 or 1994. In either case, the fragmentation of candidates and voters from parties leaves little hope for government to complete the election–government connection in ways that vindicate and stabilize voter choices leading up to the next election.

So, to respond to the critics, of course candidates will always refer to some things in campaigns as issues, but this does not mean that voters (or the press, for that matter) should immediately pounce on them as the basis for making choices. Perhaps it is more accurate to think of issues, like the other features of election communication these days, as the products of campaign strategies, not the driving forces behind campaigns or candidates. In this sense, the biggest change in the new system of elections is that ideas do not drive the process. Rather, they follow behind, catching stray voters, and do not lead them together into government. Campaigns continue to serve up a daily issue menu, a sort of "conviction du jour," as cartoonist David Wiley Miller characterized it. "Speaking out on the issues" enables candidates to strike leaderly postures, to pontificate, to parade their styles before the voters, and, not least of all, to fill an otherwise embarrassing amount of dead space during our year-long campaigns. Knowing all this at some fundamental, ritualistic level, most people don't have to take the issue posturing seriously just because the candidates are saying all those things with a straight face. Behind the glazed eyes, the voters are not necessarily stupid; they're just dazed.

A classic anthropological fable tells of an anthropologist asking a local informant to explain about the earth and the cosmos. Well, says the informant, the earth sits atop a large bird. And the bird? the anthropologist asks. Ah, the bird stands atop a huge lizard. And the lizard? You see, the lizard rests on the back of an elephant. But the elephant, what does it stand on? A turtle, of course—a large and sturdy turtle. But the turtle? On what does it rest? Ah, my good anthropologist, it's turtles all the way down from there! So, too, with elections these days we might ask about that pledge to keep the economy strong. On what does that rest? On a promise to keep our defenses strong. And the defense issue, what does it stand on? On the appearance of being a good leader, of course. And that appearance, on what does it depend? Ah, there we have a big symbol showing moral superiority over the opponent. And beneath that symbol? Another symbol showing we can take the opponent's symbolic attacks better than he takes ours. And beneath that one? Ah, my good candidate! From there, it's symbols all the way.

IT HAS JUST ALWAYS BEEN LIKE THIS

But that's the way it's always been, and there never was anything more to American elections than that. This is in many ways the most stubborn knee-jerk response to the decline of elections thesis. As this and the last chapter make clear, the elections of the 1980s and 1990s depart in many ways from more typical patterns of the past. Still, it is often said that, historically, elections in America have amounted to little more than symbol-waving and flimflammery. Out of a deep cultural mix of political festival and farce comes the selection of a leader who has withstood the rough-and-tumble of a campaign to emerge victorious as the best of the competition. In this view, the campaign is an elaborate character test, and negative campaigning is simply the custom by which candidates subject each other to withering fire to see who is left standing when the smoke lifts on election day. Central to this perspective is the proposition that eloquence and political vision are rarities in an election campaign.

As indicated earlier, however, the difference in years past is that, in addition to the festivities and familiar posturing, competing social visions have been central to many elections in American history in ways that make today's politics disappointingly empty. It is probably true that eloquence, detailed issues, and inventive rhetoric may be the exceptions rather than the rule in American political campaigns. However, this does not mean that simple words and deeds cannot represent a clear vision or a decisive policy course for the nation to take. A couple of extreme examples will illustrate what I mean here. Neither Andrew Jackson nor Abraham Lincoln uttered a single word in public during their respective elections, yet the voters had little doubt about what these candidates stood for or that the nation would embark on a decisively different course if they were chosen over their opponents.

Neither Lincoln nor Jackson said *anything* in public during their respective election campaigns because for almost the first hundred years of the Republic, it was regarded as unseemly to campaign for oneself.

The practice of candidates touring the country and speaking in their own behalf did not begin until Lincoln's opponent Stephen Douglas did it in 1860—and he was soundly criticized for doing so. This is how an editorial in an Illinois newspaper characterized the outlandish idea: "Douglas is going about peddling his opinions as a tin man peddles his wares. The only excuse for him is that since he is a small man, he has a right to be engaged in small business, and small business it is for a candidate for the Presidency to be strolling around the country begging for votes like a town constable." An Iowa paper chimed in, saying that Douglas "demeans himself as no other candidate ever yet has, who goes about begging, imploring, and beseeching the people to grant him his wish."[22]

As for Lincoln, he stayed at home in Springfield, Illinois, during the convention and during most of the election, vowing not to "write or speak anything upon doctrinal points."[23] The campaigning was left to his seconds who secured the nomination and arranged for local celebrities to make the speeches. A stickler for detail, Lincoln went so far as to cut his own name from his ballot before voting a straight Republican ticket. The point is that Lincoln didn't need to say a word in order for voters to know what his election meant. He was among the most outspoken opponents of slavery in the years before his nomination. Among the nation's most popular speakers, he drew the healthy sum of $200 per appearance. Moreover, he had already publicized his views by debating Douglas in an earlier Illinois Senate race. By campaign time, Lincoln saw no reason not to honor the customary dignified silence of the aspiring candidate. As for Douglas, he faced competition from three sides and decided to risk campaigning for his own election. The point is that there was little doubt about what Lincoln stood for; ideas need not be finely detailed during a campaign in order to be clear and consequential.

In 1832, Andrew Jackson also spoke no words in his political behalf, but he took a political action that spoke louder than words about where the country would go if he were reelected. He opened the presidential campaign in July with a veto of the congressional bill rechartering the Bank of the United States. Mindful of the symbolism, he then retired to his home in Tennessee, the Hermitage, making a show of paying for all his expenses along the way in gold. Ever a popular symbol, the precious metal became known in the campaign as "Jackson money."[24] As for the seconds his managers sent out to speak for him, Jackson doubted the need for them, remarking to a friend that the campaign "will be a walk. If our fellows didn't raise a finger from now on the thing would be just as well done. In fact . . . it's done now."[25]

Campaign Communication Has Changed

These examples show that complex rhetoric and expansive articulation of issues are not required to make an election significant. Neither, of course, is there a taboo on eloquence, as the cases of Woodrow Wilson and Franklin Roosevelt illustrate. What matters is that candidates offer, *by whatever means,* clear alternatives to the voters. This is what makes for meaningful elections: clear alternatives that would send the national destiny in one direction or another, offering voters reasonable hopes of alleviating the strains that plague society. When such an election comes along, people vote in great numbers because they see the alternatives as clear and the consequences as great.

For much of the nation's history, presidential candidates said little in their own behalf because local representatives of the candidates' parties spoke the party positions for them. Moreover, the debates held in these local settings often drew large crowds that listened attentively to the exchanges of ideas. True, there were bands, parades, picnics, and all the other trappings of a major public ritual. While the hoopla may have helped draw the crowds and sustain interest in the campaign, the center of attraction was often the echoing of ideas. With the fragmentation of parties and the rise of electronic communication, ideas have dissolved into more personalized messages delivered more personally by candidates who proudly proclaim that they speak for none other than themselves. As Bruce E. Gronbeck explains it,

> Certainly the most visible and even ordinary activities that comprise a presidential campaign are those generated by candidates and their staffs. . . . this was not always so. For most of America's history, campaigning was a party activity. The assumption was that groups of like-minded *citizens* should articulate sets of ideas and policies (platforms) and then ferret out *representatives* who would further those ideas and seek to enact those policies when victorious at the polls. Such campaigns were viewed as "the largest folk festival in the world" by the nineteenth century—testament to the centrality of the citizen role in electoral politics.
>
> But . . . by the early twentieth century the center of the process had moved; platforms were built as much for particular candidates as for the parties, and soon candidates took responsibilities for constructing many of the major planks in those ideological structures. Franklin Roosevelt, in particular, took over party and campaign structures for his party in 1936 and perhaps was determinatively responsible for the emergence of candidate-centered campaigns. And with the growth of the so-called imperial presidency in the electronic age, the *president* clearly controls the presidency and runs campaigns in most ways independent of party. . . .[26]

What we have in this overview is a gradual transformation of the political process from a party-centered contest of ideas to a highly personalized, candidate-centered battle of images. What remains constant across time are the ritual trappings of celebration, hype, and hoopla—albeit from a more distant electronic remove in recent times. There is no reason why candidates cannot introduce ideas into the process as Roosevelt did in an earlier time and Reagan did more recently. However, with the decline of parties and voter loyalties, and the shift to short-term communication strategies, there is less opportunity for those ideas to generate broad understanding and continued acceptance. The irony of the last great hope for a political realignment is that, for all his rhetorical skills, Reagan did not win large and enduring majorities to his side, much less to his party. Meanwhile, the Democrats proved even less successful at mobilizing popular support for any competing rhetorical vision. Yet both parties succeeded in using the new electoral system to capture one of the branches of government (and then trading branches between 1992 and 1994), giving each party an appreciable power base from which to draw and from which to reward its supporters. At the same time, the electoral methods used to secure power have left both parties lacking the capacity to generate the ideas (and the organizational commitment to them) necessary to govern.

WHAT HAS CHANGED?

The transformations outlined above, though gradual, are also profound. The ways in which elections connect the people with their government are simply different than in earlier times. The reasons have to do with the changes in the broader political system outlined in Chapter 4, as well as the resulting changes in campaigning and political communication noted throughout this book. The recent period of American politics is defined by the following factors that have undermined the citizen–representative–government connection:

- *Power has become personal, for both voters and representatives.* Politically independent voters expect candidates to speak personally to them, and politically independent candidates oblige. Those politicians who win public approval find others flocking to their side. Yet when the approval fades, so fade their influence and their political agendas.
- *Issues have become subordinate to short-term communication strategies.* It is nearly impossible to generalize about the role of issues in today's campaigns simply because issues evolve as small elements in larger communication strategies designed to respond to the daily fluctuations in poll results on which candidates and politicians have come to depend. In

this perverse form of democracy, leaders and followers chase each other in often-wild cycles of approval, favor-seeking, and condemnation.

• *Political communication strategies drive larger governing ideas out of the political process.* Whereas ideas may once have drawn people to parties and guided parties in the selection of leaders to represent them, leaders now announce themselves, and hire marketers to find the messages that will attract people to them (without alienating wealthy political backers). The easiest message is simply to raise doubts about anything that may look like a thoughtful proposal or idea from the opposition.

Thus, it is not relevant when critics say that American politics has never been given over to deep intellectual pursuits. The more important point is that the history of elections has witnessed a wide range of communication styles, some of them achieving rhetorical eloquence and perhaps most of them not. What matters is whether voters find a political vision credible enough to support. Credibility depends not only on capturing the political imagination in words, but also on getting institutions to turn those words into actions. In recent years, neither political parties nor elected leaders have been successful in either endeavor. The result is that America has entered what may turn out to be one of its most challenging decades without governing ideas at its disposal. Running out of ideas is neither a failure of creativity nor a sign that today's problems are unsolvable. Rather, the historical forces described in Chapter 4 have eroded the communication process between leaders and followers, leaving candidates these days with little to say and with few people who want to listen.

CHAPTER 6

The Big Buydown: Media, Money, and Marketing at Work

Elections these days are big business. . . . To win a seat in a state legislature, a big city council or the U.S. Congress these days takes not only an attractive candidate, but a good organization and plenty of advertising. And that takes money. . . .

No one today is surprised that it takes a multi-million dollar effort to run a presidential campaign. But in the four decades since the first "I Like Ike" TV commercials hit the air, the business of political advertising and consulting has penetrated to nearly every level of office-seekers. These professionals don't come cheap, so candidates are spending more and more of their campaign time dialing for dollars, and hawking their talents (and electability) before a never-ending parade of business, labor, and ideological groups that can provide campaign cash. —*Larry Makinson, Center for Responsive Politics*

Prospects for governing ideas and for spontaneous glimpses of candidate character have been reduced by pressure from campaign contributors and have been kept to a minimum through a combination of Madison Avenue-style marketing and media control strategies. This blunt statement may sound harsh, but if there is even a grain of truth in the idea—and this chapter intends to demonstrate more than that—then the shock value of saying it straightaway may motivate the kind of public debate needed to begin the process of reform. The following analysis explains how the system works behind the scenes. Specifically, it details the ways in which money influences what candidates stand for, how campaign consultants construct winning images, and why advertising has replaced news as the citizen's primary information source. Indeed, the replacement of solid journalism with insubstantial advertising images is so important in contemporary politics that we begin by looking at what happened to the press as guardian of the public interest.

THE NEWS MEDIA AS BIG BUSINESS: CLOSING THE MARKETPLACE OF IDEAS

In recent years, there has been growing concern that the all-important marketplace of ideas in American society is becoming monopolized and closed to many viewpoints worthy of public consideration. Ben Bagdikian, former dean of the Journalism School at the University of California at Berkeley, has followed this trend through multiple editions of his appropriately titled book, *The Media Monopoly*. He traces this development to the frightening rate at which the national news and communication media have been monopolized during the merger mania and leveraged buyout craze that has had Wall Street steering the national economy in often crazy directions over the last fifteen years. As of this writing, twenty-three large holding companies own the majority share of the mass communications industry. Many of these companies are oil and defense industry giants with economic interests and image concerns that may not always be conducive to the free flow of ideas. As Bagdikian puts it, "Today, despite more than 25,000 outlets in the United States, twenty-three corporations control most of the business in daily newspapers, magazines, television, books, and motion pictures."[1]

In the newspaper industry, the number of firms controlling the majority of national circulation has shrunk from twenty to eleven in the past decade. In the same period, the twenty companies that once competed for the majority of the magazine market have been gobbled down to two.[2] At the same time, these giant firms are crossing over the traditional media boundaries to buy pieces of every communication form and forum, from books to film, papers, cable channels, video rental outlets, electronic equipment factories, and news production companies that now simply generate raw generic news products for sale and distribution around the world. Imagine, as Bagdikian encourages us to do, that there were 25,000 independent owners of the proliferating media outlets in this nation. Instead of the present handful of owners and business executives who could fit in an average-sized room, there would be many different viewpoints, with different agendas, and more diverse understandings of what information and entertainment products could and should be. Would it be a violation of economic freedom to severely restrict media ownership? Perhaps it would, but it may be an even more serious violation of freedom of information not to do so.

Small media companies committed to traditional journalism and public service norms have been replaced by large conglomerates that have diversified their investments by buying into the media and information sectors of the economy. As a result, the news has become a business much like any other. Journalists are increasingly overworked, underpaid, told not to rock the boat, and encouraged to produce the largest volume of the easiest-to-sell news product.[3] At the very time that more critical discussions of political matters need to be heard, Americans hear less from journalists. With some justification, most citizens regard the press as part of the national political problem.[4] As for becoming informed, people increasingly prefer to hear themselves talk on call-in programs and to have politicians deliver their goods personally to them through commercials.

The link between the ownership of mass communication companies and the content of the news and entertainment they produce is not always direct or, at least, not easily documentable. It is not enough, however, just to point to the media monopoly as a disturbing sign and leave it at that. Whether directly discouraging critical investigative journalism, or indirectly doing so through cutbacks and efficiency measures in news rooms, the result is the same: the journalism that reaches most Americans has a greatly diminished sense of the public interest. Daily newspapers, local television, and the struggling networks all put greater emphasis on personalized, dramatized, and generally sensationalized news content than at any time since the professional press emerged more than three-quarters of a century ago.[5]

Here we begin to see some additional reasons for the patterns of political information cited earlier in the book. Recall from Chapter 1 Thomas Patterson's findings that since 1968 issue coverage has declined, while horse race themes and negative personal attacks on candidates have risen steadily. In addition to the collapse of parties and the emergence of entrepreneurial candidates cited by Patterson, we must acknowledge changes in the news business as a factor in the governing crisis. For the most part, today's news emanates from an industry that produces the lowest cost, least demanding product possible. Thus, for example, a study of the 1994 campaign news content conducted by the Center for Media and Public Affairs found that fully 52 percent of the stories on television network news (CBS, NBC, and ABC) dealt primarily with the horse race. Another 21 percent emphasized candidate character or personal impressions in polls or with voters. Only 11 percent of TV election news addressed stands on issues, and an equally small percentage put the spotlight on the candidates' records.[6]

An earlier study of 1992 election coverage by the same media watchdog group found that the length of candidate sound bites continued its stunning decline, sinking to a record low of 8.4 seconds in 1992, compared to 9.8 seconds in 1988—down from 42.3 seconds in 1968. Perhaps the most distressing news of all for the world of ideas was the finding that in 1992, only 67 out of 1,024 network news stories contained candidate statements that were longer than 20 seconds, and just 19 of those were longer than 30 seconds.[7]

What Politicians Don't Say, the Press Seldom Reports

These trends do not mean that journalists are part of some overt censorship system in which they are conspiring to keep politicians' ideas of substance out of the news. For reasons explained throughout this book, politicians in the new American politics are voicing fewer ideas of real substance that journalists can report. What we are witnessing here, then, is an all-too-convenient silence among politicians, reporters, and the corporate interests that increasingly finance politicians and own the press. News, talk shows, and pundit programs alike are downplaying any detailed analysis of how campaign finance procedures take important issues and ideas out of circulation through pressures on candidates who take interest group money. Even when some candidates do promote ideas, conflicting money pressures wear down the political coalitions needed to convert campaign promises into government action, reinforcing the public's skepticism of the very representatives they have elected.

The problem is so pervasive that journalists may be discouraged from singling out any particular case; after all, everyone is doing it. Even the freshman congressional class of 1992 that came to Washington determined to reform the corrupt money system quickly discovered that taking the money was the easiest way to stay in Washington. Not only did campaign finance reform die another slow death in Congress, but also the freshman class of 1992 set an all-time record for cash intake by first termers.[8] The moral of the story is that they learned the game quickly enough to decide not to change the rules. Would they have so easily abandoned their promise to the voters if the media had kept election reform at the top of the news agenda and turned up the heat on those who made the promise? The reluctance of news organizations to report complex issues or to crusade for the public interest keeps national media attention on such important matters just below the level at which it might make a difference. Thus, the news provides a weak echo of public anger at money in politics with occasional stories and pundits nodding sagely at the problem—all without offering much analysis that points to a clear solution. Captivated by drama and scandal, and led to most stories by politicians themselves, journalists seldom hold the promises of elected officials to the fire of public scrutiny long enough to motivate those representatives to find serious solutions.

What Would Serious News Coverage Look Like?

Enough public interest research groups and think tanks are studying money and power in Washington that it would not take more than a phone call or two for an enterprising reporter to tell the story. Indeed, Larry Makinson, the research director at the Center for Responsive Politics in Washington, has provided journalists with a "how to" book called *Follow the Money,* in which fully one-third of the pages are devoted to step-by-step tracking procedures available to anyone with a computer. The procedures are applicable right down to local campaigns. The book even contains a section called "Reporting the Story."[9]

For journalists whose habitual resort to the horse race and personality plot formulas may have left them imagination-impaired, the newsletter of the Center for Responsive Politics has even published a blueprint of what a media campaign on money in politics might look like. Imagine, say authors Jeff Cohen and Norman Solomon, that the media took the money issue as seriously as they take crime or the drug problem. We might see NBC's Tom Brokaw running a weekly (or even nightly) feature on "greedlock" in Washington, with stories on how agribusiness interests defeated nutritional ingredient labeling on food products, aided by contributions to named members of key congressional committees. The Sunday pundits would explain the methods of key players in the Washington power game. Lobby-czar Tommy Boggs, for one, has computer programs that match client donations to congressional committee members at times when key legislation is beginning to move through their committees. Or reporters could be assigned to follow the donations patterns of a captain of industry such as Dwayne Andreas, chair of the Archer-Daniels-Midland grain company. Andreas secured favorable environmental rulings from the Bush administration at the small price of just over $1 million in soft money (see p. 136) donations to the Republican party; he kept his insurance premium paid up by giving over $250,000 to the Democrats in the 1992 election—just in case Bill Clinton won. And what about a news roundtable program on how General Electric helped write a corporate tax law that reduced its taxes to zero?

All of these stories would be interesting and dramatic for many of those who now tune out the news as being unworthy of their time or attention. With audience interest piqued, journalists might even introduce expert views on just what kinds of reforms would solve these problems.[10]

Since this is clearly not the kind of political reporting available in the mainstream news media, some systematic reason must explain why such media crusades in the public interest remain fantasies. Let us now look at one more example of the media breakdown suggesting that the news media are not on the outside of the new American politics looking in. On the contrary, they sit squarely inside the new power system that most Americans would like their elected representatives to change.

The News Scandal You Didn't See: Who Stole Health Care Reform?

There are many ways in which the press tacitly reinforces the growing distortions between power and representation in the new American politics. Consider, for example, coverage of the defeat of health care reform on the eve of the 1994 election. First, the defeat was reported largely as a failure of political parties, particularly the Democrats, to deliver on their promises of reform to the American people. Second, and more importantly, most of those stories failed to emphasize the uneasy reason why those political promises to the voters were not kept: because politicians were keeping their promises to the health care industry interests that were paying the costs of their reelection campaigns. The various interests who competed to defeat key provisions of every coherent reform proposal spent more money in their efforts than any presidential candidate spent trying to get elected in 1992! This stunning fact did not stop the politicians who appeared in the news during the health care battle, and, shortly afterward as candidates in the election, from presenting their various irreconcilable positions as being in the best interests of the American people. Meanwhile, journalists continued to report the surface of the story: gridlock, party infighting, and the personal defeat of Bill Clinton. It is as though the rest—and by far the most important part—of the story could not be reported until members of Congress stepped forward and confessed their personal conflicts of interest. Yet it is hardly surprising that politicians do not come forward and say things like

- "Hi, I'm Dave Durenburger, Republican senator from Minnesota, and I took a record eleven trips paid for by health care interests in order to help me think more clearly about the public interest on health care."[11]
- "Hello, I'm Pat Schroeder, Democratic representative from Colorado, and I placed second with ten trips paid for by other health care interests to help me see their side of things more clearly."[12]
- "My name is Tom Daschle, Democratic senator from South Dakota, and I took over $400,000 in campaign contributions from health care interests alone, and that was just between 1991 and 1992. Like many of my

colleagues on the Senate Finance Committee, this really helped my thinking about how to pay for health reform."[13]
- "My name is Jim McCrery, Republican representative from Louisiana, and I accepted more than $65,000 in health industry money on the House Ways and Means Committee. I can't wait for the even larger amounts that will come my way now that we are in the majority. Surely this will help me see the national interest on health care even more clearly."[14]

Politicians do not say such things because it would be politically suicidal for them to do so. However, the journalists who report on campaigns could say these things about candidates and sharpen the focus of issue coverage in the process. As with the more general patterns of money in politics discussed earlier, facts about the health care money taken by key members of congressional health care committees were available well in advance of the 1994 elections, yet few of them worked their way into news reports on particular races. For example, the Center for Public Integrity released a study to help reporters cover this most important issue. Among the many rich findings in the 200-page report was this:

The Center for Public Integrity has found that during 1992 and 1993, members of Congress were busy traveling across the United States and even abroad at the expense of the health care industry. Over 85 members of Congress participated in 181 trips sponsored by the health care industry to 73 cities in the United States, as well as San Juan, Puerto Rico; Paris, France; Montego Bay, Jamaica; and Toronto, Canada. Of those trips, half were to the popular vacation destinations of California and Florida. Members brought their spouses on 73 of these trips.
   The largest trip giver, by far, was the American Medical Association, which sponsored 55 trips in two years. According to the AMA, these trips were held primarily to "educate" members on health care issues.[15]

Although this report received some general play in the few days after it was released, few journalists utilized it as the basis for sustained coverage of individual political races. Indeed, with reporters cranking out the formula story of the campaign horse race more than 52 percent of the time, there was little room left for issues, much less investigation into how particular candidates' stands on those issues reflected the preferences of their financial backers. That is a political can of worms that politicians and their backers, together with journalists and their corporate owners, would prefer not to open for all to see in the news. Unfortunately, when people find the news to be of little use in their final voting decisions, they have nowhere to turn but to campaign ads and candidate appearances on talk shows. It is ironic that people find these controlled political communication experiences to be more useful than news.

What Happened to Public Interest Reporting?

The question of what happened to the press's responsibility to the public requires us to examine several factors. Communication scholar Robert McChesney suggests that we begin our inquiry by reviewing the decisions politicians made during the 1930s to give away most of the public airwaves freely to private corporations to use for profits, with only small and underfunded space allocated for public broadcasting organizations that would be free of commercial pressures.[16] (The political attack on public broadcasting has continued with renewed vigor following the Republican ascendancy in Congress.) After the critical policy decisions of the 1930s, the next fifty years saw the increasing weakening of the few regulations placed on broadcasters, with the result that less obligation was imposed on the press to present informational programming and competing points of view. The final factor in this mix was the recent buyout of the nation's media by distant corporate conglomerates with primary loyalties to shareholders, together with executive-level doubts that serving the public interest makes sense either economically or politically.[17]

Thus it was that news organizations had little incentive to engage in critical, enterprising, or investigative reporting. Fading from the nation's memory is the spirit of public interest journalism. Even worse, at a time when angry citizens are short on good explanations for their anger, critical journalism has been smeared with the "liberal" label by the very interests that least want to have their political dealings exposed in the press. Replacing the vanishing ideal of a watchdog press is an evolving industry norm that might be called "presumed democracy." This everyday working agreement between press and politicians can be stated simply as follows: Elected officials are presumed to represent the broad public interest, and if for some reason they don't, it is, after all, a free country in which disgruntled citizens have no complaint. They are free to elect representatives they like better. In effect, this assumption allows politicians to set the daily tone of most of the news: scandals, policy debates, election campaigns, and all. The trouble with presumed democracy is that it is too simple to be true. This course of least resistance for news organizations favors government-issued news, which is more efficient, easily gathered, standardized, and less subject to politicians' charges of press bias.[18] In the process, the resulting news downplays the new power system in Washington. Press scandals involve the personal foibles of politicians, not their debts to narrow interests. This information system makes it difficult for independent-minded leaders to enter politics in the first place. And if they do get in, the same system makes it difficult to promote the new ideas that got them there.

In the end, the convenient working relations between reporters and officials overlook the key question that any democracy must face: *Who Will Tell the People?* Reporter William Greider, who wrote a book with that title, concluded that in present-day America, neither journalists nor politicians can be relied upon to tell the people just what has gone wrong.[19] In the current information system, many citizens rely on talk show diatribes and campaign commercials to figure out what has gone wrong. For example, people may hear that money has corrupted the system, but they are unlikely to hear how the campaign finance process works, which makes it difficult to think about workable solutions for the money problem.

MONEY, MONEY, MONEY

"I've raised millions upon millions for the Democratic Party and I've never seen this happen," said [M. Larry] Lawrence. The 61-year-old chairman of the fashionable Hotel del Coronado in Coronado, California, donated $100,000 of his own to the Democrats in the primaries, and has pledged to raise an additional $1 million for the general election. "We're raising money like it's going out of style. It's beyond comprehension. It's gorgeous. It's so exciting."[20]

In at least one respect, this wealthy businessman and long-time Democratic fundraiser was right: "It's beyond comprehension." Creative interpretations of the Federal Election Campaign Act have showered more money than ever before on the nation's politicians. More importantly, there are now so many points of entry and uses for these huge sums that it becomes difficult to fathom the total effect. In this section, we explore the combined effects of three important money channels into the political process.

- Soft money: The great loophole in campaign finance reform law allows unlimited donations to political party organizations (with a wink) as long as those funds are not placed in the budget of any particular candidate's campaign. These staggering sums are to be used for general party-building activities, such as get-out-the-vote efforts, polling, and state campaign coordinating operations (all of which, of course, can be conducted with an eye to particular presidential or congressional candidates).

- PACs, of course: Although individual contributors still make up the majority of funds raised in elections (an estimated 55 percent of all national campaign income in 1992), PACs deliver a hefty and predictable base on which politicians come to depend (32 percent of total money in 1992 and 42 percent of the winners' campaign budgets).[21] More importantly, PAC money is targeted to particular members of Congress and to the legislation they are encouraged to sponsor or defeat, making PAC money the greatest lobbying tool ever invented.
- Personal wealth: The costs of the election game have soared to the point that American politics is becoming the exclusive playing field of the rich—perhaps more so than at any time since the Gilded Age of the robber barons a century ago. Congressional candidates who can finance large parts of their campaigns by writing personal checks have an edge on those who simply try to break into politics because they have ideas about how to make the system work better. Personal wealth also operates prominently behind the scenes as candidates line up the wealthy backers needed to get their campaigns started and to keep them going in the crucial late stages. Repayment of these personal debts may range from ambassadorships to favorable policies affecting backers' industries.

These money flows operate differently in congressional and presidential politics, as shown in the following sections.

Padding the Presidency

Today soft money contributions to candidates' parties commonly rival the amounts raised by the campaigns themselves, even with the public matching money offered to qualifying candidates. The point of public funding, of course, was to equalize the competition and keep spending within reason. According to one expert, the soft money frenzy drove costs of presidential campaigning to $500 million in 1988, up from $325 million in 1984.[22] Estimates for the presidency topped $600 million in 1992 (helped, of course, by third candidate Ross Perot who spent more than $60 million of his personal fortune to run). Nowadays, the paltry $100 million or so given in federal funding to the candidates is dwarfed by the soft money escalation. The limit on how much the candidates can accept from their parties (under $10 million in the last two presidential elections) if they "voluntarily" take public funding has become a joke.

These soft money bank accounts can be spent on a wide array of vote-getting activities as long as the candidate's name is not specifically mentioned. Thus, soft money can be used for voter registration, get-out-the-vote drives, primary and caucus politicking, the conventions (now costing tens of millions), alliances between candidates and state and local party organizations, and on and on. Indeed, if the money game is played well, as it was by Reagan in 1980 and 1984, Bush in 1988, and Clinton in 1992, there is no need to spend all that soft money on specific name-identification advertising. The money ties can end up personalizing the entire party structure. As the price of such personalized presidential politics, various issues that once gave substance to party platforms may well be auctioned off. As we will see shortly, an even more personalized and fragmented money system has emerged in Congress in the form of members' personal PACs (or "leadership PACs" as they are known euphemistically).

Following the Money Trail

As noted in Chapter 4, the Democrats learned to play the money game in the mid-1980s, when they caught up with and then passed the Republicans in congressional wealth and ran close to and sometimes ahead of the GOP in the presidential money race. For example, at the presidential level in 1984, the national party campaign was deeply in debt going into the months just before the election. By 1988, the Democratic soft funds easily exceeded the amounts of hard money provided by federal funding. This fact led Bush's chief fundraiser, Robert A. Mosbacher, Jr. (later rewarded with a cabinet post), to remark, probably with tongue in cheek: "The Democrats are saying they're going for the big money. And I don't think there's much we can do about it but match them."[23]

Mosbacher had the plan to do it: the Team 100 club. The membership fee was merely 100 (thousand) dollars to the Republican National Committee (the soft money holding company for the Bush campaign). *Common Cause Magazine* called Mosbacher's Team 100 a veritable who's who of American business:

> The $100,000 contributors include 66 in the investment and banking community, 58 in real estate and construction, another 17 in the oil industry, and 15 from food and agriculture. Team 100 also includes members from the entertainment, cable, insurance, steel and auto industries.
>
> Almost across the board, Team 100 members or the companies they are associated with want something from the government—whether it's broad policy initiatives like Bush's proposed reduction in the capital gains tax or favors more specific to a company or industry. Many gave their $100,000 at a time when they had significant business or regulatory matters pending with the federal government—or knew they likely would under the Bush administration.[24]

Once these donors were on the team, they kept on giving, to the tune of $25,000 a year between elections and another $100,000 in 1992. Thus, each Team 100 member signed checks totaling at least $275,000 for the two Bush elections.[25] Meanwhile, the Democrats weren't doing too badly either. Although slowed somewhat in 1988 by Dukakis's reluctance to solicit corporate funds, the state parties finally decided to join the money fest. At one point, the California party chairman boasted that the state campaign was being financed by "every big California corporation you can think of."[26]

These backers (wealthy business elites, groups of executives from particular industries, rich individuals who seek political appointments) place bets on candidates likely to do them favors if they are elected. Since incumbents have an election edge, the flow of money follows the winners. Thus, when Bush lost and Clinton won in 1992, the soft money flowed to the Democrats. Bill Clinton's answer to Team 100 was even grander. The Democratic party elite club was called the Managing Trustees, and its members gave or raised over $200,000 each for the privilege of joining.[27] This grand financial scheme came from the same president who pledged on the night of his election "to reform the political system, to reduce the influence of special interests."[28] Like the Republicans who had won the money game before him, the politician newly crowned "king and protector" of the money system by Common Cause president Fred Wertheimer pointed to his opponents as the reason for playing the soft money game with a vengeance. Clinton said that he could not "disarm unilaterally" when the Republicans were out there playing by the old rules. Mastering the line heard by leading figures of both parties, Clinton advisor George Stephanopoulos explained that "The President has called for real reform. When the reform has passed, he will live under the rules."[29]

During the Republican soft money heyday from 1991 to 1992, the top soft money donors were: Archer-Daniels-Midland ($1.1 million); American Financial Corporation ($715,000); International Marketing Bureau ($633,770); Philip Morris ($589,000); Atlantic Richfield ($579,000); and RJR Nabisco ($529,000).[30] When the money flow favored the Democrats from 1993 to 1994, the top soft money sources (based on incomplete figures through June of 1994) were Beneficial Management Corporation ($397,250); Archer-Daniels-Midland ($261,500); American Financial Corporation ($250,000); Atlantic Richfield ($240,500); and the National Education Association ($239,000).

Although many big donors obviously hope their checks will get the attention of candidates, party fundraisers walk (and talk) a fine legal line, claiming that these generous souls and corporations are simply overwhelmed with party loyalty. There are several reasons to be skeptical of such assurances. Many signs point to soft money as little more than a quasi-legal laundering operation for individual candidates. First, the parties are often so personalized around a particular candidate's politics (and political staff) that giving to the party amounts to giving to the presidential campaign. Second, the key soft money fundraisers are usually insiders in the candidate's campaign. Third, and most importantly, national campaign strategy for candidates ends up being calculated around how to divide up the hard and soft money expenses. In practice, the "ground war" (registration, get-out-the-vote drives, etc.) in a campaign is waged primarily with soft money—money that individual campaigns otherwise would have to spend. Diverting most of the soft money to ground-war activities allows candidates to spend more of their personal campaign accounts on the "air war." This blatant calculation of soft money into campaign strategy drives up the budgets for advertising and marketing, and leads candidates to rely increasingly on the air war as the heart of the campaign.[31]

Cashing In on Congress

The most glaring fact about money on Capitol Hill is that more of it pours in every year. The most visible source is PAC funding, which escalated from $55 million in 1980 to a record of more than $169 million in 1994, with the vast majority each year going to incumbents.[32] The figures for PAC contributions to congressional candidates during this period are as follows.

1980	55.3 million
1982	83.6 million
1984	105.3 million
1986	130.0 million
1988	150.0 million
1990	150.0 million
1992	161.9 million
1994	169.5 million

As described in Chapter 4, the deluge of PAC money allows incumbents to keep their seats by greatly outspending their opponents (by a 2 to 1 margin in the Senate and a 3.5 to 1 margin in the House in recent elections). So many interests now walk the halls of Congress that money is handed out even to those legislators who may not vote the right way. A director of a business PAC described this goodwill strategy in these terms: "First, you get to everyone on Ways and Means whether they're for you or against you. Secondly, there's a presumption that we look seriously into giving to incumbents where we have a major facility unless the guy has gone out of his way to urinate on us. And we give money to guys where we have major facilities who vote against us nine times out of ten."[33]

The PAC deluge has atomized Congress. In a column pointing out the broad bipartisan agreement with this assessment, David Broder quoted a former member of the House as saying that Congress "is a rudderless ship, that its members are squabbling all the time and that they are afraid to bite any bullets or make any hard choices."[34] Broder's recommendation, passed along from a number of former solons, is to sweep out the cash. It will take a lot of sweeping because the cash is not delivered solely in the PAC bundles discussed so far.

Freebies and Fringe Benefits

In addition to the rain of PAC dollars, members of Congress have to cope with another temptation created by their special interest clients: favors and other considerations such as the free trips showered on key players in the health care reform fiasco of 1994. This "ethics swamp" has swallowed one representative after another in recent years. The political treats they are given—the breakfast clubs, party boats, golf trips, book publishing deals, and the like—have become so routine that many representatives seem unaware of their corrupting influences. For example, one of the loudest critics of the savings-and-loan scandal that rocked the economy at the close of the 1980s, and still consumes millions of taxpayers' dollars in an ongoing industry bailout, was Massachusetts Senator John Kerry. While lashing out at S&L kingpins who stole the nation's savings accounts, Kerry turned out to be a frequent guest of one of those kingpins. According to a *Wall Street Journal* report, one of the S&L operators charged with egregious misuse of over $30 million of his bank's funds was David Paul, the man named by Senator Kerry to chair the Democratic Senatorial Campaign Committee Majority Trust campaign fund. In addition to giving more than $300,000 of his own money to Senate campaigns, Paul personally hosted Senator Kerry a number of times, including several trips on his private jet. At one particularly memorable dinner in Miami, Senator Kerry and the other guests were treated to a meal prepared by six chefs flown in from France, a ten-piece orchestra, and caviar, all of which added up to a check for $129,000 picked up by Paul. Although several news reports had surfaced on Paul's growing legal problems by that time, Senator Kerry saw nothing amiss with the dinner, which he thought was a charity affair. "Who could know?" he asked. "In life there are some people who turn out to be bad apples."[35]

And then there was the $4.5 million book advance accepted by first-time suspense novelist Newt Gingrich. Following his ascension to power in the Republican landslide of 1994, Gingrich met with media mogul Rupert Murdoch, who faced critical regulatory problems with his Fox television network, and also happened to own the publishing company that offered Gingrich the Stephen King-sized advance. Both parties denied any conflict of interest in the dealing. Gingrich decided not to accept the money only after Senate leader Robert Dole joined other Republicans in raising questions about the propriety of such a move following an election in which the Republicans promised to clean up the mess in Washington. While decrying abuses by others, politicians have found ever more creative ways to block meaningful ethics and lobbying reform legislation.

Capitol Hill Potentates: The Personal PAC System

With so much money flowing so freely around them, many members of Congress have more than they really need to win elections. Some of the serious players have opened up special money funds that they use to spread their influence more broadly in Congress and in their parties. These so-called leadership PACs allow established politicians to offer money and management services to build bases of influence with less secure candidates for Congress, and state and local offices as well.

These elected fat cats, as political scientist Ross Baker has dubbed them, reward and punish their colleagues as party power brokers did in the old days.[36] The competition to rule the roost in Congress is stiff, with some forty-two members of Congress having their own PACs during the 1991–1992 election cycle. (The number of leadership PACs is sixty-two if one counts those still run by former members of Congress who remain active in national politics.) None of these PACs is called by the name of its owner, of course: the Robert C. Byrd PAC is known as the Committee for America's Future; Jesse Helms presides over the National Congressional Club; Newt Gingrich controls the purse strings of GOPAC; and so on. Behind the noble names are large reserves of dollars that multiply the divisions of the PAC system as a whole, splitting Congress internally and further undermining the traditional role of parties and party leadership. In the 1991–1992 election period, Robert Dole's Campaign America distributed over $388,000 to Republican candidates.[37]

The Gingrich operation, GOPAC, is the model for a new generation of leadership PACs. Instead of winning friends on the Hill with cash donations, Gingrich helped engineer the entire Republican congressional campaign of 1994 by hiring centralized campaign consultants (who produced the Contract with America, for example) and donating campaign strategy and management services to state campaigns. Just 1 percent of GOPAC spending was in the form of cash contributions, while fully 24 percent went to political consultants retained by the PAC. The dozen full-time employees of GOPAC spend its $2 million annual budget mailing out training tapes to grass-roots candidates and running campaign management seminars that show candidates how to raise money, develop campaign strategies, hire consultants, manage budgets, and master the art of the sound bite.[38]

Despite being an open critic of Washington insider politics, Gingrich refuses to disclose his original backers, saying only that future donors to the $10,000 "charter member" club may be named. In fending off requests for lists of contributors, PAC officials have cited a loophole in reporting requirements, claiming that only contributors to federal election campaigns must be identified. Since GOPAC claims to spend 90 percent of its budget on state and local races, it disclosed a selected list of only 10 percent of its donors. In addition to avoiding the disclosure of backers, the state and local strategy personalizes the Republican grass roots around Gingrich, preparing his national presidential base when he decides to make a bid for the White House.

Personal Wealth

Add to these money forces the increasing leverage of individuals who can write big political checks. Michael Huffington nearly bought a California Senate seat in 1994, spending almost $30 million, much of it from his own personal fortune. His opponent, Dianne Feinstein, also went to her own substantial bank account to run a competitive campaign. The Massachusetts Senate race featured two financial heavyweights as well, Ted Kennedy and Mitt Romney, whose personal fortunes fueled expensive media campaigns. The list of rich candidates grows longer each year, from Ross Perot funding his own national movement to Herb Kohl in Wisconsin and the Bush brothers in Florida and Texas.

According to one estimate on the eve of the 1994 election, "millionaires are at least 30 times more common on Capitol Hill than in American society."[39] The infusion of personal wealth in campaigns to buy seats on the nation's political governing board has escalated dramatically over the last several elections, from less than $25 million in 1990 to $54.4 million in 1992, and more than $100 million in 1994.[40] It is unlikely that sweeping political reforms will come from a class of elected officials who began their careers making huge profits from the economic system and ended up taking seats in the governing bodies that regulate that economic system, write the tax laws, and determine the rules for winning public office. Even if such legislators passed laws changing minor aspects of the election system, would they ever think of placing fundamental limits on private spending in politics or shifting to a public funding system, knowing that their own political advantages would be eliminated in the process?

Where the Money Goes: Spending Patterns

Money from all of these sources, along with the all-important small contributions raised in sophisticated direct mail appeals, goes to pay for the huge costs of running campaigns. In 1992, for example, the average incumbent in the House spent more than $571,000 in campaigning for reelection (compared to an average of just $173,000 spent by House challengers), while the average Senate incumbent spent over $4.1 million (compared to just over $1.9 million by Senate challengers). According to preliminary Federal Election Commission reports, the challenger-to-incumbent gap narrowed in 1994, as Republicans ran more well-funded campaigns against incumbent Democrats than ever before.[41] The favorable Republican results add more weight to the first principles of the new American politics: (1) the more money invested in campaigns, the greater the chances of winning, and (2) political backers invest their money in parties and candidates that look like winners.

How is the money allocated? Below is a fairly typical budget for a Senate campaign. These expenses were not for an incumbent's campaign but for a challenge by Harriet Woods of Missouri, who raised enough money to put on a credible, though losing, campaign in 1986.[42] Though somewhat dated, this profile of income and expenses remains fairly typical of today's Senate contests. Perhaps its model qualities help explain why Harriet Woods went on to head up EMILY's list (for: Early Money Is Like Yeast), a finance operation for women candidates.

Sources of Money		*Expense Breakdown*	
Individuals in Missouri	$1,150,000	TV time & ad production	$2,550,000
Individuals outside Missouri	600,000	Polling	200,000
Direct mail & phone solicitation	1,200,000	Staff & operations	875,000

"Bundling" (outside groups collecting individual money)	$300,000	Fundraising costs	$775,000
Political action committee	800,000		
Democratic party funds	350,000		
TOTALS	$4,400,000		$4,400,000

In the 1992 House races, incumbents spent an average of 30 percent of their budgets on polling and electronic advertising alone, with the marketing figure going over 42 percent once mail advertising is factored in and jumping to nearly 60 percent when the costs of telemarketing and fundraising are included.[43] Senate campaigns (by incumbents) begin at over 43 percent spent on just polling and electronic advertising, with an increase to 46 percent with mail advertising included; over 66 percent of the average budget is accounted for when fundraising costs are added.[44] Thus, raising money and spending it on candidate marketing consume over 60 percent of campaign costs in both House and Senate races.

The other major cost of campaigning is the often vague category of "overhead," which includes rent for offices, salaries of campaign consultants and staff, and daily expenses. Campaign analysts explain the soaring overhead costs in elections as indicators that the campaign never stops. Incumbents now wage what Dwight Morris and Murielle Gamache call the "permanent campaign," with full-time staff, fundraising activities, and polling that helps politicians calculate their actions in office against the reactions of potential voters in future elections. Incumbent senators now spend an average of more than $500,000 on overhead, with New York's Alfonse D'Amato claiming the title of king of the permanent campaign by spending nearly $4 million in overhead to keep his campaign organization up and running all the time. In the House, Dick Gephardt of Missouri reported that fully 53 percent of his budget went to a combination of overhead and fundraising costs. It is no wonder that the average senator had to raise $14,000 every week of his or her elected term in office, while the typical representative looked at a $5,000 weekly fundraising obligation.[45]

Running for office, whether on the executive or legislative level, leads candidates into the world of high finance and special interest temptations. Money, not ideas, has become the greatest challenge and obstacle to national leadership. Since there are differing views on how the competition for money affects the production of ideas in Washington, it is worth considering the leading theories carefully.

Two Theories about How Money Affects Politics

The money system has atomized the nation's leadership, eroded the party system, and turned elections into just another part of a grand veto system, eliminating new governing ideas as quickly as they begin to develop. This view is expressed in David Broder's image of the rudderless ship cited earlier. It is stated cogently in the conclusion of Ross Baker's study of "The New (Congressional) Fat Cats":

> PACs generally absorb money that has traditionally gone to political parties. More important, perhaps, PACs also absorbed much of the energy of those who formerly worked through the parties to influence public policy. If parties with their comprehensive agendas designed to appeal to the broadest segments of the population stand at one end of the spectrum, PACs with their narrow focus tailored to appeal only to those with a special interest stand at the other. PACs have, by their very nature, a fragmenting effect on politics. They enable groups with narrow interests to contribute money to politicians who have single-issue agendas. Members of Congress are held to no overall philosophical account by most PACs. And PACs lavish on legislators the money needed to win campaigns at a time [of soaring campaign costs].[46]

The fragmenting influences of money are multiplied many times over when this influence of PACs is compounded by special favors, the divisiveness of leadership funds, the covert uses of soft money, and the pressures of wealthy individual backers. One significant consequence of this fragmentation of party power, of course, is the vastly diminished production of governing ideas around which leaders and citizens can develop or sustain mutual commitments.

Contrasted with this view is another thesis that states the case somewhat differently: The American parties still represent coherent ideas, but they are ideologically conservative ones that appeal only to a minority of voters, leaving the silenced majority without representation or leadership. In this view, attracting the big money required to win elections has thrown the whole electoral process into the hands of moneyed interests who have exacted a right turn in the flow of public debate as the price for their contributions. As with the fragmentation thesis, the trouble here also begins with money. But in this view political campaigns can be regarded as investment opportunities for more ideologically organized financial interests—perhaps one of the best investments around. As political scientist Thomas Ferguson and sociologist Joel Rogers' investment theory of elections explains it, the traditional party conflict during the first half of the century between multinational corporate interests (the old Democratic backers) and domestic manufacturers (the old Republican money) has been resolved, more or less, over the last few decades.[47] The multinationals are the big players in the election game today, which means that they don't need the Democratic party to fight their old free trade and nonisolationist foreign policy battles against the Republicans. (Witness, for example, the strong bipartisan support for recent trade agreements such as NAFTA and the latest round of GATT.) The Republicans have come around to the free trade position so completely that the Democrats now must make increasingly large concessions, selling out the interests of their traditional labor and social constituents just to compete for money they once attracted with relatively little effort.

Despite a clear market of voters who are responsive to jobs programs, more favorable labor and minimum wage laws, health protection, environmental actions, budget cuts in defense, and a whole range of other issues, the Democrats have rolled over and played these issues in much the same way as the Republicans. In 1984, Walter Mondale became the first Democrat in modern times to run for office without a jobs program. He proposed a tax increase, but he offered no program of national revitalization to justify the extraction of money from weary taxpayers. In 1988, Dukakis turned his back on the party's traditional constituency of black voters after Jesse Jackson went to the trouble of bringing large numbers of them to the polling place door. In that same year, Dukakis took a weaker environmental program to the voters than did Bush, and neither candidate said anything harsh about corporate polluters, who just happened to be paying the campaign bills. In 1992, Bill Clinton also ignored the African-American vote and aimed his entire campaign at the middle class, while neglecting the traditional Democratic blocs of labor and the poor. While he did offer a jobs program, it was to retrain workers thrown into unemployment by multinational corporations moving manufacturing operations offshore—a development that Clinton accepted without question. Clinton's buildup to the 1996 campaign featured a "Middle Class Bill of Rights," suggesting that the neglect of the party's left wing would continue.

Can these and a long list of other Democratic right turns be attributed to a rising conservative tide among voters? To the contrary, say Ferguson and Rogers, many government programs on the chopping block ever since the Reagan revolution would have been spared the ax if left to the voters' decision. At critical moments when cuts were made, sizable opinion margins favored holding the line on environmental regulation (49 to 28 percent), industrial safety (66 to 18 percent), teenage minimum wage (58 to 29 percent), auto emission and safety standards (59 to 29 percent), federal lands policies (43 to 27 percent), and offshore oil drilling restrictions (46 to 29 percent), among others.[48] Yet government retrenchments in these and dozens of other areas were made with barely a whimper from the Democrats, and virtually no effort was made to rally this opinion in subsequent elections.

The right-turn thesis argues that popular anger at "corporate welfare" from the government could be turned into votes by the Democrats if the party could afford to turn its back on big corporate contributors. For more than two decades, polls have shown a growing public outrage at the favoritism granted to the corporate sector.[49] The most revealing statistic of all is the percentage of people who believe that the government is run for the benefit of a few big interests at the expense of the public interest: the figure grew from less than one-quarter of the public in the rosy days of the 1950s to fully three-quarters by the mid-1990s.[50]

According to this view, then, it seems that the Democrats are a party on the run—on the run from their own voters! As recently as the 1994 congressional elections, Thomas Ferguson pointed to a sudden money flow away from the Democrats, creating a communication whiplash in their campaign. Democratic candidates ran scared in the money race and ended up emulating Republicans, whose Contract with America promoted a minority view that "government should leave people alone to solve their own problems." The result, argues Ferguson, is that the Republican "landslide" of 1994 was produced by a mere 21 percent of the eligible electorate.[51] The voters needed to boost the Democratic totals simply stayed home because their party offered few appealing ideas.

The Ferguson and Rogers right-turn thesis is a provocative way of thinking about what has happened to American politics. However, there are several troublesome points that seem inconsistent with other trends on the national political scene. To begin with, the stubborn plurality of independent voters suggests that no existing ideological program is likely to attract majority voter support. Whether the Democrats return to their old liberal agenda or whether they articulate the new Democratic agenda more clearly, it is unlikely that they will find a loyal voter following waiting to send them back into power with a stable mandate. What Ferguson and Rogers are probably right about is that there is little basis for arguing that a solid conservative majority has emerged over the last twenty years. Even a Republican presidential victory in 1996 would not imply a consolidation of voter support behind a set of governing ideas, any more than the Democratic control of government from 1993 to 1994 meant a consolidation of power behind some Democratic governing vision. Even when parties are given the reins of government, interest fragmentation (the veto system described earlier) breaks down consensus within them.

These considerations suggest at least a couple of changes in Ferguson and Rogers' investment thesis. First, it may be too simple to say that the

Democratic party, as some coherent whole, has moved to the right along a neat ideological continuum and that its salvation requires only sliding back to the left again. Second, and related to this point, is a perceptive critique by sociologist William Domhoff, who argues that the real problem with campaign finance is not moving policies in or out of ideological alignment with the public, but, more generally, disrupting any systematic connections between policies and elections, or voting and government, as it were.[52] This is occurring in a system where vote–policy linkages are already weakened by a winner-take-all, two-party system that works against dramatic candidate differences and ideologically unified parties.[53] In the end, the fragmentation thesis may fit more of the data about elections and the national political decline.

One conclusion is clear: no matter what view of campaign finance we take, structural changes in the electoral system must occur if the parties are to work out anything resembling a broad political vision shared by voters.[54] Until such reforms occur, the whole spectrum of big questions on which candidates might stir the public interest shrinks to petty niggling and unconvincing blustering in 8-second communication bites. The overall result of the great political buydown is simple. Candidates just don't have much to say; indeed, they have far less to say than voters would like. Not surprisingly, many voters tune out and leave the political arena altogether. As for those who remain, they represent a tough sell, withholding their preferences, refraining from strong displays of party or candidate allegiance, and requiring all the marketing talents that Madison Avenue has developed through years of selling damaged goods to skeptical and weary consumers.

THE MARKETING CHASE

The arguments on marketing presented in earlier chapters can be summarized quickly. Once most of the governing ideas have been wrung out of a campaign, the management team is left with a tricky problem: how to sell what's left to the people. Selling damaged political goods isn't easy. First, voters must be convinced that they have a choice that means something. This is a choice that fully half the electorate won't buy at all, preferring to do something else with the ten or fifteen minutes out of their lives that voting consumes every four years. If we were talking about cars, soap flakes, or deodorants, the marketplace would be in a shambles by now. For better or worse, the voting market doesn't respond like other markets do to declining product quality and resulting consumer unrest.

Politics today, even more than cars or underarm deodorants, is the realm of illusion. When signs of political illegitimacy begin to appear, image-making techniques can create the illusion of legitimacy to dispel serious consideration of the underlying problem. Elaborate Hollywood productions create the illusion of enthusiasm at the conventions, even as viewers at home wonder what all the excitement is about. All that needs be done is wrap the candidate in the flag and have him promise to be more patriotic than his Brand X competition. Viewers at home can only shrug their shoulders and wonder if *they* missed something—if something is wrong with *them*.

Democracy as a Marketing Problem

The question of what this means for democracy is lost on the marketing experts who, after all, are only doing a job. It is a job that may not be pretty, but, as they say, somebody has to do it. The first blow to democracy comes with the recognition that since the electoral arena differs from the economic one, the problem of damaged goods isn't so overwhelming. The whole democratic marketplace has been refigured in order to turn the seeming liability of consumer defection into an advantage. All this requires is lowering the value of democratic participation, and the first big hurdle is cleared easily. Recall here the earlier words of Republican strategist Paul Weyrich, who ushered in this democratic devaluation as bluntly as can be imagined: "I don't want everyone to vote. Our leverage in the election quite candidly goes up as the voting population goes down."[55] This is a key principle of the new politics.

Noting this fundamental shift in the democratic tradition, political scientist Benjamin Ginsberg observed that "politicians of both parties have turned away from mobilizing voters in an effort to win elections." With predictable, if ironic, results, as Ginsberg points out: "The upshot of all this is that in the United States today the electoral process itself seems to be declining in importance. The electoral arena seems less decisive than we assume it to be under most democratic theories and less decisive than at any other time in our history. We are entering what could almost be called a post-electoral era in the United States."[56] Aiming similar concerns at the wholesale entry of campaign consultants into elections, political scientist Mark Petracca said: "The United States faces a monumental challenge to the practice of democratic governance. The challenge stems, in part, from significant changes in the conceptualization and practice of political campaigning and from the revolutionary effects of the technology deployed in contemporary campaigns."[57]

Beyond turning the decline of participation from a problem into a virtue, campaign consultants exert a number of other worrisome influences on the quality of national political life. First, they boost levels of ambiguity and symbolic abstraction in a system already burdened with plenty of both. As Petracca suggests, campaign consultants have turned an annoying tendency toward empty rhetoric into standard, institutionalized procedure.[58] Alongside this trend is a second development of equal concern. In a survey of campaign consultants, Petracca found that candidates have abandoned the content side of campaigning to an alarming extent. Forty-four percent of the consultants said that their candidates were neither very involved nor very influential in setting the issue priorities in their own campaigns. Moreover, 60 percent of the consultants revealed that their clients were neither very involved nor influential in the tactical side of the campaign.[59] Perhaps it isn't surprising to learn that when politicians hire consultants, they abdicate much of their control over campaign content, but it is nonetheless disturbing to think about the implications.

The direct marketing of candidates has dealt a possibly fatal blow to the health of political parties in America. Several prior factors account for the decline of parties as ideological melting pots, grass-roots forums, and leadership development pools. For example, the direct financing of campaigns by PACs and the resulting lack of political competition owing to high incumbency rates greatly reduced the dependence of politicians on parties.[60] However, the dependence of candidates on marketing consultants has blown open the gap between politicians and the last vestiges of ideologically coherent, disciplined, broadly representative party organizations.[61] In the words of former campaign consultant Walter de Vries, perhaps the most important consequence of the new politics is this weakening of the two-party system: "Candidates now deal primarily with consultants. They seldom deal seriously with the parties. . . . During my 25 years as a campaign consultant, I was responsible only to my clients."[62]

The Selling of American Politics

The communication between citizens and representatives in today's politics has become a highly managed affair, following closely the growth of the political marketing industry itself. The American Association of Political Consultants was founded in 1967 with fewer than forty members. Today, there are 800 members representing 400 firms, and this is just the tip of the iceberg. When we include the large number of freelancers and unaffiliated consultants operating in smaller political campaigns, there are, according to de Vries, some 12,000 people earning part or most of their incomes from political consulting. The growth in this industry has been exponential. According to Petracca's survey, fully half the firms have been created since 1980, up from one-quarter in 1974 and rising from the tiny 8 percent of today's total that were in business in 1964.[63] With this growth of the industry has come an increasing specialization of political management services, aimed at greater control of the relationship between people and politicians. Here is how de Vries describes these developments:

> The early consultants—in the campaigns of the 1960's—were generalists. They knew something about every piece of a campaign and advised candidates on everything. What you have now increasingly is more and more specialized consultants who deal only with television production, media buys, fund raising, polling and so on. Today, a campaign can have as many as three, four, or five consultants and I'm not just talking about presidential campaigns; I'm talking about statewide and even lesser campaigns.[64]

What exactly do these communication and marketing specialists contribute to a campaign? For starters, they accept the limitations on what candidates are willing to say to voters, while taking up the challenge those limits pose for creating voter enthusiasm. Next, they size up the population of people likely to vote and apply basic marketing techniques (polling, focus groups, "people meter" sessions) to evaluate the relative strengths and weaknesses of the client and the opponent, along with themes that generate public interest within the range of topics left open for discussion. Finally, a marketing strategy is devised to deliver favorable candidate images, unfavorable opponent images, and salient themes to key segments of the voting market. These key voter blocs, or target audiences, are determined by applying four criteria.

1. Are they already likely to vote? (There is no point in complicating an already difficult job by stirring up dormant voters.)
2. Are they undecided? (It is nearly impossible to get people to change their minds if they are strongly committed to the opposing candidate or party.)
3. Is it possible to appeal to the resulting groups without creating a backlash in some other group already likely to vote for the candidate? (This would be a very poor return on the marketing dollar.)
4. Which of the finalist groups are located in key states in sufficient numbers that winning their support could make a difference in the outcome of the electoral college vote? (There is no point in turning out people whose votes would not tip the final outcome.)

Running the voting population through these screening criteria helps explain why campaigns can take such strange forms, sometimes seeming out of touch with a candidate's most loyal supporters. "How could

Dukakis shrink in shame from the 'L-word,' and sell out the minority vote?" wondered many staunch Democrats in 1988. On the other side of the fence, many Republicans fretted over Bush's apparent softening on defense and the budget, not to mention his dangerous flirtation with environmentalism. In 1992, the Clinton campaign began to narrow the social appeal of its ideas when Ross Perot dropped out of the race and expanded it again when Perot reentered. And Clinton's commitment to the Middle Class Bill of Rights as the preamble to his 1996 campaign raised questions about where those at the lower end of the economic spectrum would turn for ideas that made sense to them. The defection of former party loyalists is understandable when elections boil down to spending hundreds of millions of dollars to make delicate marketing pitches to groups that may be as small as 10 percent of the total electorate. Yet, in the view of consultants, it is worth it if this tiny percentage of the population meets the four criteria on which campaign strategy is based. Thus, a relatively small number of voters often becomes the focus of the entire election.

The Permanent Campaign

The ripple effects of the strategic communication industry are beginning to reach well beyond elections into the day-to-day operations of American politics. The services provided by political consultants seldom end, as they once did, on election day. Having abandoned programs and philosophies to the marketing magic used to win elections, elected officials realize that they have trouble sustaining the public relations atmosphere of the campaign after reaching office. This can be more than a little frightening to the politician who realizes that he (and most of them are still men in this world of power) is in danger of revealing himself to be someone other than the image that was just elected. This moment of shock sends most well-financed politicians back to their consultants for advice about what to do in office—and how to do it. This last trend goes well beyond the effects that political consultants may have on participation, parties, and programs, and into another, perhaps deeper, area of concern about their impact on the quality of leadership itself.

Related to this addiction of leaders to their public images is a still deeper problem for democracy: the conversion of the national political scene into an endless election in which the goal is to dodge the problems and issues of the day, keep one's image strong, and make it to the next election with a full campaign chest and no mistakes to live down. In this system, politicians no longer campaign to win elections and get on with the business of governing. Rather, they govern much as they campaign: to be assured of winning the next election and getting on with the business of staying in office.

Recalling that time not so long ago when consultants assumed their jobs were over on election night, former consultant de Vries writes: "Consultants did not expect to be part of the governing process—to go on to the White House, the State House, or other governmental positions. Now, many consultants are retained to advise their candidate/office holders in the course of governing as well as in campaigning. This, to me, is a disturbing trend that raises all kinds of ethical questions. This trend has accelerated during the 1980's elections, and I think it is one that will certainly continue."[65]

As an example, de Vries cited the elevation of George Bush's 1988 consultant/campaign manager Lee Atwater to the chairmanship of the Republican party. (Atwater later stepped down when he became ill with cancer.) While Atwater was left to run the party (presumably without damaging the interests of his man in the White House), the political vacuum inside the executive mansion was filled by appointing glitzy image-maker and former Bush campaign TV producer Sig Rogich to the position of special assistant to the president for activities and initiatives. The job, according to one observer, resembled the same post "raised to a cynical art form in the Reagan years by Michael K. Deaver, [and] entails shaping the president's message and themes, planning his travel schedule and crafting how what he does looks for television."[66] Who was Sig Rogich? During the campaign, Rogich brought much of the Roger Ailes vision to life in the form of tough attack ads, including his work on the prison release ads and the legendary Willie Horton commercial. Before joining the Bush team, he ran the largest advertising firm in Nevada, worked for clients including Donald Trump and Frank Sinatra (helping Sinatra win a gambling license), served as a Nevada boxing commissioner, acted as a director of Bally's Casino, and helped the Stardust Hotel improve its image after it had been linked to organized crime. With all that behind him, Rogich rose to the challenge of democracy by saying, "I know it sounds corny for someone to tell you they're patriotic and that they feel honored to do something like this. But I believe deeply in this president because he's a good guy."[67] After the campaign and his tour of duty as a Bush handler in the White House, Sig Rogich became the ambassador to Iceland.

The 1992 campaign was dominated by James Carville, chief strategist for Clinton, and Mary Matalin, Bush's top strategist. After the election, the two opposing political managers were married. They then wrote a book that received extensive media play from all their friends in the press, and Matalin became host of a political talk show on Roger Ailes's CNBC channel. In a bit of news hype for the stunning couple, a *Newsweek* cover story began with a picture of the two lovebirds hugging themselves between a live elephant and donkey. The article reached a breathless level of tongue-in-cheek candor with this assessment of campaign consultants as the new Washington celebrities: "Carville and Matalin have become more than just another Washington power couple. They've become talk-show proxies for the trials of the two career life, the incestuousness of Washington elites, the vacuousness of campaigns, and the cynicism of handlers who run them."[68]

In a town that buzzes over money, sex, and power, the new political management moguls are at the center of the buzz. Many of them are the envy of the journalists who cover their campaigns, and, increasingly, their personal lives. After all, they not only put the spin on the news that gets reported, but they also make far more money than those who dutifully report it. In 1992, for example, consultants billed candidates $165,589,508, and that does not count the $27,212,742 billed to the parties.[69] What do candidates and parties get for their money? For the answer, we return to the aspect of our framework that began this chapter, the media.

Media Control

"Damage control" has taken its place alongside "spin doctor" and "sound bite" as the favorite phraseology of contemporary politics. Many journalists understand that the contemporary election has made the final transition from logos to logo, from the spontaneous to the contrived, from real to realistic. They lament covering "The Speech" day in and day out while searching desperately for something new or interesting to offer their audiences. They write increasingly of how candidates and their consultants try to manipulate news content. They note declining voter registration and growing distress among those who remain in the voting ranks. They grow angry and frustrated, waiting to pounce on a candidate mistake—eager for a chance to unleash a spontaneous question-and-answer session with the candidate.

If the marketed candidate is to survive in this volatile atmosphere, the name of the game is to control the media. The good news for campaigns is that the press is easily controlled because it depends on content generated by the candidates themselves—a dependence reinforced by the growing conservatism in corporate media ownership. As journalist Mark Hertsgaard has noted, contemporary campaigning follows the media control strategy developed in the Reagan White House: "Control your message by keeping reporters and their questions away from a scripted candidate;

capture TV's attention with prefabricated, photo-opportunity events that reinforce the campaign's chosen 'line of the day.' "[70] This strategy only works, however, if the media remain willing to let the politicians dictate the content of the news.

The result of this syndrome of a restless but often controllable press is that we enter an Alice-in-Wonderland world where the media savage the candidates who can't control them, while offering grudging respect for those who can. The spin doctors, marketers, handlers, and other damage control experts have become the political antiheroes of the age. In this upside-down world, the campaign becomes evaluated according to a perverse aesthetics of media mastery. And so it goes. The press complains, the consultants calculate, the spin doctors spin, and the candidates are wheeled out on cue in front of the visual backdrop of the day. The difference between the campaign stories of the day is that one candidate may have a better sound bite written for a more carefully selected occasion and may manage to look more comfortable with the part. That's all.

In the end, the values that have become most prized in this process are not social values or ideals, but media production values. And the best way to secure good production values is to neutralize the news and take the campaign into the video studio for the 30-second spots that drill the messages home to voters. In the Pennsylvania governor's race in 1994, for example, the image-makers worked overtime to create the right illusion around their candidate, Tom Ridge, a little-known Republican member of Congress from Erie. As a journalist covering the campaign noted, "The work of these image makers is serious business. Winning a statewide election can have as much to do with the quality of the advertisement as the quality of the candidate."[71] A trip to the video editing studio found the image masters working feverishly to add more treble to the candidate's commercial voice. The finishing touch was to adjust his skin color to a more pleasing hue. As an electronic technician put it, "he seemed overly ruddy, so I took a little of the red out and added green."[72]

We come full circle. In the end, the election process falls under the political loophole of presumed democracy. No matter how they are financed, marketed, or mediated, the electoral choices presented to the public are presumed to constitute some outpouring of democracy, and if there is something amiss, it is for the public to fix. One wonders, however, who will finance the popular reform movement, how it will be marketed to politicians, and who will publicize the efforts. And who *will* tell the people?

PART III

Political Culture at the Crossroads

CHAPTER 7

Running on
(Empty) Ritual

From the White House to Capitol Hill, the critical weakness of American politics and governance is becoming woefully apparent: a frightening inability to define and debate emerging problems. For the moment, the political culture appears to be brain-dead. —*Kevin Phillips*

Society revolves around a calendar of rituals: planting and harvest; birth and death; graduation, career, and retirement; marriage and family-building; gift-giving and economic exchange; power-sharing and political succession; religious worship and spiritual rebirth. These ritual events mark the passages and cycles of life. From grand public occasions like coronations and elections to the private celebration of bar/bat mitzvahs and weddings, rituals mark time, create order in moments of change, and recall the meanings and messages of civilized life.

Rituals suspend the ordinary course of daily existence and invite us to become spectator-participants in larger-than-life events. Well-performed rituals are at once familiar in script and caricature, and at the same time full of drama, mystery, and surprise. Actors who are given over to the dramatic possibilities before them call up the great traditions and truths of society with an eye to the contemporary concerns of the participants. Taken seriously, these dramatic affirmations of society and culture bring the wisdom of the ages to bear on thought and action in the present. Creative leaders speak the emerging truths of the day, sowing the seeds of myths for future generations to live by. Yet rituals also can fall victim to cynicism and neglect, becoming little more than instruments to manipulate people. Brittle and transparent, they break apart under the strain of apathy and popular disbelief.

WHY THE ELECTION RITUAL HAS FALLEN APART

The trouble with rituals, then, is that they can be neglected or manipulated until they are reduced to empty exercises in which people simply go through the motions. The actors become cardboard characters—objects of secret scorn and mockery (the fates of most politicians today) rather than the embodiments of wisdom and virtue. When leaders no longer bring new life to old litanies, prayers, vows, and myths, the meaningful links between past and present, society and the individual, are broken. Contemporary problems and concerns are paid lip service. Visions for the future grow dim.

The new American election is a ritual that has begun to fall apart, above all, because its content and spontaneity have become thoroughly manipulated by polling, marketing, and controlled communication that leave voters and candidates wary of each other. Rather than joining enthusiastically in the ritual that renews government, citizens and politicians keep each other at a distance, avoiding the risky and chaotic exchanges required for new ideas to rise up from society and for leadership to be tested around those ideas. Today's ideas are produced in focus groups and delivered in canned commercials, predetermining the scope and seriousness of the nation's exploration of its problems. Leaders are similarly manufactured as celluloid images with a repertoire of 8-second rallying cries—people who rise rapidly to power through the light and magic of the media rather than as social role models widely recognized for their exemplary deeds. Whereas money has pulled at the system from behind the scenes, marketing and mediated politics have placed limits on what goes on in public, in the rituals involving citizens and representatives that constitute the core of the civic culture.

The contemporary election is an increasingly controlled image forum that has lost important elements of spontaneous play and open communication that allow society to explore problems in ways that satisfy voters (rather than in ways that political consultants deem safe for their candidates); to find divisions and alliances at the grass-roots level (rather than as marketing constructions); and, ultimately, to select representatives who stand on principle (rather than on the latest poll results).

Decaying rituals are confusing to people who still try to find meaning in them. Like fading images whose parts remain clear enough to suggest the whole, they are still reminiscent of something meaningful but are ultimately elusive and unsatisfying. In American elections, the party conventions still have the balloons, the music, and the demonstrations, but political conflicts are suppressed in favor of harmony for the television cameras. Platforms have dissolved into so many words on paper, binding no one to their spirit. Meanwhile, on the campaign trail, candidates continue to invoke themes and symbols from the grand American mythology, while dodging the commitments to action later on in government that might convince people that the election ritual was more meaningful. In short, the new election process is pitched almost entirely toward winning elections, not toward governing afterward. This is a classic case of the breakdown of the meaning and credibility required for rituals to create effective links between people and government.

The Dangers of Dysfunctional Elections

In an age when political consultants regard voter apathy as a strategic advantage, there is no reason to revive the grand dramas of the political culture. The need to control communication frustrates bold ideas that might breathe life into a dormant citizenry. Thus, the grand problems and promises that might inspire and ignite a people are ignored in favor of the low-cost, manageable symbols—prayer, abortion, race—that discourage and divide. Low-powered groups—the poor, the minorities, the elderly—are eased out of the political picture. Society becomes an awkward place in which public life finds disparate groups moving uneasily around each other.

This is not to suggest that well-functioning rituals are celebrations of peace and harmony. Embedded within most cultures are conflicting traditions, class and ethnic differences, and competing human values. Yet it is within the familiar confines of ritual performances that these tensions can be expressed, explored, and, sometimes, resolved. When they are working, rituals permit people to engage in play, fantasy, and dramas that excite the imagination and transcend the limits and frustrations of everyday experience. The problem arises when rituals are no longer used as important contexts in which to explore social differences and problems. When constituent groups and their pressing concerns are ignored, as has been the case in recent elections aimed almost exclusively at the concerns of the middle class, the social fabric begins to tear apart. The transformation of elections into marketing situations has reduced the grand ritual to a propaganda battle that is often cynically narrow in its social appeal. Worse, when the select voter groups that are targeted by campaigns see little government action following from election promises, hostility toward government and politicians grows even among those who continue to participate. Rather than renewing faith in government, as a well-functioning ritual would, the new American election has undermined it.

When people sense that rituals have become empty, whether through corruption or neglect, they hear the familiar words and see people going through the old motions, but doubt their relevance to the everyday life of society. The steady decline of voter satisfaction and participation is probably the most important indicator that elections as rituals have become dangerously empty experiences. As the dramatic turnabout in the 1994 election indicated, voters have become increasingly impatient with the disconnection between elections and government. However, anger and vote switching are not enough to fix the ritual. The dysfunction is structural, having to do with the breakdown of parties and political communication due to the corrosive forces of media, money, and marketing.

The Old Order and the New: An Historical Transition

In charting the decline of the election ritual, it is useful to analyze a transitional contest that displays traditional patterns but also reflects emerging forces of historical change. The election of 1976 was such a contest. In that year, the rules and well-known litanies of campaigning chafed against the pressures of marketing and media control that have since come to define American political life. In this election year, Jimmy Carter and Gerald Ford battled for the nation's top office. In the primaries, Ronald Reagan challenged Ford, his party's incumbent president, and learned the hard lessons about avoiding spontaneity and controlling communication—lessons that enabled him to emerge four years later as president.

Perhaps more than any election since, 1976 swirled with clearly defined conflicts and crises that split the nation: the divisive ending to Vietnam, the Watergate corruption scandal, a global economic whiplash from surging Asian and European economies, rising Middle East oil powers, and on the domestic front, the unfulfilled promise of civil rights and poverty programs from the 1960s. All of these issues could have electrified the campaign and sent a government to Washington with a vision of national renewal. Instead, we saw the rise of outsider, entrepreneurial candidates who found messages that played with different market segments of the public. We saw the growing emphasis on candidate marketing and media control that came to dominate later contests, especially the 1988, 1992, and 1994 campaigns. At the same time, we also saw examples of candidates who were not trying to control and manipulate the ritual in the ways of these more recent campaigns. We saw in 1976, then, an uneasy mixture of the old and new systems, from the bold statements of a Ronald Reagan who was allowed by his handlers to speak his own mind to the carefully managed image of Jimmy Carter who convinced voters to trust

him in troubled times. Indeed, Carter presaged the coming electoral breakdown by selling himself convincingly in the election, only to fail in office
because he did not have a plan of action or the party support to chart a
satisfying course for government. Ironically, it was the Reagan primary
campaign in 1976 that most resembled the old, pre-marketing, pre-media
control election, with its risky ideas and minimal regard for their strategic
effects on voters. Reagan's failure to win the Republican nomination with
his shoot-from-the-hip style led him to accept a much more tightly managed image campaign in his successful bid for the presidency in 1980.

Even the personal attacks and leadership displays that have always
defined the American election ritual showed signs of losing their traditional qualities as marketing introduced a calculating and controlled element into exchanges between candidates and their followers. At a superficial level, even today the candidates may seem to be attacking each other
much as candidates have done since the beginning of the Republic. However, as explained in Chapter 5, personal attacks once followed highly
patterned (i.e., ritualistic) codes of proper and improper conduct that
those who sought the nation's highest office were expected to observe.
Recall that these candidate codes of etiquette were once so strict that the
candidates themselves did not even participate directly in campaigns,
much less fling personal insults at one another. In later elections, these
codes of ritual combat changed to involve candidates more directly in
campaigning—initially with the more dignified postures of debaters and
leaders who remained above the political fray. In recent times, these codes
of candidate conduct have crumbled, with marketers using their clients as
delivery systems for almost any kind of attacks deemed likely to work on
the emotions of voters. This trend has not been lost on the voters who
complain that the dignity of both the contest and the contestants has been
undermined. A simple explanation for why politicians have lost public
respect in recent years is that they have allowed their political consultants
to corrupt the dignified elements of our political rituals.

In the following analysis, we will look at three defining features of the
American election ritual that mark a transition from a more spontaneous
to a more controlled political event: the presentation of political ideas by
candidates, the exchange of personal attacks, and the display of leadership
qualities. Most candidate–voter communication in campaigns falls into
these three general categories. The very process of defining the election
ritual and getting the people to participate in it generally involves familiar,
highly patterned exchanges in each of these three areas.[1]

While following this analysis, it will help to remember that the gradual
breakdowns in each of these areas followed the historical changes outlined
in Chapter 4: the rise of independent voters, the decline of parties, the

emergence of independent candidates, and the reforms in the campaign finance system, among others. It will also help to think about the general question: What makes some rituals full of meaning and others empty? Let's drop in on Election '76 for a look at a political culture at the crossroads.

HOW CANDIDATES PRESENT IDEAS

In the midst of the 1976 presidential campaign, senior American states-man W. Averell Harriman journeyed to the Soviet Union to brief Soviet premier Leonid Brezhnev on the election. The major purpose of the visit seemed to be to assure Brezhnev that he need not take the candidates' statements (particularly Ronald Reagan's calls for more confrontation) too seriously. Harriman said of his mission: "It's awfully hard to under-stand the workings of an American campaign, but I think I did some good. I think he was somewhat relieved by what I had to say. I'm sure he wasn't totally satisfied. I'm not sure I was able to persuade him that everything that was said was of no importance."[2]

It is unlikely that Harriman meant that the candidates' pronounce-ments on various subjects during the campaign were of *no* importance. However, as everyone knows, candidates often say things just to win votes. Moreover, they have to say things just to appear plausible as people engaged in a familiar ritual. In other words, the same symbolic appeals that win or lose votes for the candidates also establish the election ritual itself. All this means that the candidates' vote-getting or pragmatic lan-guage (campaign rhetoric) must also serve as the ritualistic symbols through which citizens work out tensions and satisfy needs for security, order, leadership, and control over the future. These basic human con-cerns are addressed by elections and all other rituals of political succes-sion. Yet 1976 provided an interesting contrast between the things all candidates say just to reassure voters that they have a reason to run for office and the widely different abilities of the candidates to develop and present their ideas.

A Reason to Run: Policy Stands and Position-Taking

Participants in a ritual must first of all establish the ritual itself by adopting the tone, language, and litany of familiar ideas that let people know that a particular ritual is underway and that it is worth their time to join as participants. A ritual is properly established when the actors are able to communicate through their ordinary dialogue (1) that they are engaging in some familiar social activity, (2) that they are doing it in a competent fashion, and (3) that the participants and observers, therefore, can respond properly to the situation by assuming familiar roles. In other words, as candidates go about the business of getting elected, the way they do it reminds voters—if the ritual is still healthy—that an important opportunity for the exchange of ideas and the evaluation of leaders awaits their participation.

A concern with policy problems is the most acceptable, if not the only, justification for a candidate's entry in a race. This invocation of concern for the issues can be quite direct, as it was in most of Ronald Reagan's justifications of his candidacy. For example, in Reagan's first nationally televised speech during the 1976 primaries, the candidate began his campaign by saying simply, "Good evening to all of you from California. Tonight I'd like to talk to you about issues. Issues which I think are involved—or should be involved—in this primary election season."[3] Reagan used this often repeated theme of concern about "neglected" policies to legitimate his challenge to the incumbent president of his own party.

The following statements illustrate Democratic challenger Jimmy Carter's embrace of the issues: "I don't make these commitments [on the issues] idly. . . . When I say we need a national health insurance program, I mean to do it. Nobody's ever done it. It's been talked about by very fine Democratic presidents ever since as early as Harry Truman. That will be the difference,"[4] and "I'll never tell a lie, I'll never make a misleading statement, I'll never avoid a controversial issue. . . . Watch television, listen to the radio. If I ever do any of those things, don't support me."[5]

As far as establishing the election ritual is concerned, just claiming to have positions on "the issues" is what matters. Yet the convincing articulation of ideas becomes very important when the time comes to fill the ritual with meaning, generate enthusiasm, and send representatives to government with some mutual understanding of what they will do. Jimmy Carter satisfied the ritual requirement of posturing on the issues without articulating much of a vision that united large numbers of people behind his presidency. He failed in the second area because his campaign communication strategy fragmented his issue appeals into the different media audiences to which they were directed.

In the days before TV news provided instant accounts of what candidates told followers, candidates could try out ideas and experiment with appeals at relatively low risk. With the rise of the nightly news and instant electronic communication, candidates began to be more careful about what they told diverse audiences. As marketing and media management techniques have improved over the years, campaigns have developed rhetorical strategies to make special appeals to target audiences whether or not the candidate has a governing vision to integrate all those vote-getting statements into a coherent whole (i.e., a governing program). In 1976, the Carter campaign succeeded in making effective special appeals to different segments of the voter audience, without offering an integrating political vision in the bargain—unless, of course, we consider themes such as "trust me" and "a government as good as the people" to be visionary.

This fragmentation of meaning in pursuit of isolated votes continues to operate in today's campaigns based on three related communication strategies that enable candidates to say often contradictory things and defend them against press criticism. These media control strategies were evident in 1976, particularly in the Carter campaign:

- *Selective appeals:* through which focused but potentially volatile appeals were constructed for homogeneous and isolated audiences.
- *Disclaimers:* through which these special appeals were qualified or given "tag lines" that made it difficult for opponents to take them out of context. This allowed candidates to advocate different, often contradictory, policies to different audiences.
- *Vague generalities:* through which special appeals were summarized in broad or vague terms that allowed diverse constituencies to form different interpretations of the candidate's position.

Selective Appeals

Carter's critical upset victory in the 1976 Florida primary may well be credited to his judicious use of selective appeals. The Carter campaign spent more than a year before this primary isolating different media audiences and designing appeals for them. For example, a tape of Carter saying that the Civil Rights Act was "the best thing that ever happened to the South in my lifetime" was aired on black radio stations through the state. This message was withheld from other audiences. The rationale is obvious: Carter had a good chance of attracting black voters but did not want to risk losing conservative whites to George Wallace, the front runner. Spots showing Carter talking about togetherness and the mood of the country were regularly aired on *Sara*, a television program with a middle American audience. Liberal renditions of Carter's stands on welfare and employment were broadcast during episodes of *Maude*, a program with a young and comparatively liberal following. Other selected appeals were presented to blue-collar audiences on *Hee Haw*, to professional viewers on *Today*, and to senior citizens on *Lawrence Welk*.[6] As this list indicates, care was taken to target programs that attracted fairly homogeneous audiences and that had relatively little overlap of viewership.

Another good example of selective rhetoric also comes from the Carter campaign. In the early primaries, polls showed that opponent Henry Jackson, a powerful senator from Washington State, had attracted the majority of Jewish Democratic voters. A Carter speech writer reported that after this pattern crystallized, his candidate issued an instruction saying, "I don't want any more statements on the Middle East or Lebanon. Jackson has all the Jews anyway. It doesn't matter how far I go, I don't get over 4 percent of the Jewish vote anyway, so forget it. We get the Christians."[7] When Jackson withdrew from the primaries following his defeat in Pennsylvania, Carter began to make special appeals to Jewish audiences once again. For example, he appeared before a large Jewish audience in New Jersey. Wearing a blue velvet yarmulke[8] for the occasion, Carter said, "I worship the same God you do. We study the same Bible you do." He also noted that when the United States recognized Israel in 1948, "the President of the United States was Harry Truman, and Harry Truman was a Baptist."[9] In this and other speeches following Jackson's withdrawal from the race, Carter began making major policy statements on the Palestinian question, the Middle East situation, the status of Jews in the Soviet Union, and other issues of potential concern to Jewish voters.

Carter was not, of course, the only candidate to engage in the standard practice of appealing directly to special interests. For example, Gerald Ford told the convention of the California Peace Officers Association that he favored a mandatory death penalty "upon conviction of sabotage, murder, espionage, and treason in certain circumstances."[10] Two days later, Ford's opponent Ronald Reagan told the same convention that "Piously claiming defense of civil liberties and prodded by a variety of bleeding hearts of the society we have dismantled much of the intelligence operations of law enforcement that we must have if we are to protect society."[11] When Ford addressed the San Diego Council of the Naval League, he criticized Congress for its "political interference with our national security needs."[12] When Reagan spoke to the Economic Club of Detroit, he said that "The automobile and the men and women who make it are under constant attack from Washington."[13]

Not all selective appeals are politically risky. For example, Reagan's remarks to the auto workers were fairly safe. They were also open to more diverse interpretations than most selective appeals. In contrast, Carter's statement on the Civil Rights Act and Ford's pronouncement on the death penalty could alienate potential supporters if they were taken out of their initial contexts.

Disclaimers

The volatility of selective appeals can be reduced by affixing disclaimers, or tag lines, to them. These symbolic appendages have little impact within the immediate context, but they make it possible for a candidate to defend a statement if it is taken out of that context. A classic example of the use of tag lines was Richard Nixon's political abdication speech of 1962. In this speech, delivered after his loss in the California gubernatorial race (which followed his earlier loss of the presidency in 1960), Nixon claimed that he was leaving politics and that the press would not have him to "kick around" anymore. The speech was both emotional and bitter. In 1968, however, Nixon returned to politics as a candidate for president, claiming there was a "new Nixon."[14] Strategists for his Democratic opponent, Hubert Humphrey, hoped to use excerpts from the 1962 speech in commercials designed to combat the new Nixon image. However, upon close attention to the speech, they discovered that, despite the obvious sentiments of the performance, not a single damaging line could be taken smoothly out of context. Each of Nixon's charges against the press was coupled with some statement of faint praise.[15] This was all the more remarkable since the speech was both spontaneous and emotional, attesting to the degree to which some political actors may internalize the use of disclaimers.

Disclaimers and tag lines were numerous in 1976. For example, Gerald Ford's rather extreme statement on the death penalty carried the tag line "in certain circumstances." This disclaimer was rather simple in comparison to many of Jimmy Carter's uses. In one speech, Carter told a group of wealthy oilmen at a Houston, Texas, fundraising banquet that he perceived an "unwarranted inclination on the part of politicians and the people to blame the oil industry for inflation and fuel shortages."[16] In the same speech, he also addressed the sensitive issue of governmental regulation of oil monopolies. He said that he would support a partial breakup of the oil industry "only as a last resort." These sentiments could have been perceived by other Democratic groups as direct contradictions of two major planks in the party platform concerning the protection of consumers and the breakup of oil company monopolies. As if to guard against this interpretation, Carter included two tag lines in the speech. The first one stated that, unless he was satisfied that adequate competition existed in the industry, he would favor legislation divesting the big companies of their wholesale and retail outlets. The second tag line was even more subtle: "I want to be sure we have a minimum of interference of government in the affairs of business provided we can assure that consumers are adequately protected from a violation of the competitive commitment that's got to be part of all our lives." Should the occasion arise, it could be shown that these lines were virtual quotations from the Democratic party platform. One plank in the platform read: "When competition inadequate to insure free markets and maximum benefit to American consumers exists, we support effective restrictions on the right of major companies to own all phases of the oil industry."[17] Thus, the speech could be defended as a statement of party policy, even though the contextual references to oil policy were a considerable departure from the party line. Carter's rhetoric showed that the party platform had become another empty element of the ritual that was not worth fighting for, much less introducing into the campaign itself.

Vague Generalities

The use of tag lines permits candidates to make fairly pointed statements to isolated audiences with relatively little risk that the statements will alienate other groups. However, candidates must present their policy positions to a broad spectrum of voters on numerous occasions. Covering specific appeals with a rhetoric of vague generalities allows the consensual requirements of American democracy to be affirmed, even as the emptiness of those generalities raises public doubt about the grounds and quality of the consensus.

Vague generalizations depend on two categorical properties of language. First, words that appear together in the same grammatical context lead people to search for (semantic) relationship categories that provide common meaning for the words. Sociolinguist Harvey Sacks illustrated this principle with his analysis of a child's statement, "The baby cried. The mommy picked it up."[18] In this simple categorization problem, the terms *baby* and *mommy* can be located, in the abstract, within several different categories of relationship: family, stage of life, human beings, and so on. Their particular relationship in this context is best satisfied by the interpretive use of the category family. Sacks claims that as a result of this categorization we "hear" that the "mommy" in this utterance is the mommy of the baby, even though their relationship to one another is not stated explicitly. The second property might be called the projection principle: while highly specific words restrict people to a small number of possible categorical relationships, more general words invite people in heterogeneous audiences to project multiple interpretations that fit their different political circumstances.

As an example of the first principle, Jimmy Carter referred to George Wallace in the Florida primary as the perennial candidate who would run until 1988 if he was "able." Carter did not have to specify precisely what he meant by "able." In the abstract, a number of links can be drawn between the symbols "run" and "able." For example, we might think of such connections as financial support, age, political backing, physical health, and mental health. In referring to Wallace (who had been partially paralyzed after being shot in an earlier campaign), it was clear that the state of the candidate's physical health was the most appropriate connection to draw. Since this was the connection most interpreters were likely to make, it was one that Carter did not have to specify. As a result, if challenged he could defend the statement by substituting other category connections to change its meaning.

The second (or projection) principle is well illustrated by a variety of policy statements made on the issue of turning control of the Panama Canal over to Panama. Consider Ronald Reagan's ill-fated suggestion that we should stop responding to blackmail (i.e., stop negotiating) and simply tell the Panamanian dictator that we own the canal and "we're going to keep it." Compare this highly specific usage to Jimmy Carter's categorically more general position that he opposed "relinquishing actual control of the canal." This usage permits a large number of inferences to be drawn (through the symbol "control") about possible relationships between the United States and Panama.

An effort to shift the definition of an issue from specific and politically damaging terms to more general symbols occurred during the Reagan–Ford primary contest in 1976. Ronald Reagan had succeeded in making an issue of the defense and foreign policies of the Ford administration. At the core of Reagan's attack was his criticism of the conciliatory foreign policy of Secretary of State Henry Kissinger. Reagan referred to this policy of détente as "a one way street," "a concession of weakness," and an "approval of Russia's enslavement of captive nations."[19] In the face of the popularity of Reagan's definition of détente, Ford made a curious speech in which he revealed the recategorization process at work: "I don't use the word 'détente' anymore. I think that what we ought to say is that the United States will meet with superpowers, the Soviet Union and with China, and others and seek to relax tensions so that we can continue a policy of peace through strength."[20]

Jimmy Carter clearly made the best use of categorical generalizations in the 1976 campaign. For example, in his standard campaign statement on welfare, Carter began by referring to specific conditions in the welfare system. He noted that there were 12 million people "chronically on welfare and 2 million welfare workers, one worker for every 6 recipients." He also cited the figure of the 1.3 million people who "should not be on the welfare rolls at all." Then, on the other side of the issue, he cited the specific problem of the "unfortunates" who deserved welfare and deserved to be "treated with respect, decency and love." He then invoked the general reference for his welfare policy by saying that when he became president he would "reform the welfare system."[21] The term *reform* in this context clearly means many different things politically. This general tactic was very successful: opinion polls taken during the primaries showed that conservatives viewed Carter as conservative, moderates saw him as moderate, and liberals identified him as liberal.[22] During his presidency, Carter discovered that he could not sustain this image of being all things to all people, and many of his policy initiatives suffered as a result.

In contrast to Carter's skill at turning special appeals into vague generalities, the leading Republican candidates, Ford and Reagan, showed ineptitude in this area, each taking advantage of the other's rhetorical vulnerabilities. Reagan's greatest triumph was a national television speech in which broad generalities contrasted markedly with his string of shoot-from-the-hip specifics in other, less controlled campaign appearances. By 1980, Reagan's handlers had convinced their man to stick to the script and avoid thinking on his own in public, giving most of his 1980 performance the tone of broad generality achieved in this carefully crafted early 1976 speech:[23]

"Our nation is in danger and the danger grows greater every day."

" 'Wandering without aim' describes U.S. foreign policy."

"We're Number Two in a world where it is dangerous, if not fatal, to be second best."

"We're Americans and we have a rendezvous with destiny."

However, as Reagan's success in the primaries grew, he began to make an increasing number of specific policy proposals. As often happens under such circumstances, his opponent was able to take advantage of these statements. Among Reagan's violations of the generalization rule that Ford was able to turn to his advantage were the following:

January 15, 1976, on Angola: "[Tell the Russians to get] out. We'll let them do the fighting, or you're going to have to deal with us. . . . It's time for us to straighten up and eyeball [the Russians]."

February 27, 1976, on Panama: "I don't understand how the State Department can suggest we pay blackmail to this dictator, for blackmail is what it is. When it comes to the canal, we bought it, we paid for it, it's ours, and we should tell Torrijos and company we are going to keep it."

May 22, 1976, on Vietnam: "Never again should this country send its young men to die in a war unless this country is totally committed to winning it."

May 31, 1976, on Vietnam: "Can anyone think for a moment that North Vietnam would have moved to the attack had its leaders believed we would respond with B-52's?"

June 2, 1976, on Rhodesia: "Whether it will be enough to have simply a show of strength, a promise that we would [supply] troops, or whether you'd have to go in with occupation forces or not, I don't know."

These statements were of such categorical specificity that they permitted dispute on ideological, logical, and even empirical grounds. Toward the end of the primary season, the Ford staff built an effective propaganda campaign around these statements. An important element of the campaign involved a number of conservative Republicans attacking Reagan's policy statements as irrational, extreme, and factually incorrect. For example, in a series of radio commercials aired before the important Nebraska primary, Arizona senator (and former Republican presidential candidate) Barry Goldwater told Nebraska voters: "I know Ronald Reagan's public statements concerning the Panama Canal contained gross factual errors. . . . He has clearly represented himself in an irresponsible manner on an issue which could affect the nation's security."[24] The categorical difference between saying that we owned the canal and saying that we had interests or rights in the area allowed Reagan's opponent to make this effective attack on his ability to take competent and responsible positions on foreign policy issues.

Taking advantage of Reagan's increasingly open communication style, Ford strategists produced a series of radio and television commercials that were aired during the California primary. These ads ended with the admonition: "When you vote Tuesday, remember: Governor Ronald Reagan couldn't start a war. President Ronald Reagan could."[25] Although these commercials did not keep Reagan from winning the California primary,[26] for the first time in the campaign, Ford was able to assume an offensive posture. This turnabout was crucial for persuading uncommitted Republican delegates to support him at the nominating convention. The irony here is that while the Republican candidates were waging a fairly traditional election battle, Jimmy Carter was running a much more controlled, marketed, and mediated campaign. And he won.

HOW CANDIDATES ATTACK EACH OTHER

Beyond taking stands on the issues, candidates must dramatize the competitive aspect of an election. The practice of attacking the opponent's record, views, or competence is a traditional aspect of the ritual that has undergone dramatic changes. In the traditional exchange of ritual attacks, it was important to choose carefully between defensive and offensive delivery formats. Offensive formats directly accuse an opponent of taking an irresponsible stand on an issue or of exhibiting some undesirable personal trait (lack of candor, indecisiveness, fiscal irresponsibility, membership in an ineffectual party, etc.). Defensive formats respond to a prior (and, no doubt, uncalled for) attack by calling into question the opponent's motives or honor. As a rule, underdogs are granted more latitude with offensive formats, and front runners generally utilize indirect or defensive formats. In recent years, the etiquette about when to be above the mudslinging and when to engage more directly in it has fallen apart under marketing strategies that favor no-holds-barred exchanges among candidates that have elevated attacks above issues in campaign strategy.

The traditional rules for exchanging campaign attacks can be regarded as similar to many cultural rituals in which limited and stylized displays of aggression serve to defuse social tensions or to convey status recognition. Many cultures practice the exchange of ritual insults. Consider, for example, the insulting practice of low-status chiefs giving lavish gifts and feasts to higher status chiefs in the potlatch ceremonies of the Kwakiutl Indians of the Pacific Northwest. Or the pattern of insulting rhetoric in the complex verbal game called Playing the Dozens, played, among others, by urban American youth who vie for status and membership in street gangs. In another historical time, chivalrous knights of inferior status challenged knights of superior status by throwing down a gauntlet. All these symbolic exchanges involve the initiation of a personal challenge by a lesser contestant and the opportunity for the higher status recipient of the challenge to respond in a manner befitting his dignity. The point is not that candidate attacks during elections are just like gift-giving by tribal chiefs or exchanges of insult by urban youth, but that they may once have been governed by ritual conventions that had important meaning in campaigns.

Jimmy Carter's use of personal attacks in the 1976 campaign illustrates the rules governing ritualized personal attacks. To begin with, Carter pledged to conduct a campaign that was above personal attacks. Such pledges, of course, are obligatory for those planning to engage in personal recriminations. In the Michigan primary, Democratic opponent Morris "Mo" Udall, a colorful member of Congress from Arizona who also pledged a campaign based solely on the issues, challenged Carter by running an intensive media campaign that accused the front runner of being fuzzy on the issues. The ads labeled Carter "The Waffler." As an underfunded underdog in the race, Udall utilized an appropriate offensive format for these attacks. As the front runner, Carter responded appropriately by defending his honor and accusing the opponent of vindictive and vituperative campaign practices. The advertisements, he said, represented a "breakdown in the relationships that have been maintained between candidates."[27] Even though everyone knew what candidate he was referring to, Carter felt it would be improper to mention him by name. This is a good example of an indirect attack on an opponent that defended Carter's honor while remaining consistent with his front runner's claim to being above personal concerns.

Carter's reluctance to mention names also permitted him to generalize his attacks to other opponents who, he claimed, sought only "to maintain at all costs their own entrenched, unresponsive, bankrupt, irresponsible, political power."[28] It is noteworthy that these speeches were delivered in Ohio, a state where opponents Jerry Brown and Frank Church were not on the ballot. When asked if he referred to all his opponents in these speeches, Carter preserved his claims to being above petty personal concerns by saying, "I don't attribute that kind of motivation to Jerry Brown or Frank Church." These opponents, he argued, were "very good men and very worthy candidates."[29] Despite this caveat, Carter had encountered one of these "worthy opponents" (Brown) in the Maryland primary ten days earlier. In that primary, Brown was the front runner and Carter was the underdog. Carter assumed an offensive posture by airing a statewide television commercial containing a direct attack on Brown and his entrenched power motive: "My opponent has the backing of almost every machine politician in Maryland. They want a brokered convention where powerful people can horse trade in the back rooms and pick the nominee. They don't want to let the people of Maryland make that decision for themselves."[30] In each race where he ran as an underdog, Carter followed the basic rules for direct personal attacks.

In general, the use of personal attacks by all the candidates in 1976 conformed to the three basic rules that (1) underdogs use the offensive format, (2) front runners use the defensive format, and (3) candidates claim to be above these personal concerns at all times. The dramatization of personal competition is so basic to an election ritual that candidates who choose to be largely unresponsive to the attacks of opponents (e.g., Eisenhower in 1952 and Nixon in 1972) generally find it necessary to send their running mates into personal skirmishes with opposing candidates.[31] A failure to observe such norms can throw the ritual out of balance, resulting in damage to social understandings about the proper personal code for a leader.

The deterioration of the rules for ritual insults in recent elections may explain why many candidates have had trouble convincing voters that they have leadership potential, relying instead on the negative appeal that they are simply less weak than their opponents. For example, in 1988, George Bush began his negative campaign against Michael Dukakis as a proper underdog, issuing direct attacks on Dukakis's liberalism, patriotism, and religious convictions. Also befitting the front runner, Dukakis chose to ignore the mudslinging, maintaining the image of being "above it all" (an acceptable alternative to the indirect counterattacks issued by Carter when he was the front runner in 1976). However, after Bush took a commanding lead in the polls, he continued to push his negative offensive against Dukakis—an approach that disturbed many voters seeking a degree of decorum in an otherwise empty ritual. To compound the problem, Dukakis finally launched his own negative campaign against Bush but did so in the rhetoric of the front runner, appearing stoically above the fray despite a seventeen-point deficit in the polls. It is worth considering that public dismay at the negativism of the 1988 race was due not so much to the spectacle of the candidates attacking each other, but to their disregard for the etiquette that once governed the exchange of ritual insults.

HOW CANDIDATES DISPLAY LEADERSHIP

The electoral drama resolves candidate battles by designating a new leader or affirming faith in the old one. The familiar litany of leadership is therefore a basic component of campaign discourse. If elections are about nothing else, they entail the dramatization and resolution of voter concerns about security, governmental succession, and the future. In order for candidates to play their roles properly, they must address these concerns by defining leadership as a basic campaign issue and by transmitting personal images of leadership in the process. The rhetoric of leadership is so standardized that a few examples are adequate to illustrate it:

"The American people deserve a leader they can trust."[32]

"A president should describe a future."[33]

"I want to lead our country away from a wasteful preoccupation with what's wrong with America and get on with the job of making things right with America."[34]

These banal words hardly display the sophistication normally associated with persuasive appeals.[35] It makes more sense to think of such standard pronouncements as the sort of thing one must say in order to establish the proper definition of the election ritual. Yet there is more to leadership in the eyes of voters than just hearing candidates pronounce the litany of the ritual. Leaders also convince people with their actions, including their ability to respond appropriately to the attacks of opponents, as well as to face the people under tough campaign conditions and appear able to handle the pressure. In recent elections, spontaneous glimpses of leadership have all but disappeared under the inhibiting effects of candidate marketing and media control strategies.

The representation of leadership in a campaign evolves through actions and through displays of skill or virtue that invite the attribution of competence by the followers. A common pragmatic approach to leadership occurs when incumbents blur the distinction between their images as candidates and their images as public officials. For example, the majority of Republican incumbent president Gerald Ford's television spots during the 1976 primaries showed still shots of Ford acting as president (holding conferences, signing bills, studying reports, giving speeches, etc.) within official settings like the Oval Office, aboard Air Force One, and in the chamber of the House of Representatives where he served before being appointed vice president by soon-to-resign President Nixon. Included in the soundtracks were excerpts from Ford's 1976 State of the Union Message and the recurring strains of "Hail to the Chief." In some of these ads the word "president" was used more than a dozen times, including the repetitious closing lines that ran, "President Ford is your President. Keep him."[36] In addition to such advertising, the president's official activities were exploited for their leadership imagery. The most notable of these activities was an international economic summit conference that Ford initiated and hosted shortly before the Republican nominating convention. Relatively little was accomplished at this conference, but front-page pictures appeared almost daily in which Ford was shown in the company of the leaders of the major capitalist industrial nations.

All of this pomp and ceremony rang a bit hollow, however, since Ford had not been elected president, but was appointed by the disgraced previous occupant of the Oval Office. Using incumbency as an effective leadership claim may require more than just a slick advertising campaign. Yet many candidates have little more than an advertising image to offer as leadership credentials. Even when the Ford campaign abandoned its Oval Office advertising format late in the primaries in response to gains by challenger Reagan, it resorted to a new marketing strategy with the focus on *President* Ford. The new ads were created around a slice of life format. The basic Madison Avenue scenario for such commercials involves a friend giving an enthusiastic recommendation for a product to another friend. The recipient of the recommendation then becomes converted into a satisfied buyer during the course of the commercial. In the commercials run by the Ford campaign during the June primaries, the product was Gerald Ford and the satisfied buyer was a housewife who was pleased with lower food prices. The commercial began with two women (carrying bags of groceries) meeting in front of the supermarket:

Friend: Ellie! Are you working for President Ford?

Ellie: Only about 26 hours a day. Notice anything about these food prices lately?

Friend: Well, they don't seem to be going up the way they used to.

Ellie: President Ford has cut inflation in half.

Friend: In half? Wow!

Ellie: It's just that I'd hate to think where we'd be without him.

Announcer's Voice: President Ford is leading us back to prosperity. Stay with him. He knows the way.[37]

Even though the format is a radical departure from the Oval Office motif, the basic symbolic appeal is much the same. Candidates who lack this symbolic resource (incumbency) must develop other devices if they are to strike a leadership pose. Endorsements by other political leaders and celebrities are among the most familiar devices used. However, more novel formats may surface in the course of a campaign. Among these were Jimmy Carter's efforts to develop an image as a national leader and a foreign policy expert. An ingenious tactic was a leak from his staff claiming that Soviet officials had made repeated efforts to contact and consult with the candidate. A Carter aide was reported as saying that "Since February or March, and especially in the last month or so, they have been lighting up our switchboards and coming over regularly."[38] This leak came on the eve of a speech on international nuclear energy policy that Carter delivered at a privately sponsored conference held in the United Nations Building. The leak drew considerable attention to both Carter and his speech. In news reports, the speech became "a major policy statement" that was delivered "at the U.N." The leak also gave Carter the opportunity to respond to reporters' predictable questions by saying, "They [the Soviet officials] believe I have a good chance to be the Democratic nominee, the next President."[39] He added that he didn't think it would be appropriate to hold direct negotiations with foreign governments until the nominating process was over. The moral of this scenario, it would seem, is that short of being the president the next best strategy is to act in a presidential manner.[40]

Whether being president or acting like one, it makes a difference if the postures the candidate strikes have any connection to actual skills and accomplishments. In the 1976 campaign, the candidates invoked images that had little substance beyond the ads and news articles that conveyed them. In this regard, Jimmy Carter may have been the first of the new breed of anti-Washington candidates to run on the claim of being an outsider—someone whose strengths included the lack of high-level leadership experience. In subsequent elections, many candidates have rushed to this anti-leader position, competing with each other for outsider status. The irony in this perversion of the leadership ritual is that many politicians who might offer solid leadership credentials have either been driven out of public life or have (mistakenly, perhaps) concealed some of their own political abilities by campaigning as outsiders themselves.

RUNNING OUT OF RITUAL

Despite the clear influence of marketing and media control in the 1976 campaign, there were still moments when the ritual threatened to become meaningful for its voter audience. Election '76 witnessed a constant tension between meaning and marketing, with the edge going to marketing in issue presentation and leadership, and to more traditional ritual forms in the exchange of personal attacks. By the late 1980s, that tension had disappeared, and marketing held nearly complete sway over issue discussions and candidate attacks. Not surprisingly, the display of political leadership, one of the most important elements of the ritual, has become thoroughly corrupted in this process.

Even though Carter was cautious in his appeals to minorities and the poor (hedging them with disclaimers and vague generalities), he still made those appeals. As a result, the Carter victory in 1976 came without completely sacrificing the party's traditional constituency. By contrast, Mondale in 1984 and then Dukakis in 1988 and Clinton in 1992 all but abandoned appeals to traditional groups of poor and minority voters. The result was not just a loss of meaning for many potential participants, but a sacrifice in the broad democratic appeal of the election ritual itself.

Beyond narrowing the appeal and relevance of elections to broad voter groups, there has also been a notable decline of spontaneous, lively debate among candidates since 1976. For all the use of marketing and media control techniques in 1976, there was still a tentativeness about their intrusion into the nation's most sacred political context. Reagan actually spoke his own mind on a number of occasions. Ford actually shifted his foreign policy position during the campaign in response to Reagan's criticisms. These glimmers of open debate offered voters the hope that something meaningful might be taking place on the political stage.

After 1976, the role of political consultants and candidate handlers became unashamedly intrusive. George Bush's 1988 claim that Michael Dukakis was a liberal was probably effective only because Dukakis took the advice of his handlers and denied it for months. It did not require a particularly enlightened voter to see that Dukakis was denying the obvious. Adding insult to injury, the Democrat finally took the advice of a new consulting team and admitted that he was, after all, a liberal and proud of it. Such slavish scripting robs terms like liberal of any meaning or vision, while turning elections into painfully staged affairs.

What about the electronic town halls of 1992 and the Republican landslide of 1994? The increased levels of debates, television appearances, and voter call-in programs in 1992 did produce higher levels of reported voter satisfaction than in 1988, but the overall level of participation was still just 54 percent of eligible voters in a three-candidate race! While voter enthusiasm is an important indicator of the health of the ritual, so are the numbers of people infected with it. In 1994, the Republican landslide was produced by just 21 percent of the eligible electorate. The change in Congress produced by that election is important and worth noting, but it is difficult to argue that the vitality of the ritual has been restored in light of the narrow range of ideas expressed in most of the campaigns, the tastelessness of what some observers regarded as the most negative campaigning yet, or the nearly universal stampede of candidates to abandon traditional leadership displays in favor of advertising themselves as inexperienced outsiders.

The overriding problem is that contemporary candidates are ordered to stick to their scripts, while avoiding spontaneous outbursts of public thinking and shunning contact with the media. These dictates of campaign strategy may enable campaign consultants to apply their techniques with greater precision and effect, but the resulting damage to the ritual is great. As campaign content is increasingly filled with the results of marketing research, the central ritual of American democracy grows increasingly empty.

CHAPTER 8

Failing the Presidential Character Test

In certain important aspects, the American presidency bears some comparison with the principate of Imperial Rome. . . . Dignified and efficient functions of government are not sharply separated [as they are elsewhere] but are here fused in a single person. Americans vote for a political leader who, in addition to his other functions, is the *pontifex maximus,* not so very different, perhaps, from Augustus Caesar. . . . Theodore Roosevelt, a particularly adept practitioner . . . had the insight to refer to the presidency as a "bully pulpit." . . . Closely connected to [the religious role of the presidency] is that elusive quality, presidential "vision," through which focus on "the good society" is attempted and often achieved. —*Walter Dean Burnham*

More than any world leader, short of a full-fledged monarch, the American president is party chief, legislative advocate, ceremonial figure, spiritual guide, and spokesperson for the national vision—all in one person. The curious system of government set forth in the Constitution assumed that clashing parties and sharply drawn interests were negative elements, while deliberation aimed at broad consensus around core values was the secret to stable government. It turned out that this vision was a bit idealistic, as the rapid rise of parties would attest, but its legacy of slow, deliberative government is with us to this day. When that government works best, the president is generally at the helm, offering wisdom, spiritual uplift, and broad visions about where the nation should go, and what laws and actions will best take it there. When this system works well, as it often has, citizens are drawn to presidents with an appealing vision fashioned from familiar cultural values and with the strength of character to embody that vision in both word and deed.

Vision and character are delicate qualities on which to base government. They can easily be overlooked in the rush to win elections using the latest technologies of persuasion and short-term emotional appeal. Even worse, it is tempting to think that character and vision can be manufactured with electronic light and sound, assisted by good scripts and drama coaching. When voters contemplate candidates who are hiding behind managed images, there is little choice but to make the best judgment about who the real leader may be. To their credit, those citizens who continue to participate manage to do it. Yet, confidence in those judgments may be weak. Presidents who receive large majorities in an election may find themselves rudely rejected if, after they take office, they reveal that they have no vision, or worse, that they have no character.

The image techniques that increasingly dominate campaigns may work well enough to get someone elected, but they are not easily sustained through all the crises, scandals, and genuine tests of character that every modern president has endured in his years in office. The manufacture of character and political vision may have done more to undermine the delicate balance of leadership in the American political culture than anything else. In this chapter, we explore the presidential campaign as a grand national character test, and we examine the presidency as, more than anything else, a national pulpit to which people look for insights about how to adapt the great wisdoms of the political culture to new challenges. The media, money, and marketing forces that drive the new election system not only make the character test less reliable, but also undermine the vision of leaders who short-circuit the process by using polls to see what their often confused followers want today.

THE PRESIDENTIAL CAMPAIGN AS CHARACTER TEST

Most students of the presidency stress the personal qualities of candidates. In one view, even if candidates have a vision, they must be evaluated in terms of their strength of character to carry it out.[1] In another analysis, the lack of a vision (or credible issues) may not prove fatal if the candidate communicates personal qualities worth voting for.[2] The trouble is that the new electoral system plays havoc with these personal considerations in voter choice. Not only do money, media control, and marketing undermine political visions, but they also reduce the chances that voters will catch useful glimpses of the personalities behind the campaign masks. This chapter explores how the new election system makes it difficult for voters to make satisfying judgments about candidate personalities.

A stranger to American politics might conclude that nearly everything a candidate is subjected to during an election is degrading in some way. Political campaigning is grueling. Presidential candidates often spend eighteen-hour days carrying their messages and their campaign personalities into as many media markets as possible. A typical day's itinerary may contain twenty or more entries.[3] The events on the schedule are often as tedious and humbling as the schedule itself. The time, place, supporting cast, and audience may change from hour to hour and day to day, but the activities and performances fall into a pattern. The campaign becomes a numbing blur of repetitious action.

The attention of press and public seems to shift from the monotony of the campaign to any activity that represents a departure from the routine. The most newsworthy and perhaps the most noteworthy departures from electoral routine are those occasions when candidates blunder, lose control, or otherwise reveal embarrassing flaws in their carefully staged performances. Gaffes by candidates and the often degrading episodes that follow them are a major focus of press coverage; in addition, candidates also spend a good deal of energy explaining their mistakes in efforts to repair their images. Some blunders are repaired effectively, while those handled less smoothly only seem to confirm suspicions about the candidate's incompetence or deceitfulness.

Because gaffes have been prominent features of elections, it is important to understand them. Although pundits and purists often bemoan the media fascination with candidate blunders, gaffes are not easily dismissed as trivial preoccupations of a frustrated press and a bored public. To the contrary, gaffes can be shown to be the basis of clearly identifiable character tests, or what we define later in the chapter as degradation rituals in campaigns. These rituals contribute both to the definition of the electoral process and to the information needs of voters who must make decisions within that process. The trouble is that well-managed candidates can lead voters to choose leaders whose primary virtue is having good handlers rather than good character.

PRESIDENTIAL CHARACTER ON DISPLAY

Many analysts have noted the connection between gaffes and the generally grueling and personally challenging nature of campaigns. For example, political scientist James David Barber has described the campaign as a stress test. The measures of performance on this test are the incidence and handling of gaffes. In Barber's words, "The campaign stress test reaches its apex in the gaffe."[4]

Gaffes seem to be defining features of campaigns, and the attention paid to them hints at the possibility that they convey some sort of useful information. For example, in light of all the issues, policies, and personal attacks that the candidates handled so deftly in the 1976 debates, why was so much attention devoted to Gerald Ford's gaffe about there being no Soviet domination in Poland and his unsuccessful efforts to repair it?[5] Why does a campaign event seem to have less significance if a gaffe does not occur within it? For example, gaffes did not figure in the 1980 Carter–Reagan debate, and so the press seemed hard pressed to pick a winner. *Washington Post* reporters Lou Cannon and Edward Walsh called the debates "bloodless" and noted that "each candidate remained carefully in control of his emotions throughout the 90-minute forum."[6]

Perhaps the most glaring trend in presidential debates since 1976 is their general lack of gaffes. This, it may be argued, is due less to the nomination of unerring humans than to the campaign consultants' increased control over the coaching and directing of candidates before their every public appearance. Not that we can expect complete elimination of gaffes in the race for the presidency. To err, after all, is human, and no candidate is thoroughly programmable. However, the coaching, directing, and scripting of candidate performances are making a visible impact on the incidence of candidate mistakes. The contemporary campaign is less a test of character than a display of public relations techniques.

The damage done to candidate character in recent elections has generally involved hidden secrets from the past that were dug up by the opposition or announced to the press by opportunistic enemies. In 1992, for example, Bill Clinton opened his primary campaign and immediately faced charges of sexual misconduct. As explained in Chapter 3, the candidate and his wife went on *60 Minutes* to show that they were once again a loving and faithful couple who had overcome some marital "problems" in the past. Polls showed that enough people accepted this repair of Clinton's image to allow his campaign to go on. Moreover, from that point onward, the campaign developed a media strategy that not only avoided press contact as much as possible, but that also eventually produced a whole new character for the candidate (the Man from Hope) in its effort to defeat the Slick Willie image planted so successfully in the press. The ultimate problem, of course, was that other hidden secrets continued to come out during the Clinton presidency, and the presidency itself became a continuous damage control and image management operation. The moral of the manufactured character is that it requires so much maintenance that the people eventually lose hope for convincing leadership and political vision.

Inventing a Character and Sticking to It

With the great dramatic demands of the office, presidents may always have been compelled to invent a public character and hide less attractive aspects of their private personae. Certainly this was true with Lincoln, who adopted the role of the nation's preacher, issuing sermons and moral guidelines during the spiritual crisis of the Civil War, all the while living with madness and personal tragedy inside the White House. Roosevelt endured great pain to stand on his own legs while delivering important speeches in public, although polio kept him in a wheelchair almost all the rest of the time. Eisenhower was known in public as a beloved national grandfather figure but ran the White House as the distant general, a character that had emerged in the harsh years he served as supreme Allied commander in World War II.

The public, too, understands the dramatic values of the nation's highest office and so has often invited its occupants and aspirants to assume grand stage presences. Ronald Reagan, for example, was criticized in some quarters for bringing his acting talent to the nation's great stage, but his followers revered him all the more for playing the part so well. At the same time, Reagan's image and public communication were the most thoroughly managed of any president in history, making Reagan a transitional figure between the old politics and the new.[7]

In the hundred years or so between the rise of candidates who campaigned for themselves and the recent rise of electronic politicians who campaign for their image consultants, it may have seemed natural to allow candidates to reinvent themselves when they auditioned for the nation's leading political role. After all, this is America, the land in which being born again is a good thing. Moreover, an important mark of leadership is the ability to change, adapt, and grow. Finally, if the traditional election ritual is working properly, a New Candidate who had strayed too far from real character would fall apart under the attacks of opponents and the intense scrutiny of the public, and be held accountable by voters. Or so thought the voters who elected the New Nixon in 1968—a media invention of Roger Ailes[8]—and discovered only well into his second term that they had in fact elected the old Richard Nixon, whose character flaws visited something of a Greek tragedy on the White House and the nation. Yet communication scholar David Swanson found that in the next election, invented candidate characters continued to play in the news at face value, so to speak, without much deeper criticism from the media.[9]

The Cultural Dilemma

Viewed historically, then, here is the cultural dilemma we face. Candidates have traditionally been permitted a remarkable degree of freedom to invent their campaign personalities and then are held accountable for the faithful portrayal of those characters.[10] However, in the age before campaign management had a near total grip on candidate performances, gaffes and other spontaneous displays of character gave voters an opportunity to see if candidates were truly comfortable with their transformed selves. Now, comfortable or not, candidates are taught how to play their chosen roles to the hilt. Witness, for example, George Bush who, by his own admission, felt awkward and estranged from his tough guy image in 1988, but who recited the obligatory Clint Eastwood-like lines in journeyman performances. Then, there is the continual preparation of Dan Quayle who, until his decision not to run in 1996, evolved a character that did not appear to experience so many technical difficulties before the television cameras. And what to make of Bill Clinton, whose multiple media personalities (Slick Willie, the Comeback Kid, and the Man from Hope) seemed to compete endlessly with one another for claim to being the real Bill Clinton? Authenticity in such matters is an increasingly academic question: To what extent were the personae of George Bush, or those of Dan Quayle, or each of the Clinton characters, largely (if not entirely) products of the media? Sometimes the media images are created by the politician's own marketers and image managers, sometimes by opponents, and sometimes by the press pack on the trail of a scandal or a hero for a day, but behind every mediated character there often lie others, waiting to spring on a weary public.

Now that gaffe control (media consultants call it "damage control") has become a prominent feature of campaigns, voters no longer get a candid look at leadership skills such as knowledge, sensitivity, awareness of social norms, or the ability to think and act under pressure. In traditional campaigns where candidates had greater spontaneous contact with the press and with each other, gaffes regularly became campaign issues. The success or failure of candidates in redressing the violations became a basis for practical voter judgments, while candidate responses confirmed the importance of the norms in question.[11]

Nowadays, on the rare occasions when candidates depart from their scripts or (more likely) get caught in questionable activities, they just ignore reporters' questions, while smiling over the heads of the snarling press to the viewers at home. In the congressional races of 1990, for example, incumbents accused of doing special favors for the owners of failing savings and loans responded as though there was no difference between pulling strings for fat-cat campaign contributors and helping little old ladies find lost social security checks. When Newt Gingrich decided that it was bad public relations to take a multimillion dollar book advance from a media mogul with important business pending before the government, he held a press conference and announced that all bets were off, while holding up a one-dollar bill to signal the size of his new advance. But what were the people to conclude about his character or about the clean government vision that he claimed to support? Were Bill Clinton's serial scandals the signs of a terminally flawed character or the work of a slick media campaign run by his political enemies? The danger of life in this electronic hall of mirrors is that we may be losing the all-important public accountability and sureness of leadership that keep our political norms and values (along with the rituals in which they are displayed) meaningful for citizens and politicians.

CHARACTER TESTS IN OTHER SOCIAL SETTINGS

Candidates' once-familiar efforts to restore lost status, morality, or competence in the eyes of skeptical voters are similar to what sociologists call degradation rituals; these rituals are said to occur in almost any setting in which new members are socialized, status is conferred, and character is tested. As sociologist Harold Garfinkel noted in his illuminating work on the subject, probably no society or institution with a moral order to uphold does not prescribe some sort of degradation ceremony that will test and affirm members' commitments to that order.[12] Degradation rituals literally certify that an individual's public persona meets the standards of the group or the institution. Certification is granted if individuals who violate the norms for their public roles can then repair the violation in ways that indicate understanding and acceptance of those roles. People who fail to repair their indiscretions suffer status degradation by being rejected for their chosen social careers.

Degradation rituals, according to Garfinkel, display several defining characteristics. First, other actors must regard the offending behavior as a departure from the norm and a damaging blow to proper role behavior. Second, and more importantly, the group leaves to the transgressor the task of repairing the damage. Third, and most important of all, the offender must select a rhetorical gambit (an account, a reinterpretation, or an apology) that (1) indicates recognition of the nature of the problem, (2) demonstrates an understanding of the proper behavior, and (3) indicates a convincing ability to display the proper behavior.

If concluded successfully, degradation rituals accomplish a number of important social functions: the socialization of new members, the rehearsal of social norms, the affirmation that roles and norms are binding on the individuals in the setting, the promotion of solidarity in the group, the display of command or ineptitude on the part of various actors, and so on. These social accomplishments of degradation rituals explain why they are so central to so many social contexts. For example, "total institutions" like prisons, asylums, and the military use degradation rituals to uproot individuals from former life contexts and to induce the radical transformation of identity necessary for successful conduct in the new setting.[13] Degradation rituals also occur in not so "total" institutions like street gangs, business firms, families, universities, and, of course, political campaigns.

Presidential candidates do not exchange the same insults as members of street gangs or military recruits, but they do exchange character challenges according to a very special set of ritualistic rules. At least they did before the ritual began to fall apart. In the traditional election ritual, candidates were also held accountable for alleged violations of political norms and for inconsistencies in their contrived characters. The following discussion addresses the questions of how gaffes are identified, how they are formulated into complaints, how candidates respond to them, and how political audiences assess the responses. Afterward we turn to the problem of what it means when these character tests disappear from the electoral process.

THE TRADITIONAL ELECTION CHARACTER TESTS

Turning gaffes into legitimate campaign issues is a problem of rhetoric involving language categorization: namely, finding the words to describe a questionable candidate action in a way that fits observed behavior under some relevant political norm. Testing candidate actions against various political norms enables voters to make two kinds of judgments. First, gaffes that violate important norms can be distinguished from gaffes that represent minor slips of little or no political importance. Second, finding a normative category for a particular gaffe enables voters to anticipate how a candidate should repair the violation.

As these guidelines suggest, not all candidate errors provide good material for campaign issues. Some slips and blunders are hard to categorize within accepted political norms. For example, when Jimmy Carter slipped during his 1980 acceptance speech at the Democratic party convention and referred to former vice president and party heavyweight "Hubert Horatio Hornblower Humphrey," he was not called into account for his statement. Neither was Carter made accountable following a poor performance in the 1980 presidential debate with Ronald Reagan when he thanked the people of Cleveland for showing such hospitality in the "last hours of my life." A simple slip of the tongue may blemish the delivery of a line in a speech, but it is not easily taken as a sign of serious character or leadership problems. A chronic problem with delivery, pronunciation, or coherence may, on the other hand, lead to complaints about leadership skills. Gerald Ford's slips in 1976 became notable because they exceeded what many observers regarded as normal or tolerable levels in a leader.[14]

There are, of course, no precise rules for determining exactly what constitutes a normative violation. The existence of such rules would miss the point of the gaffe-repair ritual. It is through the playing out of each situation that agreement is negotiated on the nature and gravity of violations. Without this element of spontaneity and surprise, rituals become empty.

Thus, a candidate's choice of repair rhetoric has an important effect on public judgments about the severity of the violation and the possible remedies that might be in order. For example, concern seemed to die quickly following the Carter charge in 1980 that Reagan was a "warmonger." Carter staff people answered questions about the propriety of the remark with the concession that the word may have been a bit harsh. Suggesting the relatively minor normative category "momentary loss of temper" was enough to satisfy NBC's John Chancellor, who described the incident as a mere case of the president "having some trouble with his rhetoric today."[15] In contrast, Carter's 1976 remark about the merits of preserving the "ethnic purity" of neighborhoods was less easily dismissed and, instead, was taken as a possible violation of major norms about race relations in America. A president's failure to adhere to such norms would undermine his credibility as a national leader. As a result of the more serious nature of this violation, Carter was forced to engage in elaborate attempts to demonstrate his commitment to social equality and integration. He finally surrounded himself with a group of black leaders who offered personal endorsements at a televised press conference.

Transforming a gaffe into a campaign issue requires both a linkage to some political norm and the introduction of the public as the party to whom the accounting is owed. There are various ways of doing this. For example, an opponent may discount the personal hurt of an insult and suggest, instead, that it lowers the standards of campaigning—implying that the public deserves better. In other cases, leaders of a social group may register a complaint, as when black leaders initially denounced Carter's ethnic purity statement. In still other cases, a neutral political leader may speak "in the public interest," as Barry Goldwater did in 1976 when he issued a statement (no doubt, on behalf of Gerald Ford) pointing out the factual inaccuracy and irresponsibility of Ronald Reagan's Panama Canal position. In other cases, the press may report a gaffe in such a way that its offensiveness is made clear.

The ways in which gaffes are categorized constrain effective candidate responses to them. For example, a gaffe that is poorly categorized under a norm of only minor importance leaves the candidate the option of simply denying the validity of the charge. In contrast, a clear normative violation increases the pressure for some form of apology to satisfy an offended audience. The gambit from "denial-to-apology" is, of course, very general. The art of apology involves a variety of ways to save face.

In their discussion of the rhetorical genre of apologia, rhetoricians B. L. Ware and Wil Linkugel argue that attempts to restore character and affirm social norms involve much the same techniques that are employed in resolving problems involving belief in general.[16] The voter's dilemma in elections is simply to reconcile expectations about a candidate with an apparent violation of those expectations. To the extent that the candidate's response minimizes the expectation gap, the voter's dilemma is resolved with a minimum of damage to the candidate's credibility.[17]

CANDIDATES WITHOUT CHARACTER

Candidates today still go through the ritualistic motions of exchanging attacks and insults but in ways that are far removed from wit-testing spontaneity. If voters are put off by the new negativity in campaigns, it is probably not because it is unfamiliar in form, but because its content has been so contrived as to be pointless, and the chances to witness spontaneous candidate reactions are all but eliminated. Would Campaign '88, for example, have been different had Michael Dukakis taken the risk of responding personally and emotionally to Bush's attacks on his patriotism and his state's prison release programs, or to a reporter's hypothetical question about "what if" a released prisoner raped Dukakis's wife? Instead, Dukakis pursued a rhetorical strategy of controlled, calculated responses that revealed little about his humanness.

Psychologist Harold Zullow studied the rate of verbal slips among presidential candidates in high-pressure debate situations. He found that during the first Dukakis–Bush debate, Dukakis displayed an astonishingly low verbal error rate of 5.5 percent compared to Bush who made errors in 20 percent of his sentences.[18] Such a button-down character style leaves voters little to go on and perhaps explains why by the end of the campaign Bush scored higher than Dukakis in a number of preference scenarios, ranging from being the person most preferred to handle a crisis situation to being the person most people would prefer to invite over for dinner. Voters did not label Bush's slips as serious enough to be gaffes; instead, they believed that they revealed the humanness of a candidate who was slightly shy and flustered under the television lights. Most people were evidently able to laugh with Bush rather than at him when he declared

September 7 Pearl Harbor Day, when he struggled to gain command of that elusive "vision thing," and when he made a speech to an AFL-CIO convention in which he referred to the organization in the context of its foreign labor organizing efforts as the "AFL-CIA."

As media guru Roger Ailes said, the goal of modern campaigning is to maximize visuals and attacks while minimizing mistakes. Damage prevention is the word of the day, and damage control is its constant shadow. In the final analysis, victory goes to the leader with the best director, which is hardly the same thing as the leader with the best sense of direction. In the end, voters will choose the candidate (other things being equal) who displays the fewest character flaws or the greatest skill in repairing those occasional breaches of character. The problem is that in the age of electronic character, voters' confidence in those judgments, as well as their loyalty to the leaders they select, is understandably weakened.

THE REASONS WHY RITUALS MATTER

What is the connection between the character of leaders, particularly presidents, and society's ongoing efforts to define and solve its problems? The answer begins with the recognition that elections in America were not designed with policy-making in mind. With the notable exceptions of Jefferson and Paine, most of the nation's founders lived in fear of ignorant and unruly, not to mention unpropertied, masses holding sway over the course of government. As a result, unlike most other liberal democracies, we do not have a parliamentary system. Our undisciplined and beleaguered political parties have had little success in hammering out detailed programs and holding members to the party line after the voting is over. Thus, the United States stands in sharp contrast to systems in which party loyalty is the key to power, and ideological clarity is the key to votes. Fortunately, the nation's founders also suffered an equal fear of each other. As a result, we also have a fairly reliable, if unwieldy, set of checks and balances against the rise of an enduring oligarchy. This process of eliminating the unacceptable alternatives produced a system unusually dependent on folk heroes and strong leaders to make it go. Our quadrennial political spectacle is first and foremost a leadership competition. Yet this ritual also has an important policy and agenda-setting potential if left open to spontaneous communication between candidates and voters.

When a leader's character becomes suspect, so are the visions and ideas espoused by that leader. Indeed, many of today's leaders have abandoned any idea of promoting new visions or showing how to adapt core political values to new challenges. Instead, they hire marketers to take old symbols and values off the shelf and run them through focus groups. As a result of this leadership short-circuit, when old problems come up again and again to haunt Congress and the chief executive, the remedies proposed give us a powerful sense of déjà vu. New political situations seem to fall quickly into old symbolic molds.[19] The persistence of old political solutions is remarkable in light of their repeated failure to resolve the social and economic problems they address. The difficulty is not necessarily with the values, beliefs, and myths that are, in a sense, the tools of a political culture, but with the ways in which politicians use those tools to hammer out quick election victories instead of building more lasting symbolic constructions that might rally people behind solid governing programs.

MYTH AND CITIZEN CONSCIOUSNESS

Culture consists of the basic beliefs, values, and behaviors that organize social interaction and communication. Culture produces the common social understandings that guide people through everyday life situations, help them respond to new social conditions, and enable them to accept their positions in the social order. The most important aspects of culture are the basic models of (values, beliefs, and stories about) society, called myths, and the social routines through which they are brought to life, called rituals. In the absence of formal political ideologies, another notable characteristic of American politics, political myths and rituals guide the processes in which policies are made and public opinion is formed.

Political myths are difficult to analyze because they are so integral to everyday perception. They are like the lenses in a pair of glasses: they are not something people see when they look at the world but the things they see with. Myths are the truths about society that are taken for granted. These basic cultural principles are woven throughout everyday social communication from dinner table conversation to the morals of television programs and the lofty policy debates of Congress.

In the process of growing up in society, most people encounter hundreds of myths that gradually slip into their subconscious thinking. For example, young children are exposed to a battery of folk tales through school, parents, and the mass media. Some myths recount the exploits of groups such as the Puritans, the Founding Fathers, the slaves, the western pioneers, or the European immigrants. Other myths convey social lessons through the acts of individual heroes like George Washington, Daniel Boone, Andrew Jackson, Abraham Lincoln, Eleanor Roosevelt, John F. Kennedy, Martin Luther King, Jr., Colin Powell, or even the postpresidential Jimmy Carter. Through these cultural models, people first encounter the ideals of free enterprise, honesty, industry, bravery, tolerance, perseverance, and individualism. Myths also explain the causes of poverty and other social adversities and show how people overcome them. That is, myths explain the principles of politics and the nature of society. The range of different myths allows cultural perspectives to be transmitted in ways that fit the experiences of different social groups. This mythology is the basis of political consciousness in American society.

Myths condition the public to respond to the symbols used by politicians. In times of stability, myths underwrite the status quo, and in periods of upheaval, they chart the course of change. In the day-to-day business of politics, they set the terms for most public policy debate. When mythical themes and myth-related language are stripped away from policy discourse, little of substance remains. Most political controversy centers around disagreement over which myth to apply to a particular problem.

It is difficult to talk about this underlying structure of public thinking because myths are seldom learned as complete stories that individuals can recall at a conscious level. Rather, myths are assimilated through fragments of movies, books, school lessons, news stories, and personal experiences—inputs that blend fact with fantasy and confuse history with legend. They are transmitted as much through dramatic imagery and emotional associations as through concrete words or ideas. Their core symbols are reinforced throughout the social environment where individuals continue to encounter fragments of them in books, advertising, songs, religious ceremonies, youth organizations, business associations, school, family activities, the workplace, sporting events, and in numerous other everyday contexts.

Myth-Based Thinking

As a result of their pervasive reference to life experience, myths become deeply embedded in consciousness as associative mechanisms linking private experience, ongoing reality, and history into powerful frameworks of understanding. This suggests that they are employed in communication and opinion formation through primary process thinking. In contrast to secondary process or rational thought, primary process thinking is characterized by projection, fantasy, the incorporation of nonverbal imagery, a high emotional content, the easy connection of disparate ideas, the failure to make underlying assumptions explicit, and the generation of multiple levels of meaning. The most notable features of myth-based thinking are:

- The absence of formal logical connections between political beliefs and values and understandings about specific issues.
- The power of simple political symbols to evoke strong but unarticulated mythical understandings.
- The capacity of individuals to hold divergent, even contradictory, myths, which explains American voter tendencies to switch parties and candidates, the regular mixing of liberal and conservative views on different issues, and high individual tolerance for a range of political outcomes.

Consider an example of myth-based thinking as revealed in an interview with a veteran of the Revolutionary War battle of Concord and Lexington. The following interview was conducted by a historian some sixty years after the event. The interviewer was interested in the question of what motivated the patriot to risk his life in a struggle for independence:

Q: Why did you? . . . My histories tell me that you men of the Revolution took up arms against intolerable oppressions.

A: What were they? Oppressions? I didn't feel them.

Q: What, were you not oppressed by the Stamp Act?

A: I never saw one of those stamps . . . I am certain I never paid a penny for one of them.

Q: Well, what about the tea tax?

A: Tea tax, I never drank a drop of the stuff. The boys threw it all overboard.

Q: Then, I suppose you had been reading Harrington, or Sidney, or Locke, about the eternal principles of liberty?

A: Never heard of 'em.

Q: Well, then, what was the matter, what did you mean in going into the fight?

A: Young man, what we meant in going for those red-coats, was this: we always had governed ourselves and we always meant to. They didn't mean we should.[20]

The dictates of rational or logical analysis would have us dismiss such ramblings as meaningless. However, discounting the significance of ordinary political thinking not only robs individuals of a dignified basis for their actions, but also frustrates any possibility of understanding how politicians mobilize public support. The cryptic remark about self-government at the end of the interview is the key symbol that anchored the individual's thought and action within the mythology that dominated public consciousness at the time of the Revolution. Self-government was a popular translation of the Liberty myth that mobilized public support for the insurrection. Contemporary historians are beginning to recognize that the Liberty myth was not communicated to the masses in terms of ideological analyses of stamp acts or tea taxes. As historian Catherine Albanese noted in her excellent book on the mobilization of support for the Revolution, the myth of Liberty permeated the environment through the symbolism of poems, songs, posters, emblems, statues, and, above all, religious preachings.[21] When the myth was expressed in political terms, it was generally embedded in dramatic performances at public gatherings. In a common political ceremony described by Albanese, church bells gathered the townsfolk in the village green to witness a somber funeral procession carrying the casket of Liberty to its burial site. When the first spade began throwing dirt on the coffin, the Sons of Liberty swarmed over the landscape to rescue the symbol of self-government from an early grave. Historical accounts of this oft-repeated ritual note the attention of the audience, the impact of the plot, and the emotional release at the climax.

Just as drama, literature, and other forms of popular culture are often the most profound carriers of insight in everyday life, these forms also operate in politics to leave their impressions in the deepest levels of consciousness. This is why the formal structure or logic of myth remains hidden in ordinary political discourse. Only a few key symbols are needed to evoke meaningful responses.

Myth and Leadership

Where do leaders and candidates for public office fit into this picture? They are the ones responsible for putting on the dramas, telling the national stories, suggesting the symbols through which understandings are to be found, and connecting the wisdom of mythology to the dilemmas that bedevil daily life. The fate of the United States, perhaps more than that of any other First World nation, has depended on the rise of great leaders to preside over the rituals and invoke the myths of state— especially in elections.

How candidates approach the election ritual largely determines the course the nation will take after the voting is over. Will candidates seize the chance to be creative in telling the national story—blending new insights with old wisdoms, suggesting time-honored rationales for new programs, rallying public opinion behind powerful symbols, and inviting continued support for the changes to come? Or will they choose to play it safe—reciting tired phrases with little concern about their contemporary relevance, content to turn citizens away at the door of political understanding?

The American system's curious dependence on strong leaders to articulate the consciousness of the nation is both its greatest strength and its greatest weakness. The strength lies in having a society that is relatively free of the ideological tensions that create explosive animosities and paralyzing political divisions. Leaders with an eye to national renewal and an ear for the American mythology can mobilize support across party and class lines. The weakness is its vulnerability to political candidates who have neither a vision nor an interest in mobilizing popular participation. When getting elected is the main goal and when vision is narrowed by commitments to backers, the election ritual loses its vitality. Society stagnates and people lose hope. Times of failed leadership are particularly distressing in the American system because there are no traditions of strong parties or guiding ideologies to reverse the decline. Instead, people must rely on slow and often exhausting social movements to bring about reforms. Even these movements are heavily dependent on strong leaders, although they often attract a leadership relatively free of obligations to special interests.

This overview of myth, leadership, and public consciousness does not imply that bold leadership alone is sufficient to move the nation. The irony of American politics is that effective leaders generally move the public in new directions by finding creative applications of old mythologies. The memorable failures of Barry Goldwater on the right and George McGovern on the left suggest that when radical ideas are not cloaked in the proper mythology they seldom capture the popular imagination.

The public rejects radical alternatives not because of their calculable impact on life quality, but because they cannot be assimilated meaningfully into the spectrum of myth. Intolerance in this sense is quite literally a fear of the unknown and the unimaginable. This sort of intolerance is illustrated in political scientist Karl Lamb's study of members of a wealthy conservative California community. Even though Lamb found people scattered all along the spectrum of political myth, he discovered that none of them could imagine political solutions that fell outside that range of myth. For example, Lamb concluded that his respondents "cannot really imagine a society that would provide substantial material equality." One of the people he interviewed had the following incredulous response to the idea of guaranteed economic equality: "It would be like everyone going out for a track race and saying, 'Okay, everyone can run this race in the same time,' so eventually there would be no more records to be gone after."[22]

For example, in the 1972 election Democratic presidential candidate George McGovern provoked strong public rejection by proposing a guaranteed minimum income for every American. McGovern's failure to cast his plan in familiar mythic symbols elicited a hostility based on confusion. One of Lamb's respondents expressed his confusion by posing the rhetorical question of why superwealthy people like Howard Hughes would need an extra thousand dollars. In contrast to this popular rejection of the McGovern plan stands the overwhelming public approval of Republican president Richard Nixon's earlier proposal for a guaranteed annual income. Shortly after taking office in 1968, Nixon proposed a Family Assistance Plan to the public and to Congress. The most significant difference between the Nixon and McGovern plans was not the amount of the stipends or their probable impact on society and economy, but the way in which the plans were symbolized. In his presentation of the Family Assistance Plan to the public, Nixon did not even mention the concept of a guaranteed income. Instead, he stressed the work incentives and other conditions attached to the financial assistance. Recipients were required to accept job training and a job while they were in the program. As an incentive to work, they would continue to receive a diminishing stipend until their income brought them above the designated poverty line.

The symbolism in Nixon's proposal aimed at the very center of the mythological spectrum bounded by the characteristic American themes of individualism and equality of opportunity. The result was impressive from a political standpoint. An overwhelming 78 percent of the public supported the plan.[23] Even more revealing is the fact that Lamb's respondents discussed the program and the social problems it addressed in a vocabulary of symbols that was a perfect parallel to Nixon's myth-based references.[24] This suggests that normal political communication is referenced in myth. Elites use, and the public looks for, key symbols that carry implicit mythological meanings. In the new American politics, the problem of leadership is that politicians increasingly use polls to canvass publics—and very narrow politically calculated publics at that—for clues about what *they* think at the moment, how *they* feel about problems. The rituals of the political system collapse under this reversal of traditional leadership assumptions. Publics nowadays do not hear leaders taking bold stands, educating people about new applications for traditional values and beliefs, or suggesting that times call for inventing new myths.

ARE THERE MYTHS FOR TODAY?

The contemporary political scene is fascinating because it has been dominated by politicians who are struggling to break out of this cultural short-circuit, yet seem unable to recognize the political forces that frustrate their attempts. For example, Bill Clinton had a chance to lead the nation toward major health care reform, but fumbled the attempt, in part, because he could not define his efforts symbolically in ways that would withstand the relentless attacks of various opponents. Perhaps Clinton could have used such a crucial political moment to redefine basic cultural values in support of the embattled reform. Health care might have been portrayed as a new American right. On the other hand, it might have been promoted by inventing a new myth—perhaps a story about a people who shared the gift of health for all, regardless of wealth or line of work.

At another end of the political spectrum, we have Newt Gingrich who has a conscious sense of the importance of mythology for leadership and government. Yet he used the considerable resources of his leadership PAC (see Chapter 6) to construct the mythic image of a Republican Contract with America. Although the components of that contract may be popular and genuinely meaningful with certain groups, the appeal of the values embodied in the new Republican mythology is clearly limited; it is geared to the carefully selected 20 to 30 percent of the total electorate needed to win midterm and presidential elections in a system that is increasingly incapable or unwilling to reach out to larger numbers of frustrated citizens. Of what value is a leader's understanding of the uses of mythology if the resulting myths are designed for exclusive minorities of the citizenry? The manufacture of exclusionary myths that appeal to the bare minorities needed to win elections does not bode well for the future of government.

The vitality of elections lies not just in choosing leaders, but in making those choices meaningful for as many voters as possible. Unless presidential candidates can dramatize their goals to the satisfaction of large numbers of people, the importance of elections for the political system is greatly diminished. Without strong leadership emerging from the electoral arena, and without continuing popular support for the political vision embodied in that leadership, the curious and cumbersome American system of checks and balances remains unworkable.

The dilemma of American politics lies in finding strong, creative leaders at the precise time we need them. In the past, the nation has been blessed with a remarkable number of visionaries who emerged from the wings to mobilize both Congress and the people through crisis and change. The question today is whether the current system of campaigning discourages strong leaders from seeking office in the first place or, if they do run, from taking the risks necessary to mobilize people behind bold courses of action. We may have reached an impasse in which the very leadership qualities necessary to the functioning of the system have been screened out by the rules of the contemporary campaign game. Even when promising leaders choose to play the game, they may have to bend their rhetorical talents and ideas to the dictates of campaign consultants who are, after all, the experts on how to get elected these days. And when those candidates are elected, they face the unhappy prospect of having failed to cultivate the public understanding and support necessary to carry out their political goals effectively. If the rules of the current election game systematically work against the rise of leaders with clear and sustainable visions for future action, what will the future bring for a nation poised on the brink of great historical changes both at home and abroad? This is the question to be explored in the next part of the book.

PART IV

The Future of Electoral Democracy

CHAPTER 9

Leadership, Symbolic Politics, and the Struggle for Democracy

Once there was a time when the dome of the Capitol was a symbol of something good, a majestic backdrop for commercials in a re-election campaign. . . .

[In the ads that contributed to the Republican landslide of 1994] the dome of the Capitol is often used as a symbol of corruption and government gone awry, even by incumbents. Clinking champagne glasses are superimposed on it, dark limousines pull up at its steps. —*Robin Toner*

The Republican landslide of 1994 came wrapped in contradictions, paradoxes, and ironies. The contradiction was that of an election that promised (really, this time) to clean up the mess in Washington, while setting an all-time congressional campaign spending record and reaching new levels of negative campaigning. Then there is the paradox of an election called a landslide when the winning party was supported by just 21 percent of the eligible voters. Finally, we have the irony that the struggle between the two political parties has become so intense at a time when many observers and most voters consider the two parties to be hopelessly weak and ineffective, if not politically dead.

These and other aspects of the new American politics can be seen most clearly in election contests between dinosaur parties that seem unable to settle on agendas that appeal to more than bare voting majorities. Even the Republican "Contract with America" was recognized and supported by a minority of the 38.5 percent of the eligible electorate who voted in 1994. Leadership has become a battle of images among politicians whose personal ambitions (and marketing strategies) often compete with the good of their own parties. Issues in such fragmented and calculating politics are often the symbolic sort that move voters emotionally in the short term without leaving much of a lasting mark on social problems. All of the changes add up to a system that is rapidly undermining the basic assumptions of democracy itself.

ELECTIONS AND REPRESENTATION: REVERSING THE BASIC ASSUMPTIONS OF DEMOCRACY

Perhaps the most troublesome development of the new politics is its role in reversing the very idea of elections and representation. Traditional assumptions about democracy describe a system in which representatives are sent back to the seat of government to push for issues that won them votes in the last election. As we have noted, we are now approaching a system in which promises from the last election are routinely sacrificed to strategic calculations about how to win the next one. Issues that matter to people—health care being a good example—often become chewed up in calculations about how to make opponents in government look weak and ineffective in the eyes of their former voters. The irony, of course, is that "playing politics" with important issues makes all sides look bad. Perhaps the ultimate irony is that these same politicians campaign against the very ills of government that they have helped create. This political world has become a dizzying play of symbols in the news and advertising, with the Capitol being condemned most vigorously by those who most want to work there. As one top campaign consultant described the symbolic uses of the Capitol building in 1994 campaign ads: "It rattles, it shakes, it opens up, money is poured into it; it's clear that it has become demonized."[1]

In this upside-down world where parties may regard issues as opportunities to defeat each other rather than as a means of delivering government to the people, one might even ask why parties bother to contest elections at all. Yet the obvious answer in the new American politics is that parties remain the strategic mechanisms for handing out power to individual members who still need political bases from which to reward their financial backers and continue advancing their careers.

CHAMELEON PARTIES, INDEPENDENT POLITICIANS, AND THE NEW POWER GAME

The unexpectedly quick return to gridlock following the Democratic sweep of power in 1992 in part reflected the fact that the political fortunes of individual members of Congress depend less on loyalty to party or president than ever before. Congressional careers today develop through the efforts of individual politician-entrepreneurs who attract financial support from organized interests, deliver government services to states and home districts, and proclaim their allegiance to parties and presidents when it seems politically expedient to do so. During the 1994 California Senate race, for example, Democratic incumbent Dianne Feinstein recognized Bill Clinton's appeal to wealthy liberals by embracing him at a Beverly Hills fundraiser that produced nearly $1 million for her expensive campaign against Republican challenger Michael Huffington, who was spending a sizable portion of his personal fortune to get elected. Yet Feinstein later withdrew as a legislative sponsor of the Clinton health plan after polls showed that the president's name on the plan caused public support to "sink like a rock," as one health care analyst put it.[2] Another example of the absence of party loyalty was provided by the congressional campaign brochure of Georgia Democrat Craig Mathis, which according to one observer offered "prospective voters no clue as to whether Mr. Mathis is a Democrat, a Republican, or some kind of hybrid."[3] As *Time* magazine observed, the casual observer of the 1994 campaigns might "suppose that no one is a Democrat—especially the Democrats."[4]

In fact, the 1994 elections saw the president's pollster, Stanley Greenberg, advising Democratic candidates to emphasize their own records rather than their ties to the president or the party. He even issued a memo advising candidates how to respond to Republican attacks that they were liberals, Democrats, or Clinton supporters. In his "Strategic Guide to the 1994 Election," Greenberg advised candidates to make campaign issues of "their accomplishments and their agenda to help people at home." Greenberg continued, "There is no reason to highlight [your accomplishments] as Clinton or Democratic proposals."[5]

Typical of the new electoral politics, this advice echoes a similar warning issued in the previous midterm election in 1990 by Edward Rollins, then chair of the Republican congressional campaign committee. President Bush had damaged his popularity by agreeing to a tax hike that toppled his famous 1988 campaign pledge: "Read my lips. No new taxes." Rollins bluntly told candidates that inviting President Bush to help them campaign or otherwise identifying with him could "fatally wound your campaign."[6]

Chameleon candidates, disappearing parties, and fears of voter backlash against incumbent presidents—these features of recent midterm elections reflect more than just the historical fact that the party holding the White House nearly always loses seats in the midterm election. Changes in the relations among voters, candidates, and parties described throughout this book signal new patterns of power in the American political system.

As noted in Chapter 3, the conventional wisdom in Washington today is that political clout is directly linked to media images and public approval ratings. Recall here the view of CNN pollster and pundit William Schneider, who describes Washington as a town of individual political entrepreneurs who rely less on parties for their political support than on their own media images, along with the popularity of visible politicians like the president.[7] Consider, for example, the decision of Representative Lee Hamilton (D-Indiana) to vote with those who temporarily blocked the president's 1994 crime bill at a crucial moment in both Clinton's and the party's effort to make good on campaign promises from the last election. Hamilton, a key "player" in Washington and a prominent member of the Democratic party establishment, defected from the party leadership on a key election year issue with this explanation:

> The basic nature of American politics has changed. I don't get elected because of what Bill Clinton thinks or what the House leadership thinks. The electorate makes up its own mind. That inevitably means that presidents have a lot less clout with Congress than they used to have. All presidents, I mean.
>
> It's also true that when a President is riding high his influence goes up, and when a President is in the dumps the way Clinton is, his influence declines.[8]

PARTY POLITICS AND THE 1994 ELECTION

Entrepreneurial politics were evident in how members of Congress approached the issues of crime and health care on the eve of the 1994 election. One House vote involving the crime bill saw some liberal and conservative Democrats joining a number of conservative Republicans to block consideration of a bill endorsed by the Democratic leadership and the White House. In what congressional scholar Norman Ornstein described as a "failure of followership," fifty-eight Democrats—including three committee chairmen, seventeen subcommittee chairmen, and a chief deputy whip—in effect voted against the president's crime bill.[9] Even greater disarray swirled around health care, including a half dozen different proposals from the Democrats and a late-arriving Republican plan—all opposing key provisions of the legislative proposal from the White House. Both the crime and the health care debates were complicated by the constant hum of interest group lobbying and electoral campaign strategizing that shaped both the legislation and the votes cast in Congress.

Party Fragmentation and the Struggle for Power

Glaring legislative failures signal a breakdown in the ideas and ideologies that bind parties to governing programs, yet the parties' struggle to control government remains an enduring feature of the political system. Today, that struggle is marked by internal divisions over ideology and the role of government in both parties. These internal struggles complicate the jobs of party leaders, who must be concerned both with internal party discipline and with appealing to voters. At the same time, shifts in their geographical bases of power are raising the electoral stakes and changing the parties' electoral strategies.

Ideological Fragmentation in the Republican Camp

The Republican party is struggling to bridge the gap between moderate Republicans and conservative Christians, often called the "religious right." At the leadership level, the split is personified in the differences between "country-clubbers" like George Bush and Virginia Senator John Warner, and social conservatives like former vice president Dan Quayle and former education secretary Bill Bennett. At the grass-roots level, religious conservatives have become a significant source of activist energy and electoral strength for the GOP. In many locales around the country, conservative Christians have been remarkably successful at electoral politics, prompting the observation that "the Religious Right . . . has outorganized every other force in the Republican party, sponsored a rump attack on the governor of Minnesota, thwarted a liberal school curriculum in New York City, [and] seen its candidate receive the party's U.S. Senate nomination in Virginia."[10] Indeed, one political trade publication rated conservative Christian strength as "dominant" in state Republican party organizations in eighteen states.[11] But their ardent views on social issues such as abortion, sex education, and school prayer have threatened to alienate other Republicans, as well as middle-of-the road independents.

Thus, Republican party leaders face tough dilemmas. The party can't afford to lose the support of either group (conservative Christians make up about one-third of the Republican base vote),[12] but neither can it afford to let divisive issues like abortion marginalize the party. In 1992 some Republicans, including George Bush, proclaimed that the party could offer "a big tent" to accommodate a diversity of views on controversial social issues. But this approach has not won over some conservative Christians who believe that the Republican party needs to be less accommodating, not more. The dilemma intensified in 1994, as Clinton's presidency further energized the religious right, especially its political center-piece organization, the Christian Coalition. In turn, this spurred the creation of the Republican Majority Coalition, founded by Senator Arlen Specter of Pennsylvania, to offset the religious right's influence within the GOP. Afraid of its various powder keg issues, the party has turned to various antigovernment themes in an effort to rally diverse factions and independent voters at election time. Despite these efforts at party unity, elections bring out the party divisions. In 1996, for example, the presidential primaries shaped up as a battle between GOP moderates such as Robert Dole and Arlen Specter, and those with appeal to the Christian right, such as Phil Gramm and Pat Buchanan.

The "New" Democrats

Democrats, meanwhile, are in the midst of an ideological identity crisis of their own. With the very word "liberal" having become an effective tool of negative campaigning, many Democrats have shied away from defending that label and have instead sought an image—and an ideology—makeover. The "new Democrat" is the result: Democrats who favor much of the fiscal moderation promoted by many Republicans and who themselves attack older-style liberalism, taking carefully compromised positions on potentially troublesome social issues such as abortion and welfare. Richard Fisher of Texas, who challenged Republican Senator Kay Bailey Hutchison in the Texas Senate race in 1994, exemplified this new-fashioned Democrat. Described by a Democratic primary opponent as "a closet Republican," Fisher donated thousands of dollars to Republican candidates in past contests and worked as an advisor to Ross Perot in 1992. Explained Fisher, "The Democratic Party in Texas is dying—or put it this way, it's atrophying. Frankly it's in such bad shape it makes me possible."[13]

Although Fisher's support for members of other parties was perhaps unique, he was far from alone in his centrist outlook. In fact, he represented a movement within the Democratic party which sought to shift the party toward the center of the political spectrum. That movement is represented by the Democratic Leadership Council (DLC) which Fisher helped to found in 1985 and whose former leader was Bill Clinton. The DLC conceived Clinton's presidency as "a bridge to a new Democratic Party" and its enemies as "the old interests and the old constituencies" within the Democratic party, which "new" Democrats blame for the party's national electoral defeats throughout the 1980s.[14] Yet after Clinton was elected president, the Council found itself sometimes clashing with the very man who had represented the movement. On budget cuts, a proposed energy tax, and the president's economic plan, centrist DLC Democrats blocked Clinton's initiatives. The most notable clash was over health care, with the Council supporting the proposal authored by Council member Representative Jim Cooper of Tennessee (the proposal known as "Clinton Lite"), rather than supporting the president's bill.

Thus, the Democratic party faces an ideological dilemma of its own. Both "new" and "old" Democrats hold powerful positions within Congress. Even those without much institutional clout, like Cooper (he was eleventh in seniority among Democrats on the House Energy and Commerce subcommittee considering health care reform, and he eventually lost a bid for a Tennessee Senate seat), had proven themselves capable of re-routing a presidential program. Hence, many pundits advised Clinton—and any other Democrat who would be president—to move further to the center. Yet without the support of traditional liberals and progressives, a Democratic president would have a tough time mustering enough votes within Congress or the general population to win legislative proposals or elections. The political power of one liberal faction was demonstrated when the Congressional Black Caucus, comprising a block of thirty-eight votes in the 103rd Congress, withheld its support for the crime bill and helped to nearly sink it.

These ideological rifts and adjustments raise serious problems for party coherence on both sides of the aisle. Now perhaps more than ever, what it means to be a Republican or a Democrat is not always clear. As the 1994 elections approached, however, Republicans strove to present a unified front. Over 300 Republican congressional candidates even signed a "Contract with America," a ten-point legislative program they promised to bring to the floor of the House should they gain control of that chamber (explained in more detail below). Many Democrats, meanwhile, campaigned against President Clinton, against liberalism, and even against other Democrats as they sought office. In Nebraska, for example, Senator Bob Kerrey's campaign ads carefully listed the issues on which he and the president had taken opposite sides.[15]

Independent Voting and Volatile Voters

The practice of parties lining up behind symbolic facades that hide their inner disarray is reinforced by the growing ranks of independent voters. As noted in earlier chapters, independent voters mean more work for campaign strategists, who must figure out how to win them over aside from appeals to party loyalty. Defining government and the opposition as enemies is a common strategy, but it is not a stable one. Widespread dissatisfaction with government has combined with the tradition of independent voting to produce a particularly volatile, even fickle, voting public. As one professor of marketing observes, "Where customer satisfaction is not high, you see a lot of switching. [People say] 'I'll buy one I haven't tried recently.' "[16] In politics, there is less loyalty to "brand"—party—when people are generally dissatisfied with the political process. "Brand-switching" is one way that independent voting coupled with general frustration with politics gets expressed.

Significant dissatisfaction with the parties was expressed in a poll reported in September 1994, which showed that 53 percent of American voters believed there should be a third major American political party. It also uncovered a populace that is "angry, self-absorbed, and politically unanchored." "There is no clear direction in the public's political thinking," the pollsters concluded, "other than frustration with the current system and an eager responsiveness to alternative political solutions and appeals."[17] Their findings point to a complex and volatile combination of enduring "independent" orientations to politics and a large number of voters who are angry and alienated from the political system.

Given widespread voter dissatisfaction with Congress, both sides have made Congress and its "gridlock" an issue in recent elections. The Democrats blame Republicans for the failure of major legislation. Although they initially denied it in 1994, the GOP later deployed a novel strategy of promoting gridlock if it stopped unwanted Democratic legislation. An all too familiar campaign strategy thus becomes one of shifting the blame for what many voters perceive as a government failure.

The Republican Strategy

As congressional scholar Gary Jacobsen has observed, "Only failed administrations offer [the party out of power] leverage against those who share the president's party."[18] The 1994 elections offered Republicans an opportunity to campaign against what they tried to define as a failed administration. In trying to build a campaign around this strategic theme, the Republican party took two gambles in the middle of the campaign season: they gambled that the anti-incumbent mood among voters would help them gain seats in Congress and in state houses across the country, and they gambled that a policy of stalling major legislation until after the election would allow them to fan the flames of anti-incumbent anger and add to a negative public image of the Clinton administration. As chairman of the National Republican Congressional Committee Bill Paxon put it, "There is no doubt in the public's mind who runs Congress. Democrats are in charge. . . . And Congress' [popularity] numbers have been going in one direction: down."[19] The Republican wait-until-November legislative strategy, affirmed at the Republican National Committee summer meeting in Los Angeles in July, was the result. Party leaders argued that the country would be better off if major health care reform legislation was not passed by the 103rd Congress and was instead taken up in the following legislative session. Republicans in the Senate filibustered with relish, setting a record for using that means of obstruction.[20] Lacking the sixty votes necessary to overcome filibusters, Democratic legislation in the Senate languished.

While portraying their move as a response to public concerns that health care reform was moving too fast or even in the wrong direction, Republicans also acknowledged the electoral advantages they could gain from withholding their support for Democratic legislation. As Representative Dick Armey (R-Texas) said to his colleagues, "Why should we be enthusiastic about helping Democrats pull their political fat out of the fire with our ideas?"[21] The risks in this gamble lay in the fact that this strategy also potentially endangered Republican incumbents, who were no more immune to anti-incumbency voting than Democrats. (Of the 111 House members elected in 1992 with only 55 percent of the vote or less, almost half were Republicans.)[22] Therefore, already shaky Republican seats could be lost by portraying incumbency as the problem. There were also risks to being perceived as "obstructionists" and therefore as the real cause of gridlock. A late August *Time*–CNN poll confirmed the danger, showing that 48 percent of the public saw the Republicans as the main cause of government stalemate, with 32 percent holding the president most to blame.[23]

Republican campaign managers realized they needed to project an image of readiness to legislate so as to minimize the potential electoral costs of their strategy. They also faced the possibility that, as one Democratic pollster contended, "There is . . . no positive Republican message, and they are dependent on the vagaries of how people feel about the Democrats at any given time."[24] Hoping to convince voters that Republicans had more than stalling on their minds, the party fashioned the aforementioned "Contract with America." This was a pledge by Republican congressional candidates and incumbents to vote on a program of legislation, including tax cuts and a balanced budget amendment, in their first one hundred days in office. While seeming to offer a coherent governing vision, the Contract was simply a pledge to vote to bring such legislation to the House floor, not necessarily to vote to enact it. And some Republican representatives signed the Contract while simultaneously promising to fight against some of its provisions, especially term limits for members of

Congress.[25] The Contract, like most issues in the new election system, was the product of intensive focus group research and polling. Aimed at the middle class, it included only those issues that consistently received 65 percent or higher approval among targeted voter groups. (Thus, abortion and other moral issues were excluded.) When accused of passing off a marketing ploy as a revolutionary party program, the Contract's architect Newt Gingrich said: "Politics is about public opinion and gathering public support. It's like saying, isn't it pandering for WalMart to stock everything people want to buy."[26]

As noted earlier, most voters did not hear of the Contract until after the election, when the new Republican Congress began promoting it as the centerpiece of a "first hundred days" media campaign. However, during the campaign the national press picked up on the important fact that the party was making a national appeal in a midterm election. (Midterm elections generally focus more on local politics than on broad party strategies.) Coupled with the intensive advertising attack on the president and his party in Congress, this news script cast the Republicans as a united alternative to the Democrats. This impression of a national campaign was probably more important than the fact that the platform around which the party had united was poorly understood. Congressional races thus became votes on the president and his party.

The Democratic Strategy

The Democrats needed to show that the era of gridlock was over. Clinton and the Democratic leadership gambled early in the 103rd Congress that a flurry of legislative activism would result both in policy accomplishments and a new era of good feeling about government. The strategy was indeed a gamble; a failure to produce concrete policy results could mean disaster for Democrats. Public opinion was hard to read. The public seemed to want and yet not want major reform of the health care system. Public ambivalence increased as interest groups and prominent Republicans waged an aggressive campaign to discredit the White House health care bill. In July *The National Journal* reported: "A recent CNN–*USA Today* poll sums up the Democrats' predicament. Although a majority of Americans still maintain that the health care system is in crisis, and 62 per cent say that Clinton should veto a bill that doesn't provide universal coverage, support for the President's proposal has eroded badly (49 per cent oppose it, and just 43 per cent favor it), and support for the President himself is shaky."[27] By September, when the Senate declared health care reform dead, even the public's belief that the health care system needed fixing seemed to have faded. The increase in public confusion allowed Republicans to block legislative proposals at every turn—blaming delays on Democratic fumbling and fondness for "big government" solutions to public problems.

As is characteristic of a party in disarray, the Democrats were little help to themselves or their leader, as they consistently failed to act on their own initiatives. On every major piece of legislation, individual Democrats peeled away from their party and thus helped turn the Democratic gamble into a losing bet. With a seventy-eight-seat majority in the House, Democrats found it difficult to blame Republican obstructionism for the near-failure of the budget and crime bills and the failure of health reform legislation. In the Senate, powerful committee chairs such as Ted Kennedy and Daniel Patrick Moynihan fought over who would have primary jurisdiction over the legislation. As Republican Minority Leader Newt Gingrich colorfully put it, the Democrats would have a tough time saying to voters, "We've run the House for 40 years, we've run the Senate for eight years, we have the White House, and the Republicans are so much more clever that they've obstructed us. We need you to elect more dumb Democrats so we can overcome these clever Republicans."[28]

On September 26, Senate Majority Leader George Mitchell announced that health care reform legislation would be abandoned for the remainder of the 103rd Congress. The Republican legislative strategy appeared to have worked, as many voters reported that the failure of health care convinced them that the Democrats were unable to govern. At the same time, the fact that the Republicans had effectively nationalized the media campaign (through both the Contract and the attacks on Clinton's leadership) required the Democrats to put on a national campaign of their own. Buoyed by a successful round of foreign policy successes, the campaign strategists sent Clinton out on the campaign trail. Nearly everywhere he went, voters saw the president addressing a campaign rally for a local representative on the news, while commercials linked the same representative to the legislative failures of the Democrats under Clinton's leadership. The candidate's face was often "morphed" into Clinton's to make the psychological connection even clearer. The combination of news and advertising proved deadly, and the Republicans swept the Democratic majority out of Congress.

THE SYMBOL WARS

Perhaps the greatest lesson of recent elections is that no matter how important particular issues may be to voters, almost nothing is sacred when it comes to plotting campaign strategies. Concerns such as health care are sacrificed to party or candidate strategies that put winning elections above the preferences of majorities of citizens. Other issues, such as crime, drugs, government spending, budgets, and taxes, are so emotionally charged that candidates and parties compete to promise voters miracle solutions. Those promises, and the legislation that occasionally flows from them, seldom solve the problems, but they continue to attract the votes needed to win elections.

The War On (fill in your favorite issue, problem, or country here)

It has become part of the American way of politics to declare war on national problems. Wars on crime, poverty, and drugs have occurred and recurred in the past several decades. Wars make for good symbolic politics, at once turning public concerns about a dreaded problem into support for the leaders fighting it, and at the same time reassuring people that something is being done about those problems that aroused their fears to begin with.[29]

At least since Machiavelli began advising his prince, politics in most societies have had strong symbolic and public relations overtones. In contemporary America, however, there may not be much substance left after the election is over and the marketing consultants move into staff positions with the politicians they helped elect. Of course, lots of government activities are still going on: crises, bailouts, stopgap measures, and the like. But would there be so many crises to manage, or gaps to stop, or disasters to bail out if a bit more governing was going on at the center? Indeed, when administrations and congresses try to look ahead and take concerted action against social problems these days, the superficiality of governing becomes most apparent.

The Wars on Drugs and Crime

In recent decades, the most popular wars have been those on crime and drugs. The question is not whether these are serious problems that plague society, but whether the symbolic wars waged against them have much to do with solving those problems. Consider, for example, the last several presidential efforts to solve the drug and crime problems, beginning with Ronald Reagan and continuing through Bill Clinton. The levels of casual or recreational drug use had peaked and were in decline again by the time Ronald Reagan came into office in 1981. In the early years of his administration, the spotlight was not on drugs but on cutting many of the social programs that provided a broad policy context for the drug wars (particularly against hard-core drug use) in the decades before. Only after much of this programmatic context had been whittled away did the Reagan advisory team discover a symbolic use for another drug war. The Reagan remake of *Drug Wars* was devised in considerable part as a marketing strategy not for the popular president but for his less beloved wife, Nancy.

White House polls showed that the First Lady's reputation for designer clothing, hobnobbing with the rich and famous, and expensive White House entertainment and decorating tastes all mixed poorly with her general lack of social concerns. As a result, Nancy Reagan's negative public image grated uneasily alongside the president's easygoing popularity. Even worse, the First Lady's uncaring image seemed to be rubbing off on her husband. Marketing research conducted by Richard Wirthlin turned up drugs as an issue that could be used to reach out and touch (image-wise, that is) real people—particularly children—caught up in what was obviously a serious social problem.[30] And so Nancy Reagan was cast as the media star (with husband Ron in a strong supporting role) in a prolonged national war on drugs. The script of this long-playing political commercial was reduced to a single sound bite: "Just Say NO" (to drugs). It was simple, clear, and, above all, successful—not in reducing drug use but in elevating the First Lady's public image to its proper (positive) place alongside that of her already popular husband. For these and other masterstrokes of marketing and media manipulation during the Reagan presidency, Richard Wirthlin was crowned Advertising Man of the Year in 1989.[31] It was an industry Oscar given not for his creative work for General Foods or Mattel Toys, but for his career-capping achievements as director of consumer research for Ronald Reagan.

Next we come to George Bush and *Drug Wars, 1990*. Having little in the way of domestic programs to implement, White House media advisors and marketing specialists decided to stage yet another revival of what has become by now a modern political classic. Typical of political issues that do not have governing ideas behind them, the drug war of the Bush administration was also largely an image device. This time, George Bush replaced Nancy Reagan in the starring role, and the specific image objectives were altered to suit the new star's political needs. Mrs. Reagan was in need of warming up—an image achieved by casting her in media events surrounded by schoolchildren and rehabilitating Americans of all races and social backgrounds. Bush, meanwhile, was still haunted by his image as a wimp. Although his wimpiness was fairly well overcome during the election by negative campaigning and Clint Eastwood sound bites, drugs offered the chance to continue playing Mr. Tough Guy in office. This anti-wimp image was further enhanced by creating a special office for drug-fighting, filled initially by another tough guy, William Bennett, whom the media dubbed the drug czar. Thus, the same social problem was used to create a softer, more likable image for one political figure and a harder, tougher image for another. And both transformations were brought to the public through the wonders of market research and political advertising techniques.

For their part, the media played opportunistic roles in covering the Bush remake of *Drug Wars*. Television networks conducted their own ratings wars with dramatic and often frightening coverage of gangs, violence, drug lords, addicted children, and cities turned into murder capitals. At the same time, the news was surprisingly critical of Bush's symbolic crusade, pointing out that its law and order emphasis (including guerrilla warfare in the cocaine fields of Bolivia) was more likely to win political cheers from conservatives than to get at the roots of a serious American social problem. Thus, although the media could be faulted for turning the urban drug scene into police drama "infotainment" on the nightly news, there were also a few hopeful signs that news organizations were resisting the White House's management techniques.

One case in point was the *Washington Post*'s investigative report about a bag of crack cocaine held up by George Bush the night he first declared war in a nationally televised speech. Bush offered the bag of crack as evidence that the drug problem could be found right across the street from his own home at 1600 Pennsylvania Avenue. The president told a national television audience that the crack had been purchased by undercover agents in Lafayette Park, across the street. The *Post*'s investigative efforts revealed that even this tiny skirmish in the national drug war had been staged to bring the real world in line with the political script of the media consultants. Here are the opening paragraphs of the *Washington Post* story that received wide media play:

> *Washington.* White House speech writers thought it was the perfect prop for President George Bush's first prime-time television address to the nation—a dramatic one that would show how the drug trade had spread to the president's own neighborhood.
>
> "This is crack cocaine," Mr. Bush solemnly announced in his Sept. 5 speech on drug policy, holding up a plastic bag filled with a white chunky substance. It was "seized a few days ago in a park across the street from the White House," he said, adding, "It could easily have been heroin or PCP."
>
> But obtaining the crack was no easy feat. To match the words of the speech writers, Drug Enforcement Administration agents lured a sus-

pected Washington drug dealer to Lafayette Park four days before the speech. They made what appears to have been the agency's first undercover crack buy in a park better known for its location across Pennsylvania Avenue from the White House than for illegal drug activity, according to officials familiar with the case.

In fact, the teen-age suspect, when first contacted by an undercover agent posing as a buyer, seemed baffled by the request.

"Where is the White House?" he replied in a conversation that was secretly tape-recorded by the drug agency.

"We had to manipulate him to get him down here," said William McMullen, assistant special agent in charge of the agency's Washington field office. "It wasn't easy."[32]

All in all, when Bush took his turn at commanding the drug crusade, the press seemed more determined than usual to point out that the emperor had no clothes. Or as cartoonist Pat Oliphant parodied the president's famous "read my lips" cliché, "The emperor has no lips." The trouble was that Bush applied the Number One damage control rule to the situation, sealed his lips, and staged a diversionary media event. Shortly after the *Washington Post* story on the staged drug bust appeared, the president took an image trip to a Maine tree farm to demonstrate his environmental concern. Yet rather than conduct dutiful interviews about the president's relations with baby trees, the press hounded him about the staged drug bust that dramatized his national speech. The president suggested testily that questioning his methods in such a holy crusade made reporters antagonists in the drug war: "I don't understand," he complained. "I mean, has somebody got some advocates here for this drug guy?"[33]

In this day of managed news, it is doubtful that many people were shocked or even surprised when the bag of cocaine held up by the president turned out to be a theatrical prop. The irony of press criticism these days may be in confirming suspicions about how unresponsive leaders have become to reasonable public expectations about their conduct. There is something more the press could do to promote responsible political leadership: formulate its own agenda of national issues. Editors and producers may sense that it is risky for the press to do anything beyond allowing government officials to define the *crisis du jour,* and then respond critically if the winds of public opinion and elite opposition are blowing in the right direction. Yet, keeping the heat turned up on a few widely recognized big problems like the budget deficit, defense boondoggling, campaign financing, or rebuilding the economy just might meet with more public approval than a superstitious media establishment imagines.

Until the press ups the political ante, politicians will continue to tackle issues that are safe, surefire nonlosers. The drug war fills the bill neatly. To begin with, its reassuring familiarity makes it easy to pass off as a widely accepted problem. Indeed, almost every politician in the past twenty years has addressed it. Equally importantly, this means that few political opponents will openly expose the issue as a sham or a fruitless distraction when everybody else is scrambling to jump on the political bandwagon. If these features are not enough to make drugs the perfect "can't lose" political issue, the war imagery is rich with rhetorical possibilities ranging from poor, addicted children and terrorized neighborhoods to despicable enemies, foreign and domestic.

It is not surprising that the last piece of major legislation coming out of Washington on the eve of the 1994 election was a crime bill. The parties struggled both internally and between themselves over whose approach to crime (and its leading symbolic partner, drugs) would appear to be tougher. Bill Clinton boasted of putting more police on the streets. Republicans heralded harsher punishment. Even after the election was over, the new Congress continued to wrangle over crime and drug policies. The Republicans reopened hearings on the just-passed crime legislation to try to weed out liberal rehabilitation measures and tighten up punishment. Both parties battled to convince voters that they were tough on crime, drugs, and related social evils. The Democrats were up against the powerful symbolic challenge of trying to look as tough as Republicans in their efforts to punish dangerous criminals. All that was missing was thoughtful debate about workable solutions for real problems that many citizens live with and want to see solved in meaningful ways. In the new politics, actually solving problems is less important than creating political images that appeal to select groups of voters and that enhance the election chances of parties and their members. The real problems addressed by a symbol war are winning elections and building political images. Meanwhile, crime and drugs continue to live lives of their own in the real world, seemingly immune to government policies that have more impact on the minds of voters than on the behaviors of criminals and drug users.

A Culture Addicted to Symbols

An anthropologist would find the current symbolic scene in the United States fascinating from a cultural standpoint. The political culture has become stuck—recycling the symbolic scripts of old solutions and applying them melodramatically to new problems. The drug epidemic, like dozens of other items in the political crisis inventory, has its origins in a stagnating society burdened with serious problems at the core. Yet politicians who are both dependent on and divided by campaign financing, political marketing, and media management are unable to contemplate the programmatic reforms that might actually bring about social renewal. This is a classic vicious cycle. Because politicians are unwilling to address long-term solutions to the big social problems, they must launch ever grander symbolic crusades against symptomatic social crises, such as drugs, that spin off from the core problems. As the political paralysis worsens, symbolic crusades become the only recourse for politicians. To appear to be doing nothing would further antagonize the dwindling numbers of citizens who remain involved in the political process.

The symbolic crusades create a curious psychological state among the public—call it an addiction to more symbols. Here is how symbol addiction works: people become frightened, angry, and preoccupied with symbolic issues that seem so real and threatening, yet the failure of government to solve the problems leaves people empty and discouraged. Only more symbols can temporarily relieve these emotional downswings, even if those symbols ultimately prove to be disconnected from real solutions as well. Images of a besieged society create a fortress mentality in which the good burghers retreat behind the castle walls awaiting the daily supply of symbolic reassurance to calm their fears about the state of siege outside. Leaders bereft of hard political issues are only too happy to fill the public demand for symbols.

Thus, both parties compete to show which is tougher on crime and drugs, which can deliver bigger tax cuts to the middle class, which is really going to control the budget, and so on. These positions reflect what marketers say the public wants to hear. If one side tells people what they want to hear and the other does not, the side trying to be realistic tends to lose elections. It is hard to break out of this psychologically addictive cycle, since the more fantastic the symbols that politicians promise people, the more people expect their personal fantasies to be addressed by their representatives. Whether the politicians or the people are more to blame is beside the point. The engine that drives this symbolic spiral to ever more absurd promises and pandering for votes is the assumption that winning elections is the most important goal in politics, and that sacrificing principles and common goals is the price that must be paid to raise the money and hire the communications experts needed to win them. Meanwhile, the power in the system gradually flows away from the people who are mesmerized by the symbols and marketing campaigns to the interests who pay for them.

THE POWER OF INTERESTS IN THE NEW POLITICS:
THE CASE OF HEALTH CARE

As their importance to politicians' war chests increases, the influence of interest groups in both elections and legislation increases. In 1994, over 4,500 PACs made nearly $190 million in contributions.[34] When legislating, elected representatives are often attuned not only to what pollsters and their personal contacts tell them the public wants, but also to what lobbyists tell them interest groups want. When campaigning, politicians are empowered or constrained by the amount of money they can raise and what promises they can make to the public without alienating important sources of funding. With interest groups playing such a big role in funding their campaigns, representatives face a delicate balancing act in responding to their two constituencies: the public that elects them, and the interest groups that make their electoral bids viable.

The health care reform debate of 1994, according to many political observers, was the most heavily lobbied issue in U.S. history. Charles Lewis, director of the Center for Public Integrity, which studied the activity and impact of interest groups on the health care debate, observed that in the thick of the debate, the National Federation of Independent Business (NFIB) "has more people on the floor of the White House than the White House has. They are spending millions because billions are at stake."[35] A spokesman for the NFIB concurred, saying that his organization mounted "the largest single focused grassroots lobbying campaign we have ever done, which spans two years and two million pieces of mail."[36] But the effort to influence the outcome of health care reform was not only from the grass roots. For example, from 1993 through the first quarter of 1994, insurance companies donated $8,764,815 in PAC money to individual politicians and an additional $801,863 in soft money to the political parties. The five leading insurers alone gave nearly $2 million in PAC donations and more than a quarter of a million dollars in soft money.[37] Overall, from 1992 through mid-1994, health care–related groups made over $25 million in political contributions to legislators and parties—$23,236,199 in PAC contributions and $1,882,719 in soft money contributions.[38] (Although many of these groups had a variety of concerns before Congress, the magnitude of the dollars they spent is nonetheless instructive.)

Of course, not all interest groups wanted health care legislation to look the same. A variety of groups, some of them diametrically opposed, exerted pressure on various points of the political system. How exactly did these groups compete to influence the shape of health care legislation?

First, interests influenced the legislative agenda by funding campaigns, targeting their donations to key legislators. The Center for Public Integrity, compiling its figures from Federal Election Commission reports, found that between January 1993 and March 1994, PACs with health care–related interests contributed over $6 million to 121 members of three House committees considering health care legislation, and over $2 million to 25 members of Senate committees. (These figures don't include additional contributions made by individuals.)[39] Citizen Action, an advocacy group that supports a Canadian-style health care system, reports that members of the House Ways and Means Committee and Energy and Commerce Committee, key committees for producing health care reform legislation, received an average of $27,000 more than members of other committees received from PACs.[40]

The above study turned up some other interesting patterns. For example, as a legislator's influence in the policymaking process increases or declines, so does the flow of interest groups' dollars. Interest group contributions also vary according to the popularity of a legislator's proposals with key contributors. Finally, individual contributions from wealthy doctors and health care corporation executives magnified the PAC effect and in some cases were key sources of funding for politicians. These executive-level donations also allowed candidates to truthfully claim that they refused PAC donations without compromising their ability to amass considerable campaign war chests.

Second, interests influenced representatives by providing information. Often, interest groups provide representatives with much of their information about the issues and proposals before Congress. This is a valuable service to legislators hard-pressed for time and anxious to test the political winds before making bold moves. Democratic Representative Bill Brewster of Oklahoma told a reporter, "The best way to affect my vote is to provide me with information. And they try." In one week alone, the reporter noted, Brewster "was visited by at least two dozen lobbyists, including representatives of three drug companies, six of the largest businesses in [his] district, two unions, including the steelworkers, local health care plans, and four hospital associations—[and] he is still in search of more [health care ideas]." However, as Senator John Breaux (D-Louisiana) observed in the thick of the health care debate, "We've long passed informational lobbying; now we're at break-your-arm lobbying."[41]

Third, interest groups also powerfully affected the health care debate by going over the heads of Congress to the public. The Annenberg School of Communication at the University of Pennsylvania predicted that by the time Congress abandoned the health reform and campaigned instead on a set of marketing-generated symbols, interest groups would spend in excess of $60 million on television ads alone.[42] Most notable of these was the $10 million campaign by the Health Insurance Association of America—the infamous "Harry and Louise" ads—which are generally credited with causing a 20-point drop in public support for Clinton's health care plan.

Fourth, interests magnified their power by lobbying other interest groups. The most notable example of this "cross-lobbying" on health care occurred when the NFIB succeeded in convincing the American Medical Association (AMA) to reverse its endorsement of employer mandates, the plan to require employers to pay a portion of their employees' health insurance costs. Similarly, insurance companies and restaurant chains convinced the Business Roundtable to drop its support for Clinton's plan, while drug companies lobbied senior citizens' organizations like the American Association of Retired Persons to withhold support of the Clinton plan. The reason is simple. "When administration officials go in to talk to members of Congress, they can no longer say, 'The AMA supports what we're doing,' " says John J. Motley, the NFIB's chief lobbyist. "That's big. It removes a shield."[43]

The noisy competition among interest groups—a competition in which some groups are decidedly at an advantage in terms of resources and clout—is bound to have an effect on legislation. In the case of health care, interest groups appear to be responsible for major changes in the kinds of health care reform considered most seriously in Congress. Employer mandates, for example, came heavily under fire from business-related groups and were eventually dropped from serious consideration. Meanwhile, the competing pressures from a variety of directions slowed the progress of legislation and strained the legislative process to its limit. But interest group activities also have a major effect on elections. Some candidates whose views coincide with those of well-financed interest groups become themselves well-financed—possibly much better financed than their competition. Some politicians who otherwise might enjoy little notoriety within Congress or in the mass media can capture the limelight by promoting ideas that powerful interests favor, thereby increasing their name recognition with voters. And some kinds of public policy debates make it to the forefront of public attention, shaping voters' perceptions and expectations, while other questions remain on the back burner.

A good illustration of these possibilities is provided by the career of Representative Jim Cooper (D-Tennessee). In 1992, Cooper was a little-known congressman on a House Energy and Commerce subcommittee. By 1994, Cooper's name was on the front pages, as he successfully advanced his version of health care reform, which he dubbed "Clinton Lite." Cooper's plan rejected employer mandates and price controls on insurance companies, and proposed gradual, phased-in coverage of more Americans as opposed to President Clinton's plans for quicker and fuller "universal coverage." Nearly as many Republicans as Democrats eventually supported Cooper's bill (twenty-six to thirty-one as of February 1994), which soon overshadowed Clinton's proposal. But perhaps more importantly, a constellation of health care–related interest groups also supported the bill—and Cooper's reelection fund. Cooper accepted no PAC funds, but he received $162,956 from health and insurance executives and their families in the first six months of 1993. By mid-1994, Cooper was the top House recipient of health care–related funds.[44] This considerable war chest would be of great help in the tough race Cooper faced against Republican Fred Dalton Thompson for the open Senate seat of Vice President Al Gore. Also helpful would be the higher profile Cooper was suddenly cutting in the media. Cooper dismissed his own influence on the health care debate, saying "I feel like the Wizard of Oz sometimes. Pull back the curtain and there is this wormy little guy at the keyboard."[45] Cooper's modesty aside, Clinton Lite and its economically powerful backers had a profound impact on the shape of the health care debate and on the standing of health care reform and the Clinton administration as the 1994 elections approached. And Cooper's interest group allies provided him with significant electoral advantages over his opponent. Cooper played the money game well, while the reverberations echoed over the halls of Congress.

As it turned out, Cooper lost to Thompson, a movie actor with a large campaign fund and a sharp management team that dressed him in flannel shirts and posed him in front of pickup trucks. (Thompson proved so attractive on TV that he was picked to deliver the party response to Clinton's January 1995 State of the Union Address.) The Cooper rebellion on health care ended up looking like more ineffective government, while Thompson promised the appealing symbols of small government and lower taxes. In the era of the outsider, Thompson was sent to Washington to clean up the mess. All that was lost in the process was health care, an issue that voters cared about, but that the Democratic candidate sold out to interests and that the Republican candidate had no interest in. When given the choice between broken promises and appealing, if fantastic, symbols, most voters prefer the symbols. In this system, the only winners are the interests, and leaders have become their hucksters.

LEADERSHIP IN A TIME OF POLITICAL BREAKDOWN

Leaders require followers. This is perhaps an obvious point, but in the current political age it bears stating. Historian Garry Wills has put it this way:

We have a long list of the leader's requisites—determination, focus, a clear goal, a sense of priorities, and so on. We easily forget the first and all-encompassing need—followers. Without them, the best ideas, the strongest will, the most wonderful smile, have no effect. When Shakespeare's Welsh seer, Owen Glendower, boasts, "I can call spirits from the vasty deep," Hotspur deflates him with the commonsense answer, "Why, so can I, or so can any man. But will they come when you do call for them?"[46]

Today's leaders issue symbolic calls that are designed to attract followers for an election but that often fail to keep those followers answering their call afterward. Today's leaders are frequently unable to rally their own party to their causes, in part because those causes are narrowly defined by the commitments they have made to particular political backers. Indeed, today's leaders first must address the need to raise money before they can even think about what sort of call they are going to make for followers. This is the age of the lonely leader, competing with other leaders not for ideas but for the money needed to manufacture symbolic appeals that take the place of ideas.

It is not too farfetched to imagine the ideal candidate being selected precisely for a lack of ideas, the absence of strong personal character, and a corresponding willingness to be scripted, directed, and marketed down to the last detail. This is a frightening possibility, but it is not absurd. Former Vice President Dan Quayle offers an interesting case in point. Larry Sabato, a political scientist concerned about the growing impact of media control and candidate marketing on the democratic process, reports a story attributed to Quayle's best friend in college. Quayle and his friend had gone to see Robert Redford in *The Candidate,* which is a film about an attractive but directionless politician who is packaged and marketed all the way to the Senate. In Sabato's account, "The friend reported that Quayle said it was the greatest film he had ever seen, and Quayle was so excited about it that they talked for eleven hours straight after the movie. Of course, this movie became in some respects the story of Dan Quayle's life."[47] Upon hearing of Quayle's fascination with *The Candidate,* the film's screenwriter, Jeremy Larner, tried to point out that real-life candidate Quayle had failed to grasp the whole point of the movie. In Larner's words, "I am amazed to have inspired Dan Quayle. Inspiring such candidates was not our intention and I don't think [he] understood our movie. . . . [He] missed the irony. Unless, in a way we never could have foreseen, [he *is*] the irony."[48]

Failing to grasp the point of a simple movie may not be a political liability. To the contrary, it may represent a great advantage, rendering the candidate wholly malleable and uncompromisingly marketable. Indeed, this sort of Frankenstein fantasy may have crossed the minds of political consultants who may be tempted to test the limits of their art. Sabato suggests, for example, that George Bush's surprising choice of Quayle as a running mate came largely at the urging of Bush's managers: "It's pretty well known that George Bush did not have a close and continuing relationship with Dan Quayle; they didn't know each other very well. So how did the Quayle pick happen? Well, Bob Teeter, Bush's pollster, and Roger Ailes, his media consultant, had both handled Dan Quayle's previous congressional campaigns in Indiana. And they knew just how attractive and malleable Dan Quayle was. . . . It's clear that not only did they put his name on the list, but at least in the case of Roger Ailes, they became advocates for the candidate."[49] In this view, the only trouble with such perfect media candidates is that "they may be better at running for office than governing."[50] This only appears to be a problem, I suppose, if one insists on some nostalgic link between elections, leadership, and the idea of governing.

Perhaps the great irony in the case of Dan Quayle is that he withdrew from the 1996 presidential contest because he said he did not want to face the ordeal of raising the $20 million or so required to launch a primary campaign. Thus, even the perfect candidate may run up against the contradictions of the money game faced by players in today's elections. The strains of financing an election process are increasingly evident, as a succession of Republican contenders removed themselves from consideration in 1996 even though it appeared that Bill Clinton was vulnerable to defeat. In addition to Quayle, the money chase discouraged both Bill Bennett and Jack Kemp, who arguably had ideas worth sharing with the people, but who could not stomach the prospects of campaigning first to raise money and then spending it on symbolic appeals to win votes.

The contemporary leader faces a lonely and daunting election process, sustained mainly by an inordinate sense of personal ambition. In the case of Bill Clinton, the public witnessed a tireless campaigner (the Comeback Kid from Chapter 3) who became a leader beset with doubts and an inability to set a political course that he could defend and communicate to the people. Clinton thus fits the mold of the contemporary leader who may have had more ambition to run for election than he had clues about how to lead a nation afterward. The dilemma, of course, is that in the face of a fragmented system of power, it is not at all clear how to be an effective leader. When every politician is a self-proclaimed leader, there may be increasingly few loyal followers. The not surprising result is that institutions begin to look weak and unable to govern.

INSTITUTIONS AND THE DIMINISHED CAPACITY TO GOVERN

Increasingly fragmented parties trying to appeal to increasingly volatile voters do not make for smooth, efficient government once parties win power. As noted above, the result is that institutions become increasingly vulnerable to the inroads of interest groups. Political scientist James Thurber characterizes the proliferation of interest groups and their growing pressure on Congress as "hyperpluralism"—that is, an excess of representation and a fragmentation of political energies that jam the machinery of government.[51]

Washington columnist David Broder argues that "The reality is that we do not have two parties in Washington. We have 536. The president, the 100 senators, and the 435 representatives are each a political party of one," constituting "a system in which every office-seeker and officeholder constitutes his or her own party." Broder continues, "Framing national policy is difficult enough in an arena with 536 separate political parties. When the concurrence or acquiescence of more than twice that number of interest groups must be obtained, the task of forging a consensus becomes nigh impossible."[52] And when the interest groups provide the campaign funds that enable politicians to keep their jobs, both legislating and campaigning become intimately intertwined.

What this means is that the policy process of government has become corrupted by the strategic symbolic uses of issues to win future elections. National debates have been overwhelmed by the ease of promoting symbolic solutions over the more difficult task of exploring serious understandings of underlying problems. Politics in America today is an increasingly angry affair, as one would expect from a system that is not working very well for many of its members. The question is whether the anger will continue to be fueled and spent in addictive symbolic politics, or whether more sensible reforms will eventually begin to reach and make sense to average citizens. The fate of the democracy hangs in the balance.

CHAPTER 10

Reversing the Decline by Reforming the System

... a primal scream, a visceral response to an image of legislative bodies as being consumed with the preservation of perks and privileges enjoyed by a class of career politicians who are insulated from the concerns of ordinary Americans. —*Thomas E. Mann, on legislative term limits*

The most popular solution for reforming the system and ending the governing crisis is to limit the terms that elected representatives can serve. This backlash against career politicians quickly swept through twenty-two states by the time the first constitutional challenge reached the Supreme Court in its 1994–1995 term.[1] The term limits proposal involves a legal issue: simply put, the states may not be empowered to modify political job descriptions that the Constitution clearly sets forth with no prohibitions on length of service. In fact, when presidential service was limited to two terms, the Constitution was amended. In the discussion that follows, we look at term limits as an understandable, but dubious, idea that has distracted citizen attention from more workable proposals. Without steady citizen and media pressure behind these other measures, elected officials have quietly avoided most changes in election and lobbying rules that would upset their personal or party interests.

TERM LIMITS: THE CRY OF AN ANGRY ELECTORATE

Whether the topic is term limits or campaign finance, the reform process has become caught up in the very kinds of political maneuvering that it is intended to stop. Both parties have done their share to block election reform. Indeed, each party has claimed—with some reason—that reform proposals have been designed with party advantages in mind and that they change with the rise and fall of party fortunes in Washington. For example, the Republican Contract with America promised a vote on a constitutional term limit amendment following the party's victory in 1994. Yet one of the victorious GOP's first actions was to launch a trial balloon by House Majority Leader Dick Armey who said that perhaps term limits would not be necessary, after all, now that the people had elected a party that could actually straighten out the mess in Washington.[2] The basis of Armey's retreat on term limits eventually became clear when a formal proposal was defeated in Congress in March of 1995.

Armey's statement was reminiscent of the Democratic majority elected in 1992 that promised to clean up lobbying abuses and pass campaign finance reform. No sooner had the crusading freshmen taken their seats in Congress than they were briefed on the need to begin preparing for their next election by forming financial alliances with interest organizations. The party leadership soon carried the newfound concerns of the junior lawmakers to their own Democratic president who promised to lead the fight on reform, and they quietly lowered the priority of that promise. And so, the Democrats failed to deliver a reform bill during the two-year reign of the 103rd Congress from 1993 to 1994. Like the Republican soft-pedaling on term limits, the Democratic maneuvering on finance reform was explained as being in the interest of maintaining party power, for the good of the nation, of course.[3]

As with the strategic calculations that killed health care reform (see Chapter 9), the fate of campaign and election reforms can be better understood in terms of party positioning for the next election than as faithful attempts to carry out the promises or the mandates from the last. And so the political maneuvering continues in nearly every area of election reform. None of this posturing has been lost on the public. In a poll taken during the 1994 election campaign, a whopping 89 percent opined that when Congress cannot agree on legislation, it is "mainly because each side is trying to score political points," not because of "honest disagreement."[4] And fully 82 percent said that most members of Congress were only interested in "doing what's best for themselves politically," not "what's best for the country."[5] The important question here is whether people are channeling their anger in pursuit of effective reforms.

People at the Boiling Point

It is instructive to begin with a profile of public opinion over the thirty-year period in which the new electoral system has emerged. The most dramatic change in the polls has come in response to the question of whether the government is run for the benefit of a few big interests. The percentage of those who agree has gone up dramatically from 1960 to the present time.[6] The exact figures are as follows:

1960   25%
1970   50%
1980   70%
1990   77%
1994   83%

Accompanying these popular suspicions about whose interests the government serves are equally strong feelings about whose interests are going underrepresented. The current decade opened with 65 percent agreement that public officials "don't care much what people like me think."[7] At the same time, 79 percent of Americans looked toward their future with the common concern that their country was in "serious trouble."[8] Yet many of these citizens have become caught in the contradictions of the system itself. For example, polls continue to show that large majorities blame Congress, or the parties, or the selfishness of politicians for the problems with government,[9] and at the same time, majorities (albeit declining ones) also continue to vote for their own incumbent representatives on election day.[10] Like dieters who are tempted to lock the refrigerator door to keep from eating, term limit supporters may be trying to control their own selfish temptations as they seek to curb the corruption of their representatives.

The irony is that precisely these voter frustrations and contradictions drive up the costs and deceptions of campaigning, which in turn fuel the frustration and cynicism. As a result, the dwindling supply of hopeful citizens has to be hooked back into the system by new and more creative marketing strategies. Unfortunately, as political communication scholar Jarol Manheim suggests, it is increasingly possible to fool all of the people much, if not all, of the time—at least for the short term—in this age of sophisticated marketing and media technologies.[11] The inevitable results, of course, are more citizen anger and cynicism at being fooled into believing that the latest "war on (some major social problem)" or the latest politician was anything more than a symbol born of test marketing.

Beneath the anger may lie a more serious effect of this negative election spiral. A Times Mirror study of the electorate in 1994 found unprecedented levels of anger and cynicism, but it also revealed a symptom that was perhaps more ominous: the electorate has become frighteningly "rootless." That study failed to identify any "clear direction in the public's political thinking, other than frustration with the current system and an eager responsiveness to alternative political solutions and appeals."[12] Enter term limits as an easy emotional reaction to this dizzying situation. The question, of course, is whether term limits are more effective as feel-good palliatives than as serious solutions for a political breakdown. Would people still support them if they thought about some of term limits' potential shortcomings?

Term Limits: A Critical Appraisal

If voter anger, cynicism, and rootlessness make term limits an understandably popular reform measure, these same symptoms of emotional distress may also undermine rational thinking about workable solutions to the governing crisis. Various loopholes weaken the term limit logic.

- Limited politicians will be able to recycle through other public offices in order to keep their careers alive.
- Term limits will not in the least disturb the organized interests that help politicians fund their campaigns. Politicians who want to serve the maximum number of terms (six in the House and two in the Senate have become popular limits) will surely take the campaign money and lobbying favors just as eagerly as their longer termed predecessors—perhaps more so, since they have less time to feed at the trough.
- Inexperienced legislators will just be learning about complex issues of defense, health policy, or education by the time they are forced to leave office. This "learning curve" problem will surely increase the influence of lobbyists who are always there to lend their expertise in drafting legislation. Not surprisingly, interest sectors that see inexperienced legislators as even more desirable than the current ones have added financial support for the expensive election campaigns mounted around term limits.
- Term limits will likely make the career profiles of ex-elected officials even more distasteful to voters. A standard next move for a current retired or defeated member of Congress is to cross over to the other side of the political line and become a lobbyist or a lawyer for a Washington law firm. The term limit solution will make Congress all the more attractive as an apprenticeship program for the lobbyists and corporate lawyers of the future.
- Finally, term limits will serve as "no-brainers" for citizens, removing them from their sovereign duty of evaluating and voting for their representatives on their merits, not their longevity.

Journalist David Broder expanded on this last point by arguing that term limits send the wrong message to representatives: telling them that they will not be rewarded if they do a good job. To the contrary, says Broder, "term limits kill an incentive for officials to serve well. They also tell citizens that they can have the benefits of democracy without any exercise of vigilance over their elected officials. Term limits promise an effortless republic—democracy without active citizenship. That promise is dangerously false."[13]

Perhaps if people were moved less by anger, they might think about more workable—and less dangerous—solutions. The remainder of this chapter offers a set of simple suggestions about how to turn that cynical anger into constructive action. What reforms might make a difference in the quality of national elections? Rather than present a laundry list of reform proposals, I will suggest just five simple ideas. Each, if adopted, would go a long way toward removing the limits on national debate and candidate behavior imposed by big money, political marketing, and media control. These reforms are presented in order from the most sweeping and radical to the most modest and easily imaginable. Thus, the suggestion heading the list is likely to meet with the greatest resistance, but I offer it in the spirit of opening the marketplace of ideas to the widest possible range of considerations. ·

REFORM PROPOSAL NO. 1:
A (LIMITED) PROPORTIONAL REPRESENTATION SYSTEM

The political parties in America are moribund; no longer are they able to organize competing national agendas and push their members to support those platforms. With the collapse of the parties and the rise of a political star or personality system, the marketplace of ideas has fallen into disorder. One mechanism that might stimulate new life in the national political dialogue is a limited proportional representation rule in deciding races for Congress. (For obvious reasons, such a scheme would take root first in the House and later, if at all, in the Senate.)

What would this system look like? First, it would be less European in look than the typical parliamentary process in which the executive and the cabinet are forged from the balance of power in the legislative body itself. We could keep an elected president, while restoring a better representative balance between the people and Congress. The goal of making Congress more accountable to the grass roots would be advanced by a simple proportional representation rule granting House seats to parties whose candidates won at least 10 percent of the vote both locally and nationally. Say, for example, State X has twenty House seats up for election, and the

New Ideas party wins 20 percent of the vote in that state and qualifies nationally by winning 12 percent of all the votes cast. In this result, four seats from State X would go to New Ideas. Those representatives would join winning party candidates from other states with qualifying vote margins to form a New Ideas bloc in the House.

Imposing a national qualifying percentage minimizes the chance of elevating isolated state or local movements to national power, while favoring idea-based movements with nationwide appeal. Beginning on a limited scale, the introduction of multiple voice blocs and parties into the power structure will not disrupt the day-to-day workings of government any more than the current party disorientation has already thrown the system into a state of near paralysis.

The point of this shift in the representation process is to give voice to political initiatives that are now eliminated by a winner-take-all system in which the two leading alternatives are seldom able to join behind competing programs for social renewal. In light of what we know about the press, well-articulated and controversial viewpoints from government officials make the news. Indeed, the newness of this system alone will attract press attention. With the publicity granted to incoming idea groups, existing parties and incumbents would face stiffer competition in the vote marketplace. Moreover, voters would be given a chance in subsequent elections to reward parties whose platforms continued to make sense, while punishing those who failed to compete.

Whatever the possible outcomes of this experiment in proportional representation, we will not likely be allowed to witness them. Politicians will join ranks to protect the personal benefits that the present system confers on them. When most members of the House of Representatives can expect to be reelected, it is unlikely that they will do anything to rock the boat—much less instigate the kind of political debate that would make the electoral process meaningfully competitive.

If the public is interested in opening the party system to more competitive grass-roots ideas, help will come not from Washington but from states that offer direct popular initiatives and referendums on their ballots. State legislatures could thus become the experimental proving grounds for proportional representation schemes. Successful reforms in a few model states could lead the way for a national constitutional amendment. Even if this initiative gets off the ground, however, it is unlikely to go very far without major campaign finance reforms that would make parties with new ideas competitive nationally, particularly at the presidential level. Indeed, with or without a restructuring of the representation system, campaign finance reform is crucial to reopening American politics.

REFORM PROPOSAL NO. 2:
CAMPAIGN FINANCE CONTROL

This is the big one, both because it would make a huge difference in the quality of national dialogue and because citizens' lobbying groups are already fired up about it. When Congress became embroiled in a dangerous ethics war during the closing years of the 1980s, calmer heads negotiated a cease-fire when it quickly became apparent that ethics charges could bring nearly everyone down. One marvels at the rich array of creative financing programs the members had worked out: breakfast clubs, free air travel, honoraria, dubious book sales, huge bankrolls of unspent "campaign" contributions, questionable investment opportunities, lobbying services for clients with little or no base in a member's home district, and the list goes on. The representation system itself seemed to be undergoing a transformation from one based in geography and votes to one anchored in high finance and influence.

The erosion of party principle and political integrity has become difficult to hide, raising the continual specter of public embarrassment because lawmakers routinely find themselves in compromising positions. Take the five U.S. senators who ran interference for a bankrupt savings and loan, delaying its seizure by federal bank regulators. Buying additional time permitted the owners to drain off liquid assets, adding considerably to the astonishing $2 billion cost of the eventual government bailout. Yet all five senators denied that their actions had been influenced by the more than $1 million in campaign contributions from the chairman of the S&L. They dismissed the episode as a routine constituent service. One of them went so far as to say, "I have done this kind of thing many, many times," and likened his actions to "helping the little lady who didn't get her Social Security."[14] The whole system of political finance that gives rise to these routine activities must be reformed if politicians are to develop a healthier sense of the public interest. Fred Wertheimer, president of Common Cause (the public interest lobby that pushed for investigation of this case of special senatorial services), makes the following observations.

> Washington has become an ethics swamp. Our nation's capital is addicted to special-interest influence money, and members of Congress are benefitting professionally and personally from these funds.
> In the last six years, special interests have poured more than $400 million in PAC money, $31 million in honoraria fees, and countless additional millions in illegal soft money and other payments into our system of government. These payments represent investments in government decision making—investments which improperly and unfairly magnify the voices of special interests at the expense of representative government.

We've always experienced individual cases of corruption and impropriety in government. But today we have a system of institutionalized corruption. The rules themselves allow activities to take place legally that are improper and corrupting.

Washington insiders argue that the American people don't really care about Washington's ethics mess. They're wrong. But what's happening is even more dangerous than what they perceive as indifference on the part of the American public.

The American people are moving beyond outrage to a state of deep cynicism. They are reaching a state of "no expectations" about our government leaders. And in a democracy, that's a red flag alert. There cannot be a fundamental erosion of ethical values at the seat of government without grave consequences for the nation.[15]

Reforms in campaign finance must affect all levels of politics from the president and Congress to local offices. Since we are talking about a system of influence, it will do little good to correct one part of the problem without attending to all of it. Electing a president with his or her own ideas for a change will have little consequence if Congress throws up a wall of special interest resistance to putting those ideas into action. The same parallel applies to state and local politics.

A Brief History of Finance Reform in the New Election System

If the finance reforms of the mid-1970s and early 1980s helped create the new American politics, the political advantages of that same money machine have kept elected officials from dismantling it in recent years. The story of recent finance reform efforts follows much the same plot, no matter which party has just won power on a promise to clean up the mess in Washington: foot dragging, weak measures, lack of party solidarity, and much posturing and moralizing for the benefit of the media.

Consider the reform politics of five recent congresses, from the 100th (1987–1988) to the 104th (1995–1996). Democrats in the 100th Congress moved on legislation in the House and Senate that would have limited the amount of PAC money in individual campaigns, created more for the challengers, and set spending limits in ways designed to get around the Supreme Court's 1976 *Buckley v. Valeo* decision affirming that campaign financing is free speech. However, even these modest steps toward electoral responsibility were halted by a Republican filibuster that ended any hope for final passage. The 101st Congress (1989–1990) ended up even more divided: the House favored reduced PAC contributions and voluntary spending limits; the Senate proposed to eliminate PACs at the federal level, while imposing voluntary spending limits; and President Bush threatened to veto any bill that contained spending limits. No legislation made it out of Washington by the end of that Congress either.

The Democrats in the 102nd Congress (1991–1992) sensed rising public anger at Washington politicians (approval of Congress dipped below 20 percent on the eve of the 1992 election), and they finally passed a reform package designed to make the Republicans look bad in the election. What was more distressing than the promised veto by Republican President George Bush was the weakness of the legislation itself. Not only did the House and Senate Democrats include different provisions to accommodate their different campaign cycles and funding needs, but also the House bill set spending limits at the levels deemed necessary to maintain the party's incumbent advantages. Following the Bush veto, the finance reform issue figured prominently in Democratic election rhetoric, but the party yielded once again to the temptations of political advantage and failed to move quickly on the issue after winning the Congress and the White House in 1992. When bills finally made it through the 103rd Congress (1993–1994), the scenario was a replay of the time before, with different bills tailored to the campaign needs of senators and representatives, and voluntary spending limits so high that they would have made little difference. The hopes for even that modest reform were killed by a Republican filibuster in the Senate that was aimed in part against the idea of any spending limits. The 103rd Congress also distinguished itself by joining in an eleventh-hour bipartisan effort (in the Senate) to kill a lobbying reform package that would have restricted gifts, free meals and entertainment, and other fringe benefits that lobbyists have used to forge ties with congressional power brokers. Perhaps the greatest irony is that the lobby reform bill was defeated by a last-minute lobbying blitz. Those who voted against reform claimed that many public interest groups from both sides of the political spectrum would be disadvantaged if they were to lose their intimate access to representatives.

The reform spotlight switched to the Republicans in the 104th Congress (1995–1996). Although the Republican vetoes and filibusters that blocked campaign reforms through the four previous congresses were advertised as opposition to pro-Democratic legislation, the new majority on Capitol Hill did not leap to give up its newly gained political advantage. Their landslide in the 1994 elections was brought about in part through the hefty PAC operations of Robert Dole and Newt Gingrich, and the development of other effective finance strategies. The Republican leadership did not rush to change the system that it now controlled, while President Clinton revived his once dormant call to end big money election politics.

The most frustrating aspect of the many failed reform efforts is that even if they had been passed, they were probably too weak to make much of a difference in the election system that underlies the governing crisis. Research by political scientists Jonathan Krasno and Donald Philip Green shows that none of the reforms proposed in the last decade would have seriously altered either the incumbent advantage in elections or the huge emphasis on the monetary alliances that have warped political priorities. For example, their models indicate that spending limits of $300,000 would have to be set on House races in order to give challengers much of an assist against the incumbent advantage.[16] Yet current incumbent spending averages are over $500,000, and the spending limit proposed in the Democratic bill that passed the House during the 103rd Congress was $600,000. The Republican landslide of 1994 was produced with cash infusions that would have been hampered by more serious limits—all of which illustrates the reasons for popular skepticism about the idea of "politician, reform thyself."

Putting Some Teeth in Finance Reform

What kind of finance reform would make a difference?

First, eliminate PAC contributions to political campaigns. Contributions to party organizations might be permitted, but state and national parties should be severely restricted in soft money spending during the several months prior to election day. Let party-building activities take place between, not during, elections.

Next, set spending limits on campaigns, and index those limits according to the office and the size of the district. In order to observe Supreme Court rulings that political finance is a form of free speech, spending limits might be set on those who voluntarily accept public funding. In conjunction with the other reforms below, it is possible to imagine spending limits set at one-half or even one-third of current spending averages.

Finally, create a system of public funding for both congressional challengers and incumbents. It would be possible to modify various European models as noted below.

How would federal moneys be allocated? Under the most obvious scheme, funds could be given to parties in proportion to their strength in Congress or, at state levels, in the legislature. Party nominees would then be granted shares of the party fund based on the number of voters in their districts. This would encourage greater ideological or issue linkages between candidates and party organizations, and it would encourage parties to run better candidates against incumbents in the other party. Fancier schemes could include "incentives" based on some measure of party and candidate performance in the last election. Although no system of financing is perfect or free of corruption, a financial index based on some linkage between party programs and voter support is preferable to the current system in which candidate and party bank accounts are indexed directly to PAC and private investor support.

In this and other electoral reforms, currently successful officeholders are not likely to become advocates of change; they will prefer instead to drag their feet and throw up smoke screens of scary rhetoric. We can expect to hear about the dangers of government intervention in the free market of political ideas. Most voters, however, will recognize this for what it is: so much political self-interest on the part of politicians. Presidential candidates today, for example, are happy to take the government financing currently available after private money has narrowed the field of competition. Why not also keep the effects of PAC and private money to a minimum in the crucial early stages of all federal elections? In addition, to make this system work, the parties would have to be either prohibited from accepting soft money or at least kept from spending it during the final months of a campaign.

But, the critics will argue, the costs are too great. How can the government afford to back large numbers of political aspirants, many of whom stand no chance of ultimate victory? To put this question in perspective, the costs of financing the entire slate of national candidates, including challengers, in a presidential year would amount to about one percent of the annual defense budget—even if current high levels of spending were allowed to continue. Leaving aside the questions of what our national tax priorities ought to be and what dollar value should be placed on democratic competition, there is another, more expedient answer to this criticism. The cost of campaigning could be lowered by over half through one very simple move: eliminate the enormously expensive practice of paid political advertising on television and radio. This could be done in ways that would also end the Madison Avenue-style candidate marketing which is so damaging to the spirit of democracy. This brings us to our third proposal.

REFORM PROPOSAL NO. 3: REGULATION OF POLITICAL ADVERTISING IN THE BROADCAST MEDIA

Under the present system, the political commercial that reaches the television screen or the rush hour "drive time" radio program does little to stimulate democratic dialogue. To the contrary, the practice of candidate marketing sets in motion a whole antidemocratic syndrome. Rather than promoting dialogues between candidates and voters that might result in new political initiatives, political advertising of the sort that dominates American campaigns short-circuits the very chances for such communications. Skipping the stages of dialogue, reason, feedback, and debate, marketing techniques probe the subliminal mind of isolated segments of the voter market for images and themes that produce quick psychological responses. The resulting interactions between candidates and voters defy the clear understandings on which stable consensus and programs of action depend. Moreover, the practice of scientifically targeting small voter blocs and then aiming the bulk of campaign content at them violates the spirit of broad democratic involvement. Any practice that turns voting and citizen withdrawal into a good thing rather than a cause for alarm should be outlawed as unhealthy to the principles on which the whole system rests. Alas, cultural taboos about free speech permit no such direct solutions.

Although a ban on broadcast political advertising would probably be unconstitutional, various regulatory measures would reduce the quantity of dollars needed to mount an effective political campaign. In the process, quality ideas and flesh-and-blood candidates might be encouraged to fill the void created by the departure of jingles, slogans, subliminal images, and carefully scripted political performances.

One solution is to empower the Federal Communications Commission to include elections more centrally within its sphere of public service broadcasting. In particular, networks should be required to donate set amounts of public service air time to candidates and parties during elections, and the time issued (and used by candidates) should be in blocks of five to fifteen minutes. These two reforms would simultaneously cut the costs of campaigning and require candidates to say something meaningful in the spaces allocated to them. (Further encouragement could be added by requiring candidates to appear "live" in a substantial percentage of the spots.) More importantly, these reforms would help set in motion the right kind of electoral dynamic: free air time would cut the costs of campaigning, making strict spending limits more realistic; in turn, an additional ratcheting down of spending, beyond the costs of air time, would further discourage expensive marketing research.

Many, of course, will rally around the symbol of free speech on this issue. We can anticipate an unholy alliance of broadcasters, who profit enormously from campaign commercial sales, and candidates, who have won office through the assistance of good marketing. These forces will talk about free speech as though their lives had been totally dedicated to advancing that cause. However, the prohibition of political advertising on radio and television (the media where it is subject to greatest abuse) has at least three precedents within the liberal democratic tradition.

First, a number of thriving Western democracies as diverse, for example, as England, Germany, and Sweden, all regulate political advertising on the airwaves. Indeed, most other democracies regulate political advertising in ways that are much more drastic than the present proposal calls for. Their political processes, if not healthier than ours, are at the very least no worse for it.

Second, the United States has regulated various other forms of broadcast advertising deemed harmful to the national health—hard liquor, cigarettes, sexual services, and pornography, just to name a few. The deterioration of political life caused by candidate marketing on television and radio constitutes at least as great a public hazard as these commodities.

Finally, the free speech defense crumbles even when it is examined on strict constructionist terms. Almost nobody in public life subscribes to the absolute reading of the First Amendment clause that says "Congress shall pass *no* law . . . " Since the eminent justice Oliver Wendell Holmes developed the "clear and present danger" doctrine in the early part of this century, most reasonable people have accepted the idea that speech may be restricted if it presents a clear and present danger to the survival of the people or their way of government. Even the Supreme Court decision in *Buckley v. Valeo* granted Congress some broad regulatory powers in elections. If a better case is made for the dangers of contemporary electoral speech, perhaps the Court will see fit to expand those powers in future rulings. I would suggest that the effects of candidate marketing, as they are manifest through the commercialization of elections, represent a far greater threat to the principles and practices of our democratic government than any threat that can be conjured by domestic enemies or flag burning.

REFORM PROPOSAL NO. 4: IMPROVED NEWS COVERAGE

It would be nice if the press did more than just grumble when political campaigns manipulate news events and restrict journalistic access to candidates. True, the media are running more stories about media manipulation, empty rhetoric, and voter dissatisfaction than ever before, but they have had little or no perceptible impact on candidate behavior. (As for impact on voters, we may well be looking at a kind of media criticism that only adds to voter cynicism.) Of course, reporters cannot force candidates to ride on the press plane and talk candidly about what, if anything, is on their minds. However, new ways of reporting on campaigns could exert considerable indirect pressure on candidates.

There are some promising signs that the press is struggling to define a new election journalism. For example, the focus on political advertising has increased, and many newspapers have added "adwatch" analyses to their election coverage. Another promising move, pioneered by R. W. Apple, Jr. of the *New York Times,* among others, is the use of focus groups with a broad range of citizens to sensitize reporters to public concerns. Several other innovations might be considered that build on the idea of a critical dialogue contained within news reports.

Constructing a National Agenda in the News

To begin with, the leading national news organizations could stake their prestige on creating a national agenda that would reflect a synthesis of public opinion and the views of bipartisan experts on the major concerns of the day. This agenda could then be used as a reference for analyzing candidate responsiveness to the national interest. In other words, instead of framing the campaign story as an often baseless horse race, journalists could compare candidates on their responses to the items on the national agenda. Of course, it would still be tempting to make a horse race out of an election, for the metaphor seems to have a powerful hold in the culture. (It goes back at least as far as Andrew Jackson's acclaimed entry as the "Tennessee stud" in the presidential race of 1824.) However, the metaphor need not be as empty as it has been. Making a horse race out of candidate responses to the national agenda would turn elections into more meaningful contests than the current weekly updates based on popularity polls. As the race progresses, news organizations could update their evaluations by asking the panels of bipartisan experts for continuing inputs. Opinion polls could be figured in as well, but only after vague questions about "popularity" or "who would you vote for?" had been supplemented with questions about the credibility of candidate responses to the agenda items.

Creating national agendas and evaluating candidate credibility might break down the candidates' ability to control the content of campaign news coverage, while opening up other aspects of the press–politician relationship. By responding pointedly to poor showings against their competition, politicians might actually turn idle promises into more serious issues in the eyes of voters and experts alike. Moreover, if broadcast advertising were regulated, candidates might have to say something substantive just to stay even with each other in precious media exposure.

Holding Real Candidate Debates

The pressure on candidates to discuss the national future could also be increased by holding real political debates. As currently conceived, the debates scarcely deserve that name. Candidates do not really engage each other on adversarial terms; instead, they respond to reporters' questions that are usually based on the candidates' own agendas. A debate system in which candidates are permitted to go at each other could provide revealing glimpses of candidate character, along with insights about their ability to function under real pressure. In addition, if they are to continue playing a part in televised debates, journalists could use their national agendas to lead candidates away from the standard campaign script and the predictable posturing. The debates could offer the media opportunities to pressure candidates to address an independently constructed issue agenda (if the press is willing to construct such an agenda, that is). A promising development along these lines emerged in the 1992 presidential campaign with the addition of a debate in which candidates faced the audience directly and answered questions from ordinary people. Not only were the questions in this debate more varied, but also people reported that the debate was more useful than the familiar press panel format.

Exploring the Public Responsibility of the Press

Changing the way campaigns are covered is not likely to be a high priority with media organizations that are comfortable with big profits, smooth and relatively standardized news production routines, and the ease of traveling in a pack with other news organizations. These and other obstacles to change in the news media are discussed elsewhere.[17] The point here is that when media executives explain why they can't change their approaches to news coverage, there are notable weaknesses in the standard reasons they offer.

At issue here is the curious set of norms the press has adopted to define its role. Politicians' personal failings and scandals are fair game, not to mention great fun. The press froths at the chance to catch a candidate in a gaffe or indiscretion. Yet breaking from the pack and deciding independently what really matters blurs the neat distinction between news content that emanates from the candidates themselves (scandals and gaffes conform to this rule) and content that is injected into the news from the editorial desk. This old distinction between reporting and editorializing still holds powerful sway and accounts for the ability of campaigns to control media coverage to a remarkable extent.

Ironically, when reporters do catch politicians in some personal trouble, it is easy for the press to come out looking petty, vindictive, and overly antagonistic. As a result, the press has suffered as much as, and perhaps even more than, politicians in terms of declining popular respect and confidence. Journalists often perceive this public disapproval as a warning not to be too critical rather than as a sign of popular frustration about being critical of the wrong things (i.e., candidates' petty personal problems). If journalists shifted their priorities and held candidates accountable for ideas instead of idiosyncrasies, they just might find a resurgence of public support.

As for the problem of editorializing on the news pages, journalists can draw a distinction between an editorial, which is an in-house opinion, and an agenda of national priorities constructed from the opinions of experts and the public. Few of us want to hear personal opinions passed off as news analysis, but an analytical standard constructed from an intelligent definition of public opinion would give people a useful tool for evaluating candidates and locating themselves in the ongoing debate.

As for the objection that no two news organizations would come up with the same national agenda, so much the better. Surely there would be enough overlap to provide some continuity in the news coverage. (The tendency of the press to look over its shoulder to see what the competition is doing would assure it.) Some level of informed disagreement about the shape of the public interest and the degree of party and candidate responsiveness would introduce a necessary critical edge into the proceedings. If many societies thrive with an avowedly partisan press, surely the American people can live with media debates about national goals.

REFORM PROPOSAL NO. 5: IMPLEMENTING THE NATIONAL VOTER REGISTRATION ACT

In one of the most progressive moves in recent years, Congress passed and the president signed into law the National Voter Registration Act of 1993. The law (and its implementation rules drafted by the Department of Health and Human Services) requires states to offer voter registration forms to driver's license applicants, to accept mail-in registration, and to designate particular government agencies (the most controversial being welfare offices) as voter registration centers. This was by far the easiest and among the most effective of political reforms, yet its passage represented years of partisan struggle. And the struggle goes on: the new Republican majority in the 104th Congress began to talk about blocking the reform based on the thin reasoning that the costs of implementation will be unfairly shouldered by the states. Picking up the cry of "unfunded federal mandates," Republican governors in the three key electoral vote states of California, Illinois, and Pennsylvania blocked implementation of the act when it was due to go into effect in January 1995.

From its legislative struggle to its rocky implementation, this simple reform suffered the familiar onslaught of partisan politics. Republicans charge Democrats with trying to boost turnouts by registering currently inactive citizens who are more likely to vote Democratic. Meanwhile, Democrats charge Republicans with wanting to keep participation low because they are advantaged when fewer people vote. Both sides have a point, but a larger issue might emerge if either could step back from its political calculations: the United States ranks near the bottom of the democratic world in citizen participation levels, and such widespread citizen withdrawal does not improve the health of the political process.

Why Registration Matters

If people are registered, they tend to vote. Indeed, states such as Minnesota and Washington that implemented "motor-voter" registration procedures before the national law was passed experienced significant boosts in electoral participation. If registration to vote were easier and more uniform across the various states, more people would be introduced into the electoral arena, magnifying the effects of all the reforms discussed here. Few, if any, good reasons exist for cumbersome voter registration procedures. We are beyond the age of machine politics and the corruption of voter lists that may once have justified the ordeal of seeking out a registrar and supplying proof of identity and residence. And there is no longer room for the racial discrimination that led many states to impose one obstacle after another on the registration of black voters.

Although common sense may tell us that registration remains the single largest obstacle to voting, those with partisan reasons to limit registration have argued that the turnouts among registered voters have declined steadily since the 1960s (from 85 percent to about 70 percent). Thus, the size of the participation gain is not worth the expense of implementing the reform. A nice piece of detective work by political scientist Frances Piven and sociologist Richard Cloward attributes the apparent drop-off in turnout figures to poor state reporting practices and outdated registration lists.[18] A study cited by Piven and Cloward concludes that, conservatively, 15 percent of those reported on state rolls are either dead or gone and, thus, highly unlikely to turn up to vote. Thus, the apparent decline of voting among registered voters is just that: an appearance created by inaccurate records. For a better estimate, Piven and Cloward cite census figures indicating that over 85 percent of those registered report voting in more recent presidential elections. Although census data may be inflated by the tendency of people to tell census takers they voted even when they didn't, it is clear that state registration data are skewed even more in the opposite direction.

Like most of the reforms on the list, registration was long held up by politicians unwilling to risk their privileged positions in our elected aristocracy. Despite passage into law, the resistance goes on, with numerous lawsuits filed on behalf of the government against recalcitrant states; on behalf of those states against unfunded government mandates; and on behalf of various citizen's groups against different government agencies and officials. Thus, even when reforms are passed, they may still fall prey to political calculations designed to maintain the current election system intact.

HOPE FOR GOVERNING IDEAS

These five reforms are suggestive, not exhaustive, responses to our national political decline. They are intended as beginning points for a discussion about what can be done, and they are not hard-and-fast conclusions or detailed working blueprints. Indeed, I can think of nothing more felicitous than for others to take up this discussion and transform these ideas into more numerous and more workable plans.

The point of election reforms is not just to increase voting levels, but to improve the quality of national political rhetoric. Competition in the marketplace of ideas is the best guarantee of a healthy democracy, not to mention the best chance we have to solve problems. If people find meaning in political rhetoric, they will vote more often. More responsive voters in a more competitive electoral environment will sharpen further the quality of political debate and enforce greater commitment by candidates to their political promises. These assumptions have guided the arguments and analyses in this book.

In the words of rhetorician Paul Corcoran, political language in the contemporary era has fallen from grace. No longer does rhetoric bring to mind the refined art of persuasion through critical public dialogue. Far from stimulating dialogue between politicians and public, says Corcoran, contemporary political language is used "not to persuade, but to control, not to stimulate thought, but to prevent it, not to convey information, but to conceal or distort it, not to draw public attention, but to divert or suppress it. In short, contemporary political language may play precisely the reverse role from that classically conceived for political rhetoric."[19] That role, according to rhetorician Charles Knepper, was to challenge popular thinking through independent leadership: "The goals of Isocrates, Cicero, and Quintilian did not center on the meager goal of being persuasive for the merely pragmatic purpose of maintaining personal power. Rather, the orator was both a thinker and a speaker whose persuasion was built upon accumulated cultural wisdom in solving problems which arose and required public decision and action."[20]

Those who scoff at the idea of an ennobling political rhetoric that produces dialogue might point out that the rough-and-tumble of American politics has never been receptive to the intellectual refinements of a Cicero or a Quintilian. This is true up to a point, but it fails to account for a tradition of great oratory ranging from Thomas Paine, Henry Clay, Daniel Webster, Abraham Lincoln, William Jennings Bryan, Woodrow Wilson, Theodore and Franklin Roosevelt down to John Kennedy and Martin Luther King, Jr. The American culture is not averse to challenging rhetoric that inspires and at the same time invites controversy.

To the extent that we can imagine a more inspiring and useful way of conducting our politics, there is room in the culture for reform and improvement. To the extent that we fail to seize the opportunities for renewal and positive change, society will continue to wither and lose its political creativity. As long as we can imagine how to improve our politics, then we can take the steps necessary to bring those imaginings to life. The quality of public life and the scope of government action are limited only by the rhetorical vision that inspires them. Nowhere is that vision more important than in the electoral arena. We can begin thinking about improving our political condition with a political scorecard to evaluate future political developments.

A POLITICAL SCORECARD FOR THE 1990s

In an age of reduced expectations, the greatest danger is that people will settle for too little. After all, something is better than nothing. As a result of this natural psychological tendency, a party with an issue looks better than a party with none at all—even if that issue is only a weak adaptation from the past. Similarly, a proposal for electoral reform may be welcomed as better than nothing at all—even though weak reforms passed by a self-serving Congress will accomplish next to nothing at all.

As the drumbeat of public anger grows, parties and candidates will come under increasing pressure to do something. And do something they will. More budgets will be passed, and more legislation, too. Even election reforms are sure to come. All will be heralded as signs of political life, party leadership, and solutions to the nation's political malaise. However, a wary public should follow such developments closely, and not settle for illusions of change based on reduced expectations. In order to decide whether significant changes are under way, the reader is invited to keep score in the following categories to judge whether the changes that will come in the years ahead are positive or merely illusory ones.

The Legislative Score: Democrats versus Republicans

The challenge for the Democrats will be to push beyond weak throwbacks from the past like "tax the rich." This sort of issue may appeal to a few voters in the short run, but it does not promise to move the country anywhere. It contains no vision. In the end, this slogan will quickly lose its standing as an issue in the minds of most voters—if for no other reason than that the Democrats have been (almost) as deeply implicated in favoring the rich as have the Republicans. After all, the Democrats mastered the PAC game, agreed to the budget overruns and tax breaks of the 1980s, were equally responsible for the savings-and-loan collapse, and abandoned the poor at many key legislative junctures during the past decade.

What can the Democrats do to make a difference? They can begin with developing a party line on national economic priorities and applying it first of all to the budget. Some degree of party unity in budget priorities for the future would mean a de facto reduction of PAC and interest group influence on the party. A resulting opening up of party politics to middle-class and grass-roots interests just might generate the kind of public dialogue a party needs to figure out what its vision of the future really is. The main point of Part III of the book is that healthy rituals, including elections, require a trial-and-error flexibility and a give-and-take dialogue between leaders and followers. This is the best one can hope for in national politics: to trust a well-functioning political culture to bring people into meaningful communication about common problems. If there is a period of some turmoil and shaking out, so be it. The worst casualty is likely to be the loss of some incumbent deadwood in Washington. It is hard to imagine a reduction in governing beyond current levels. While we cannot know in advance what a politically workable and popularly supportable Democratic vision will look like, we can recognize the efforts of a party leadership to present new programs and governing ideas to voters for their approval. Such efforts should receive high scores. At the other extreme is the worst-case scenario in which a party leadership unwilling to open up a dialogue about the future forces tired visions from the past on the citizenry. The failure to take advantage of their control of the White House and Congress between 1993 and 1994 does not earn them high marks. *If future Democratic campaigns settle for single symbolic campaign issues or warmed-over Great Society visions, give them a low score (and count on the voters to do the same).*

Since the Republicans have gained a legislative majority in Congress, it is fair to hold them equally accountable for producing a legislative agenda. Simple promises to balance budgets and reduce taxes do not speak to much party vision or integrity. No amount of cutting welfare or bureaucratic waste will balance budgets—particularly budgets that are squeezed by further tax cuts. As for the Republican antitax crusade, it is as superficial as the Democrats' mirror-image version of the same issue. The Republican antitax stand is a recurring ghost of party politics dating from before the depression of the 1930s when the wealthy, conservative core of Republican ideology believed that the best way to stimulate economic growth was to create a governmental welfare state for the rich. The Reagan supply-side theories of the 1980s added a few whistles and bells to this abiding conservative belief, and the Bush pledge to impose no new taxes carried it forward into the 1990s. With the promotion of the Contract with America, Republicans continued to make taxes and budgets part of their primary domestic stands for the rest of the decade. Fully four of the ten provisions of the Contract involve some combination of tax cuts and budget-balancing promises, yet there is no explanation of how this smoke and mirrors process will work in practice. *If the Republicans can offer no greater vision than this for the end of the 1990s, score them low (as will the voters).*

Scoring the Election System: Money, Media, and Marketing

Enough has been said about these elements of the system to allow a few scoring tips to suffice here. The main *money* development to watch is the finance point spread between incumbents and challengers. In the election cycles of the future, does the campaign finance gap close, stay the same, or widen? If meaningful reform legislation is passed, the gap should close. A high score on the money game should be awarded for only two developments: (1) a dramatic closing of the incumbent-challenger gap to no worse, on average, than a 2 to 1 incumbent advantage (we are not asking for miracles here) and (2) a restructuring of the finance system so that PACs are eased out in favor of public funding of more races, thus giving idea-coalitions a chance to form among newly competitive parties and their candidates. Give anything less than this a low score.

An alarming development in the 1994 election was a narrowing of the money gap, but owing to the infusion of huge quantities of PAC money and private wealth into Republican challengers' campaigns. *Both of the above changes must take place together to create positive results and merit a high score.*

As for the *media,* we should continue to award high marks for journalistic decoding of campaign ads and behind-the-scenes looks at media manipulation. However, we must pay close attention to media coverage and editorial postures on electoral reform. In particular, editorial weakness on the elimination of PACs should be given low marks (indicating that the media have yielded to the temptation to preserve their own options as special interest organizations). Even more telling will be media reactions to proposals for government regulation of political advertising. For example, requiring that the television networks give free commercial space in longer (say, three- to five-minute) blocks would not only level the playing field for underfinanced candidates, but also require all candidates to fill the air space with something beyond 30-second subliminal pitches. Even though virtually all other democracies regulate political advertising in these ways, the U.S. media can be expected to claim infringement of free speech (translate: free profits). *If they do, give the media a low score.*

In the area of candidate *marketing,* we should expect more of the same, until reforms (like the above) change the rules of the game. It may be tempting to score declines in mean-spirited personal attacks as an improvement, but it is important to determine whether the trends are long term or whether they are simply cycles in campaign market research that shift tactics when voters become immune to particular appeals. Thus, levels of negative advertising dipped in 1990 following the bitter 1988 campaign but came back with a vengeance in 1994. *More generally, as long as our most meaningful glimpses of candidates come through commercial images and news events staged to reinforce those images, give low scores to campaign communication.*

The Voter Scorecard: Voting May Not Be the Answer

Although voter withdrawal is a distressing symptom of electoral failure, an upturn in voting rates is not necessarily a sign that the system is improving. In fact, a number of incidental factors can produce short-term increases in turnout. In 1992, the turnout was up somewhat, but not all that dramatically considering that it was a three-candidate race. The 1994 turnout of 38.5 percent was up slightly over the 35–36 percent of recent midterm elections, but it is not what one would hope for in a true "landslide." Moreover, highly emotional appeals based on racial antagonisms or moral fears with little connection to broader, policy-related programs for national renewal can bring out voters.

Even more important is the possibility that citizens cannot simply vote their way out of the current plight of electoral democracy. If people wait for incumbent politicians to reform the system that brought them security in office, we may have a long wait ahead. Similarly, trusting interest organizations such as Common Cause to wage the reform battle single-handedly risks reducing electoral reform to just another issue in the swirl of interest group politics in Washington. Citizens must begin organizing at the grass-roots level both to raise the volume of public opinion about the importance of reform and to push parties and candidates into offering electoral reform as one of their top priorities. *If voters continue to withdraw or wait for half-hearted reforms to be handed down from the powers that be, give them low marks for citizenship. If grass-roots groups begin to raise their voices in support of tough and specific reform programs, while pushing those programs onto the platforms of candidates and parties, raise the score.*

The Electoral Reform Scorecard: Rating the National Debate

Now we come to the bottom line of electoral politics. Will the effects of money, media, and marketing be checked, or will they run on until the possibility of governing society and the economy completely collapses under their disorganizing influences? The balance may well be decided by how the public participates in the reform process. Will a cynical public with low expectations settle for simplistic, "no brainer" reforms such as term limits? Or will citizens organize and raise a loud grass-roots voice in support of fundamental changes?

Part of the answer to these questions depends on how the national debate about electoral reform progresses in the coming years. This debate should be given a low score if the news media continue to report on reform efforts as just another issue on the crowded Washington agenda (as opposed to elevating political reform to a more prominent place on the news and editorial pages). If the media continue to allow politicians to drive the news (and the prominence of reform), the national debate about political change will look just like the other public dialogues of the times: lacking in political leadership, passed along with mixed signals from the media, and intellectually fragmented, resulting in a collection of poorly understood legislative proposals unrelated to broader programs or goals. *If this pattern materializes, score the chances for meaningful change zero.*

If, on the other hand, grass-roots voices begin to emerge, the media exercise their power to set the agenda in this area, and a few political leaders hear the call, the cause of electoral reform may be elevated above the buzzing confusion of special interest politics in Washington. Then the proposals of interest organizations such as Common Cause may be given a critical public hearing. And then, we may have, as a nation, a chance to think before we act on important legislation affecting voter registration, campaign financing, broadcasting, and political advertising. *If a sweeping package of reforms goes forward under the light of media coverage and through the heat of public debate, score a victory for the possibility of governing in America once again.*

THE FINAL ANALYSIS: IT'S UP TO THE PEOPLE

One can only hope that Americans will convert their anger about a failing government into action that is likely to make a difference. As noted earlier, voting for term limit initiatives and for the latest party or candidate promising to clean up the mess in Washington is not likely to make much of a difference. But how can the right reforms get started?

National third-party initiatives may be a mixed blessing. There has been talk in recent years of a women's party, a labor party, a consumer party, a "green" party, a Ross Perot party, a Concord Coalition fiscal responsibility party, and perhaps a coalition of such groups in a revitalized rainbow party. Such efforts are doomed to splinter and fail unless they all recognize that their respective issues must be subordinated, first, to the broader issue of election reform. Perhaps a broader party with a set of election reform proposals heading its platform would make a difference and win support among discouraged voters. If nothing else, a reform party would provide a focal point (and more importantly an organizational base) for the kind of sustained social movement that will have to emerge in the next decade if Americans are to have any hope of regaining control of their government.

The prospects for a social movement are reasonably good—particularly with a third party as its beacon. Indeed, American history can be viewed as a succession of social movements (the frontier movement, transcendentalism, abolitionism, populism, the progressive movement, the suffrage movement, prohibitionism, labor, civil rights, feminism, the counterculture, born-again Christianity, abortion rights and pro life movements, just to name a few). In this view, social movements are the noninstitutional "hidden hand" of change in American life. The time is ripe for another one.

Whatever methods the people settle on, the stakes have never been higher. All lesser issues, interests, and groups are affected by the governing crisis. Without a grass-roots movement aimed squarely at regaining popular, idea-based control of the government, democracy may well become an electronic echo in a marketing jingle or a nostalgic image of times gone by. Now is the time for electoral reform—now, while there is still reason to govern.

NOTES

PREFACE

1. See, for example, Murray Edelman, *Constructing the Political Spectacle* (Chicago: University of Chicago Press, 1988).
2. From an Annenberg Public Policy Center study announced in the Annenberg Center bulletin *NewsLink* 4, no. 3 (Fall 1994): 1.
3. Quoted in *Newsweek,* perspectives, November 21, 1994, p. 33.
4. Quoted in Robert Pear, "Term Limits: Questions on Legality, But Few on Popularity," *New York Times,* November 5, 1994, p. A8.
5. In a Times/Mirror poll during the 1994 election, 53 percent said that a third party was a good idea. Richard L. Berke, "From Not Quite Acceptable to Maybe Even Electable," *New York Times,* October 2, 1994, p. E4.

CHAPTER 1

1. David Mayhew, *Divided We Govern* (New Haven, Conn.: Yale University Press, 1991).
2. Michael Wines, "Who? Us? Washington Really Is in Touch. We're the Problem." *New York Times,* October 16, 1994, pp. 4–1.
3. Bruce Gronbeck, "Electric Rhetoric: The Changing Forms of American Political Discourse," *Vichiana,* 3rd series, 1st year (Napoli: Loffredo Editore, 1990), pp. 141–161.
4. Benjamin Ginsberg, *The Captive Public: How Mass Opinion Promotes State Power* (New York: Basic Books, 1986).
5. Walter Lippmann, *Public Opinion* (New York: Free Press, 1922), p. 9.
6. National survey conducted by Princeton Survey Research Associates for the Times Mirror Center, reported in Larry Hugick and Andrew Kohut, "Taking the Nation's Pulse," *The Public Perspective,* November/December 1994, p. 3.
7. Jarol Manheim, *All of the People, All the Time: Strategic Communication in American Politics* (Armonk, N.Y.: M. E. Sharp, 1991).
8. Robert Entman, *Democracy without Citizens: Media and the Decay of American Politics* (New York: Oxford University Press, 1989).
9. Walter Lippmann, *The Phantom Public* (New York: Harcourt Brace, 1925).
10. For an excellent discussion of how scientific opinion polling contributes to these features of contemporary politics, see Susan Herbst, *Numbered Voices: How Opinion Polling Has Shaped American Politics* (Chicago: University of Chicago Press, 1993).
11. Murray Edelman, *Constructing the Political Spectacle* (Chicago: University of Chicago Press, 1988).
12. Dan Nimmo and James Coombs, *Mediated Political Realities,* 2nd ed. (New York: Longman, 1990).
13. See, for example, "Advertising: Now Playing in Politics, Latest Techniques of Hollywood," *New York Times,* October 29, 1994, p. A9.
14. See Sam Howe Verhovek, "Candidate Seeks Job She Would Cut," *New York Times,* October 30, 1994, p. A13.

15. Kathleen Hall Jamieson, *Dirty Politics* (New York: Oxford University Press, 1992).

16. Thomas Patterson, *Out of Order: How the Decline of the Political Parties and the Growing Power of the News Media Undermine the American Way of Electing Presidents* (New York: Alfred A. Knopf, 1993).

17. According to Federal Election Commission statistics compiled for the 1992 Senate races in Dwight Morris and Muriele E. Gamache, *Gold-Plated Politics: The 1992 Congressional Races* (Washington, D.C.: Congressional Quarterly Press, 1994), pp. 20–21.

18. Estimate provided by Erik Asard, Director of the Swedish Institute of North American Studies, Uppsala University.

19. Quoted in Sidney Blumenthal, "The Candidate," *The New Yorker,* October 10, 1994, p. 55.

20. Ibid.

21. Quoted in Richard Morin, "Budget Czars for a Day," *The Washington Post National Weekly Edition,* November 23–29, 1992, p. 36.

22. Roderick Hart, *Seducing America: How Television Charms the Modern Voter* (New York: Oxford University Press, 1994).

23. Thomas Ferguson and Joel Rogers, *Right Turn: The Decline of the Democrats and the Future of American Politics* (New York: Hill and Wang, 1986).

24. Stephen Rose, personal communication. In a forthcoming book, Rose, an economist, explains what he calls "the bunker mentality in the Pepsi Generation" as a result of shifts in national wealth and political priorities.

25. Poll data from *Harper's,* July 1989, p. 17.

26. University of Michigan, National Election Study Data; quoted in Gregory B. Marcus, "Americans Are Increasingly Disgusted," *International Herald Tribune,* October 15, 1990, p. 8.

27. Quoted in an Associated Press wire story, "GOP Rethinking Term-limit Pledge," *Charleston Post and Courier,* November 22, 1994, p. 1.

28. Cited in Richard L. Berke, "From Not Quite Acceptable to Maybe Even Electable," *New York Times,* October 2, 1994, p. E4.

29. Richard L. Berke, "Centrist Democrats' Poll Warns Clinton of Unrest," *New York Times,* November 18, 1994, p. A10.

30. Kevin Phillips, "America, 1989: Brain-Dead Politics in a Transition," *Washington Post* feature reprinted in the *International Herald Tribune,* October 4, 1989, p. 8.

31. Results of a *New York Times*/CBS poll reported in the *International Herald Tribune,* November 5, 1990, p. 1.

32. Result of an ABC News/*Washington Post* poll, Associated Press wire, October 19, 1990.

CHAPTER 2

1. The figures cited here will be reintroduced and analyzed in more detail later in this chapter. Full source citations are available in footnotes 33 and 34.

2. John Aldrich quoted in Ralph Blumenthal, "To Many, the Best Choice on Nov. 8 Is Just Home," *New York Times,* November 6, 1988, Sec. 1, p. 18.

3. This quote can be found in Kathleen H. Jamieson, *Eloquence in an Electronic Age: The Transformation of Political Speechmaking* (New York: Oxford University Press, 1988), p. 248.

4. See, for example, R. W. Apple, Jr., "Old Pros Appraise the '88 Campaign," *New York Times,* November 6, 1988, Sec. 1, p. 18.

5. Quoted in Michael Oreskes, "Talking Heads: Weighing Imagery in a Campaign Made for Television," *New York Times,* October 2, 1988, Sec. 4, p. 1.

6. Ibid.

7. Russell Neuman, Marian Just, and Ann Crigler, *Common Knowledge* (Chicago: University of Chicago Press, 1993).

8. ABC correspondent Brit Hume quoted in John Dillin, "News Media Critique Themselves: Many Reporters Unhappy with Campaign '88 Coverage," *Christian Science Monitor,* December 9, 1988, p. 3.

9. Jeremy Gerard, "Convention Coverage: Endangered Species?" *New York Times,* July 23, 1988, Sec. 1, p. 9.

10. Ibid.

11. Jarol Manheim, *All of the People, All the Time: Strategic Communication and American Politics* (Armonk, N.Y.: M. E. Sharpe, 1991).

12. Quoted in ibid.

13. The credit for finding this gem goes to Marjorie Hershey, "The Campaign and the Media," in Gerald M. Pomper, ed., *The Election of 1988: Reports and Interpretations* (Chatham, N.J.: Chatham House Publishers, 1989), p. 83.

14. Hershey, "The Campaign and the Media," p. 87.

15. Maureen Dowd, "Bush's Top Strategists: Smooth Poll-Taker and Hard Driving Manager," *New York Times,* May 30, 1988, p. 11.

16. Ibid.

17. Eric Alternam, "Playing Hardball," *New York Times Magazine,* April 30, 1989, p. 70.

18. Maureen Dowd, "For Bush on the Campaign Trail, the Style Is First Sour, Then Sweet," *New York Times,* October 12, 1988, p. 10.

19. Ibid.

20. Hershey, "The Campaign and the Media," p. 81.

21. Barbara G. Farah and Ethel Klein, "Public Opinion Trends," in Pomper, ed., *The Election of 1988,* p. 103.

22. For a discussion of these calculations, see Gerald M. Pomper, "The Presidential Nominations," in Pomper, ed., *The Election of 1988* (Chatham, N.J.: Chatham House, 1989), pp. 50–52.

23. Ibid.

24. Quoted in R. W. Apple, Jr., "Willie Brown Sees Dukakis Errors," *New York Times,* October 31, 1988, p. 9.

25. Michael Oreskes, "TV's Role in '88: The Medium Is the Election," *New York Times,* October 30, 1988, Sec. 1, p. 10.

26. Ibid., p. 1.

27. "NBC Nightly News," March 26, 1989. See also Marvin Kalb, "TV, Election Spoiler," *New York Times,* November 28, 1988, Sec. 1, p. 19.

28. Robin Toner, "Dukakis Works at Warmth But Keeps His Sleeves Down," *New York Times,* August 8, 1988, p. 1.

29. On the Democrats, see Philip Weiss, "Party Time in Atlanta," *Columbia Journalism Review* (September/October 1988), p. 29. On the Republicans, see "Campaign Trail," *New York Times,* October 10, 1988, Sec. 1, p. 10.

30. Lynda Barry, cartoon, "The Election from Hell," 1988.

31. *New York Times*/CBS News poll reported in *New York Times,* October 25, 1988, Sec. 1, p. 1.

32. Ibid., pp. 1, 10.

33. John Dillin, "Voters on Election '88: Is This It?" *Christian Science Monitor,* November 2, 1988, p. 1.

34. E. S. Dionne, Jr., "The Campaign Has Real Issues in Spite of Itself," *New York Times*, October 30, 1988, Sec. 4, p. 1.

35. Maureen Dowd, "Bush Lays out Foreign Policy Tenets," *New York Times*, August 3, 1988, p. 8.

36. Hershey, "The Campaign and the Media," p. 97.

37. *New York Times*, October 11, 1988, Sec. 1, p. 1. See also R. W. Apple, Jr., "County That's Always Right Dislikes '88 Choices," *New York Times*, November 2, 1988, Sec. 1, p. 12.

38. Michael Oreskes, "Steel City Tires of Politics and Promises," *New York Times*, April 25, 1988, Sec. 1, p. 1.

39. Editorial, *The Nation*, June 25, 1988, p. 1.

40. William Echikson, "Difference between Bush, Dukakis Lost on French," *Christian Science Monitor*, November 2, 1988, p. 10.

41. See Bruce Gronbeck, "Electric Rhetoric: The Changing Forms of American Political Discourse," *Vichiana*, 3rd series, 1st year (Napoli: Loffredo Editore, 1990), pp. 141–161.

42. Jeffrey K. Tulis, *The Rhetorical Presidency* (Princeton, N.J.: Princeton University Press, 1987).

43. Roderick P. Hart, *The Sound of Leadership: Presidential Communication in the Modern Age* (Chicago: University of Chicago Press, 1987).

44. Jamieson, *Eloquence in an Electronic Age*.

45. Shanto Iyengar and Donald R. Kinder, *News That Matters: Television and American Public Opinion* (Chicago: University of Chicago Press, 1987).

46. Roderick Hart, *Seducing America: How Television Charms the Modern Voter* (New York: Oxford University Press, 1994).

47. See, for example, Thomas Ferguson and Joel Rogers, *Right Turn: The Decline of the Democrats and the Future of American Politics* (New York: Hill and Wang, 1986), especially Ch. 1.

48. Quoted in Oreskes, "Talking Heads," p. 1.

49. Erik Asard, "Election Campaigns in Sweden and the U.S.: Convergence or Divergence?" *American Studies in Scandinavia* 21, no. 2 (1989): 70–85.

50. Murray Edelman, *Constructing the Political Spectacle* (Chicago: University of Chicago Press, 1988).

51. Murray Edelman, *The Symbolic Uses of Politics* (Champagne–Urbana: University of Illinois Press, 1964).

52. General estimates for the United States and England are from Lewis Lipsitz and David M. Speak, *American Democracy*, 2nd ed. (New York: St. Martin's Press, 1989), p. 259. House and Senate figures are from David B. Magleby and Candice Nelson, *The Money Chase: Congressional Campaign Finance Reform* (Washington D.C.: Brookings Institution, 1990), p. 36. Figures for 1992 House races are from Dwight Morris and Murielle E. Gamache, *Gold-Plated Politics: The 1992 Congressional Races* (Washington, D.C.: CQ Press, 1994), p. 27.

53. Quoted in Thomas Ferguson and Joel Rogers, "The Reagan Victory: Corporate Coalitions in the 1980 Campaign," in Ferguson and Rogers, eds., *The Hidden Election: Politics and Economics in the 1980 Presidential Campaign* (New York: Pantheon, 1981), p. 4.

54. See, for example, Mark Hertsgaard, *On Bended Knee: The Press and the Reagan Presidency* (New York: Farrar, Straus and Giroux, 1988).

55. "This Week with David Brinkley," ABC, November 6, 1988.

56. Unnamed source, cited in Mark Hertsgaard, "Electoral Journalism: Not Yellow, But Yellow-Bellied," *New York Times*, September 21, 1988, p. A15.

57. Thomas Patterson, *Out of Order* (New York: Alfred A. Knopf, 1993).

58. Ibid.

59. Jacques Ellul, "Preconceived Ideas about Mediated Information," in Everett M. Rogers and Francis Bolle, eds., *The Media Revolution in America and Western Europe* (Norwood, N.J.: Ablex Publishing Co., 1985), p. 107.

60. Robert Shrum, quoted in R. W. Apple, Jr., "Candidates Focus on Television Ads," *New York Times,* October 19, 1986, p. A16.

CHAPTER 3

1. For a review of research on voter ignorance, see Eric R. A. N. Smith, *The Unchanging American Voter* (Berkeley: University of California Press, 1989), Ch. 4.

2. The classic work on this remains Angus Campbell, Philip E. Converse, Warren E. Miller, and Donald E. Stokes, *The American Voter* (New York: John Wiley, 1960). Smith's argument from above is that little has changed to alter this portrait of an unsophisticated electorate.

3. Nelson W. Polsby and Aaron Wildavsky, *Presidential Elections,* 6th ed. (New York: Scribners, 1984), pp. 5–6.

4. This tradition follows the work of V. O. Key, Jr. (with Milton Cummings), *The Responsible Electorate: Rationality in Presidential Voting 1936–1960* (New York: Vintage Books, 1966).

5. See Morris P. Fiorina, *Retrospective Voting in American National Elections* (New Haven, Conn.: Yale University Press, 1981).

6. See Benjamin Page, *Choices and Echoes in Presidential Elections* (Chicago: University of Chicago Press, 1978).

7. Elizabeth Kolbert, "Media Whistle Stops a la 1992: Arsenio, Larry, and Phil," *New York Times,* June 5, 1992, p. A18.

8. *USA Today,* December 28, 1992, p. 5B.

9. Maureen Dowd, "How a Battered Clinton Has Stayed Alive," *New York Times,* March 16, 1992, p. 1.

10. See, for example, Campbell et al., *The American Voter.*

11. Recall here the earlier argument of Smith in *The Unchanging American Voter.*

12. Everett Carl Ladd, "Campaign '88: What Are the 'Issues'?" *Christian Science Monitor,* June 3, 1988, p. 14.

13. Reported in *Newsweek,* Special Election Issue, November/December 1992, p. 33.

14. Ibid., p. 34.

15. Murray Edelman, "Contestable Categories and Public Opinion," *Political Communication* 10, no. 3 (1993): 231–242.

16. See, for example, the poll data presented in W. Lance Bennett, *Inside the System: Culture, Institutions, and Power in American Politics* (Fort Worth, Tex.: Harcourt Brace, 1994), Ch. 10.

17. Source: Tim Miller and John Pavlik, "Campaign Coverage by the Numbers," in *The Finish Line: Covering the Campaign's Final Days* (New York: Columbia University Freedom Forum Media Studies Center, 1993), p. 68.

18. Ibid., p. 67.

19. *Time,* November 2, 1992, p. 30.

20. Based on Gallup poll ratings in mock elections between Bush, Clinton, and Perot taken monthly from January to November 1992.

21. From Dirk Smillie, "Breakfast with Bill, George, and Ross," in *The Finish Line,* p. 125.

22. Ibid., p. 121.

23. Based on all TV appearances reported in the *New York Times* and the *Washington Post* and detected in a *Nexis/Lexis* database search from January 1 to November

3, 1993. These data were then arrayed against the Gallup poll mock election results reported in note 20 above.

24. *TV Guide,* November 21–27, 1992, pp. 14–15.

25. *Newsweek,* November/December 1992, p. 40.

26. Ibid.

27. Ibid.

28. Ibid., p. 56.

29. Richard L. Berke, "In Late Onslaught, Nastiest of Politics Rules Radio Waves," *New York Times,* November 2, 1992, p. 1.

30. Ibid., p. 78.

31. Joanne Morreale, "American Self Images and the Presidential Campaign Film, 1964–1992," in Arthur M. Miller and Bruce E. Gronbeck, eds., *Presidential Campaigns and American Self Images* (Boulder, Colo.: Westview Press, 1994), pp. 35–37.

32. See Joe McGinnis, *The Selling of the President* (New York: Trident Press, 1969).

33. Daniel Boorstin, *The Image: A Guide to Pseudo-Events in America* (New York: Atheneum, 1961).

34. Ibid., p. 55.

35. Michael Wines, "Wonked Out: It's August; How Much Policy Can a Nation Take?" *New York Times,* August 15, 1993, Sec. 4, p. 1.

CHAPTER 4

1. Quoted in Richard H. Leach, *American Federalism* (New York: W. W. Norton, 1970), p. 54.

2. Ibid.

3. See Herbert E. Alexander, *Financing Politics: Money, Elections and Political Reform* (Washington, D.C.: Congressional Quarterly Press, 1984).

4. See W. Lance Bennett and William Haltom, "Issues, Voter Choice, and Critical Elections," *Social Science History* 4 (Fall 1980): 792–817.

5. Ibid.

6. These differences will be elaborated throughout the rest of the book. For now, this simple "snapshot" will suffice to convey the basic idea.

7. Quoted in Michael Wines, "Moderate Republicans Seek an Identity for Gingrich Era," *New York Times,* December 26, 1994, p. A1.

8. See, for example, Nelson W. Polsby, *Consequences of Party Reform* (New York: Oxford University Press, 1983).

9. See, for example, Leon D. Epstein, *Political Parties in the American Mold* (Madison: University of Wisconsin Press, 1986).

10. See Michael J. Malbin, "Looking Back at the Future of Campaign Finance Reform: Interest Groups and American Elections," in Malbin, ed., *Money and Politics in the United States* (Chatham, N.J.: Chatham House, 1984). In addition, see Alexander, *Financing Politics,* in Malbin, ed., *Money and Politics.* See also Elizabeth Drew, *Politics and Money* (New York: Collier, 1983).

11. Quoted in Richard L. Berke, "Gephardt's Star Rises in '96 Scenarios," *New York Times,* December 26, 1994, p. A8.

12. Based on figures from the Survey Research Center of the University of Michigan compiled through the National Election Surveys conducted since 1952. In 1952, for comparison, the corresponding figures were: Democrats—47 percent; Independents—22 percent; and Republicans—27 percent.

13. For differing analyses of precisely how the political pie was redivided following the depression, see Thomas Ferguson and Joel Rogers, *Right Turn: The Decline of the Democrats and the Future of American Politics* (New York: Hill and Wang, 1986);

and William Domhoff, *The Power Elite and the State: How Policy Is Made in America* (New York: Aldine de Gruyter, 1990), especially Ch. 9.

14. We will return in Chapter 7 to consider some of the larger implications of this Court ruling linking political spending and free speech.

15. For a sampling of these debates, see William J. Crotty, *Political Reform and the American Experiment* (New York: Crowell, 1977); and Larry M. Bartels, *Presidential Primaries and the Dynamics of Public Choice* (Princeton, N.J.: Princeton University Press, 1988).

16. For a highly detailed account of the evolution of PAC politics, see Larry J. Sabato, *PAC Power: Inside the World of Political Action Committees* (New York: W. W. Norton, 1985).

17. Federal Election Commission figures, 1988.

18. For a detailed breakdown of the figures, see Jean Cobb, "Top Brass," *Common Cause Magazine,* May/June 1989, pp. 23–27.

19. Quoted in Katharine Q. Seelye, "Lobbyists Are the Loudest in the Health Care Debate," *New York Times,* August 16, 1994, p. A1.

20. The first four quotes are from Representatives Andrew Jacobs of Indiana, Dan Glickman of Kansas, Barbara Mikulski of Maryland, and Richard Ottinger of New York, all reported in Sabato, *PAC Power,* pp. 126–127. The last quote is from a "Democrat from the West" who preferred anonymity in a news story by Tom Kenworthy, "U.S. House Democrats Struggling with Principles vs. PACs," *International Herald Tribune,* October 31, 1989, p. 2 (from the *Washington Post*).

21. Quoted in Sabato, *PAC Power,* p. xii.

22. As with all players, the small donations are as welcome as the large. In a typical year after this statement was made, Senator Dole accepted speaking fees as small as $1,000 and $2,000 from dozens of organizations, including the American Dental Association, the American Pharmaceutical Association, the American Stock Exchange, and the American Academy of Dermatology. Source: *New York Times* data reported in the *Seattle Weekly,* December 27, 1989, p. 19.

23. Walter Dean Burnham, "The Reagan Heritage," in Gerald M. Pomper, ed., *The Election of 1988: Reports and Interpretations* (Chatham, N.J.: Chatham House, 1989), p. 15.

24. See Ferguson and Rogers, *Right Turn.*

25. Ibid., Ch. 1.

26. National Election Study data, Survey Research Center, University of Michigan.

27. For a detailed analysis of the public role in the tax battles of the 1980s, see W. Lance Bennett and Erik Asard, "The Marketplace of Ideas: The Cases of Tax Reform in Sweden and the United States," *Polity,* forthcoming.

28. For better or worse, most of the critical content of the news in the American press system is introduced when there is a strong vocal opposition (i.e., elite opinion is divided) within the government itself. (See W. Lance Bennett, "Marginalizing the Majority: Conditioning Public Opinion to Accept Managerial Democracy," in Michael Margolis and Gary Mauser, eds., *Manipulating Public Opinion* [New York: Dorsey, 1989].) In the early Reagan years, not only were the Democrats unfocused and unable to provide the media with a sustained critical voice, but also the Republicans and their independent PAC allies quickly realized the public relations advantages of silencing the opposition. Throughout the Reagan presidency, a team made up of the White House, the Republican party, and their independent PAC allies ran local campaigns in home districts against members of Congress who opposed the Reagan policy agenda. In summary, the early weaknesses in the Republican vision were disguised by one of the most sophisticated media management campaigns in history that included a three-tiered strategy: (1) almost daily White House orchestra-

tion and coordination of news events, (2) a disciplined refusal of the president and other administration officers to engage with press criticism when it emerged, and (3) the electoral intimidation of the administration's political opponents, effectively silencing the most common channel for opposing views to enter the news. For an example of one such silencing campaign, see W. Lance Bennett, "Toward a Theory of Press-State Relations in the United States," *Journal of Communication* 40, no. 2 (Spring 1990): 103–125.

29. Figures are from Sabato, *PAC Power*, pp. 188–190, and from Federal Election Commission data on 1988.

30. Quoted in Paul E. Johnson, John H. Aldrich, Gary J. Miller, Charles W. Ostrom, and David W. Rhode, *American Government*, 2nd ed. (Boston: Houghton Mifflin, 1990), p. 336.

31. Congressional Budget Office, 1977–1988, national income analysis.

32. Benjamin Ginsberg and Martin Shefter, *Politics by Other Means: The Declining Importance of Elections in America* (New York: Basic Books, 1990).

33. Jarol Manheim, *All of the People, All the Time: Strategic Communication and American Politics* (Armonk, N.Y.: M. E. Sharpe, 1991).

CHAPTER 5

1. Quoted in Charles Snydor, *American Revolutionaries in the Making* (New York: Free Press, 1952), p. 48.

2. Ibid., p. 55.

3. Ibid., p. 57.

4. Alexis de Tocqueville, *Democracy in America*, Vol. I (New York: Alfred A. Knopf, 1945), pp. 259–260.

5. Paul Kleppner, Walter Dean Burnham, Ronald P. Formisano, Samuel P. Hays, Richard Jensen, and William G. Shade, *The Evolution of American Electoral Systems* (Westport, Conn.: Greenwood Press, 1981).

6. William G. Shade, "Political Pluralism and Party Development," in Kleppner et al., *The Evolution of American Electoral Systems*, p. 81.

7. From Paul F. Boller, Jr., *Presidential Campaigns* (New York: Oxford University Press, 1985), p. 107.

8. Quoted in ibid., p. 168.

9. The term *critical election* was coined by V. O. Key. Walter Dean Burnham discusses it extensively in his *Critical Elections and the Mainsprings of American Politics* (New York: W. W. Norton, 1970).

10. In the early days of the Clinton administration, labor secretary Robert Reich did issue a number of statements about economic restructuring, yet they were aimed at intellectuals and appeared primarily on editorial pages of elite publications. While one suspects that these statements were part of the overall Clinton economic program, they were curiously detached from the president's own rhetoric about "jobs." It appeared that Clinton's communication strategists were afraid of letting the president—a notorious "policy wonk" in the estimation of the press—loose on economic matters and so gave him a script that poorly conveyed his actual policy agenda.

11. Walter Dean Burnham, "The Reagan Heritage," in Gerald M. Pomper, *The Election of 1988: Reports and Interpretations* (Chatham, N.J.: Chatham House Publishers, 1989).

12. Quoted in Marjorie Randon Hershey, "The Campaign and the Media," in Pomper, *The Election of 1988*, p. 74.

13. See, for example, Michael S. Lewis-Beck and Tom W. Rice, *Forecasting Elections* (Washington, D.C.: Congressional Quarterly Press, 1992).

14. Arthur H. Miller and Bruce E. Gronbeck, "Presidential Campaign Politics at

the Crossroads," in Miller and Gronbeck, eds., *Presidential Campaigns and American Self Images* (Boulder, Colo.: Westview Press, 1994), p. 253.

15. Everett Carl Ladd, "Campaign '88: What Are the 'Issues'?" *Christian Science Monitor,* June 3, 1988, p. 14.

16. The definitive work on this theory of voting is Morris P. Fiorina, *Retrospective Voting in American National Elections* (New Haven, Conn.: Yale University Press, 1981).

17. Data are from a Voter Research and Surveys national exit poll of 15,490 voters leaving 300 polling places on election day, 1992. Reported in *Newsweek,* Special Election Issue, November/December 1992, p. 10.

18. Nicholas von Hoffman, " 'Goo-goos' Glom onto Issues, Again," *New York Times,* October 12, 1988, p. 27.

19. "Where They Would Lead the Country: Summaries of George Bush's and Michael Dukakis' Positions on Issues Facing the Nation from Position Papers, Campaign Advisers, and Various Issues 'Score Cards'," *Christian Science Monitor,* November 1, 1988, pp. 14–15.

20. "Campaign '88: Issues Scorecard," *New York Times,* February 4, 1988, pp. 16–17.

21. Thomas Patterson, *Out of Order* (New York: Alfred A. Knopf, 1993).

22. Quoted in Boller, *Presidential Campaigns,* pp. 109–110.

23. Ibid., p. 12.

24. Ibid., pp. 53–54.

25. Ibid., pp. 55–56.

26. Bruce E. Gronbeck, "Candidate-Generated Images in Presidential Campaigns," in Miller and Gronbeck, eds., *Presidential Campaigns and American Self Images,* p. 15.

CHAPTER 6

1. Ben H. Bagdikian, *The Media Monopoly,* 4th ed. (Boston: Beacon Press, 1992), p. 4.

2. Ibid., pp. ix, x.

3. For an excellent discussion of these trends in the newspaper industry, see Doug Underwood, *When MBAs Rule the Newsroom* (New York: Columbia University Press, 1993). A detailed look at how corporate buyouts have changed television news is available in Ken Auletta, *Three Blind Mice: How the TV Networks Lost Their Way* (New York: Vintage, 1992).

4. For more detailed analysis of the transformation of the news media and the relations among press, politicians, and publics, see W. Lance Bennett, *News: The Politics of Illusion,* 3rd ed. (White Plains, N.Y.: Longman, Inc., 1996).

5. See Bennett, *News,* Ch. 1, for a detailed analysis of the reasons why these trends have developed.

6. Based on a study by the Center for Media and Public Affairs, published in *Media Monitor* 8, no. 6 (1994): 2.

7. Center for Media and Public Affairs study cited in John Carmody's (untitled) media column in the *Washington Post,* November 18, 1992, p. C6.

8. Joshua Goldstein, "The Currency of Change: The Freshmen of 1992 Now Rely on Classic Incumbent Fundraising," *Capital Eye* 1, no. 4 (October 15, 1994): 1 (published by the Center for Responsive Politics).

9. Larry Makinson, *Follow the Money Handbook* (Washington, D.C.: Center for Responsive Politics, 1994), pp. 108–117.

10. Jeff Cohen and Norman Solomon, "Just Imagine: A Media Crusade Against

Big-Money Politics," *Capital Eye* 1, no. 5 (December 15, 1994): 3 (published by the Center for Responsive Politics, Washington, D.C.).

11. But Durenburger was one of just two members of Congress to accept so many trips, according to a study by the Center for Public Integrity, cited in *Well-Healed: Inside Lobbying for Health Care Reform,* report of the Center for Public Integrity (Washington, D.C., 1994), p. 3.

12. Yet Schroeder was a second-place finisher in the free trip derby, with ten, according to the study cited in ibid., p. 3.

13. In fact, Daschle accepted $428,268 from health interests in the 1991–1992 election cycle, according to ibid., p. A–74.

14. $65,777 to be exact. Ibid., p. A–72.

15. *Well-Healed: Inside Lobbying for Health Care Reform,* report of the Center for Public Integrity (Washington, D.C., 1994), p. 3.

16. Robert McChesney, *Telecommunications, Mass Media, and Democracy: The Battle for Control of U.S. Broadcasting, 1928–1935.* (New York: Oxford University Press, 1993).

17. See Auletta, *Three Blind Mice,* for excellent case studies of how corporate buyouts changed the commitment to public interest broadcasting at each of the three major television networks.

18. For a more elaborate discussion, see Bennett, *News.*

19. William Greider, *Who Will Tell the People: The Betrayal of American Democracy* (New York: Simon and Schuster, 1992).

20. Quoted in Richard L. Berke, "Big Money's Election Year Comeback," *New York Times,* August 7, 1988, p. E5.

21. Source: Dwight Morris and Muriel Gamache, *Handbook of Campaign Spending* (Washington, D.C.: CQ Press, 1994), p. 14.

22. Herbert Alexander, quoted in *New York Times,* ibid.

23. Ibid.

24. Jean Cobb, Jeff Denny, Vicki Kemper, and Viveca Novak, "All the President's Donors," *Common Cause Magazine,* March/April 1990, p. 22.

25. Ibid., p. 23.

26. Brooks Jackson, "Democrats Outflanked in Previous Elections, Rival GOP in Financing of Presidential Race," *Wall Street Journal,* October 3, 1988, p. A22.

27. Makinson, *Follow the Money Handbook,* p. 30.

28. Quoted in Nina Burleigh, "Million Dollar Bill," *Time,* July 4, 1994, p. 31.

29. Ibid.

30. Makinson, *Follow the Money Handbook,* p. 31.

31. Cobb et al., "All the President's Donors," p. 23.

32. Source: Congressional Research Service and Federal Election Commission. In particular, for recent figures, see the Federal Election Commission report of December 22, 1994: "1994 Congressional Spending Sets Record." For an extensive discussion of the 1992 and earlier figures, see Makinson, *Follow the Money Handbook,* pp. 3–31.

33. Quoted in Ross Baker, *The New Fat Cats* (New York: Priority Press, 1989), pp. 10–11.

34. William H. Hudnut III, quoted in David Broder, "How to Clear Up Congress? Alumni Say Sweep out the Cash," *International Herald Tribune,* January 7, 1991, p. 5 (from the *Washington Post*).

35. The quote and information cited in this paragraph are from John H. Fund, "Who Drove the S&L Getaway Car?" *Wall Street Journal,* October 31, 1990, p. 10.

36. See Baker, *The New Fat Cats.* Appendix, Table 2, provides a list of some of the potentates.

37. Source: *Open Secrets: The Encyclopedia of Congressional Money and Politics* (Washington, D.C.: Center for Responsive Politics), p. 1263.

38. Jeanne Cummings, "Gingrich Wins Friends, Influence with GOPAC," *The Atlanta Journal and Constitution,* May 1, 1994, p. A 16.

39. Glenn R. Simpson, "Representative Moneybags: Will the Millionaires Turn Congress into a Plutocracy?" *Washington Post National Weekly Edition,* May 2–8, 1994, p. 25.

40. Ibid.

41. From Charles S. Babcock, "Fall Campaigns Set Spending Record," *Washington Post National Weekly Edition,* December 31, 1994, p. A 4.

42. This was for a Senate race in 1986! Reported by Richard L. Berke, "Senate Campaign Reform vs. A Senate Campaign," *New York Times,* May 13, 1990, p. E4.

43. Morris and Gamache, *Handbook of Campaign Spending,* p. 12.

44. Ibid., p. 8.

45. Morris and Gamache, *Handbook of Campaign Spending,* p. 18.

46. Baker, *The New Fat Cats,* p. 11.

47. Thomas Ferguson and Joel Rogers, *Right Turn: The Decline of the Democrats and the Future of American Politics* (New York: Hill and Wang, 1986).

48. Ibid., p. 15.

49. Ibid., p. 14.

50. See, for example, Seymour Martin Lipset and William Schneider, *The Confidence Gap: Business, Labor and Government in the Public Mind* (New York: Free Press, 1983), p. 17. Gallup Polls, 1960–1994.

51. Thomas Ferguson, "GOP $$$ Talked; Did Voters Listen?" *The Nation,* December 26, 1994, p. 794.

52. William Domhoff, *The Power Elite and the State: How Policy Is Made in America* (New York: Aldine de Gruyter, 1990), especially Ch. 9.

53. Benjamin Page addresses these points persuasively in his *Choices and Echoes in Presidential Elections* (Chicago: University of Chicago Press, 1978).

54. *New York Times,* November 3, 1988, p. 14.

55. Quoted in Thomas Ferguson and Joel Rogers, "The Reagan Victory: Corporate Coalitions in the 1980 Campaign," in Ferguson and Rogers, eds., *The Hidden Election* (New York: Random House, 1981), p. 4.

56. Benjamin Ginsberg, "A Post Election Era?" *PS: Political Science & Politics,* March 1989, p. 19. See also Benjamin Ginsberg and Martin Sheffer, *Politics by Other Means: The Declining Importance of Elections in America* (New York: Basic Books, 1990).

57. Mark Petracca, "Political Consultants and Democratic Governance," *PS: Political Science & Politics,* March 1989, p. 11.

58. Ibid., p. 13.

59. Ibid.

60. See Ginsberg, "A Post Election Era?"

61. See Walter de Vries, "American Campaign Consulting: Trends and Concerns," *PS: Political Science & Politics,* March 1989, pp. 21–25.

62. Ibid., p. 24.

63. Petracca, "Political Consultants and Democratic Governance," p. 12.

64. de Vries, "American Campaign Consulting," p. 21.

65. Ibid., p. 23.

66. Maureen Dowd, "New Today at the Bush 'Beige' White House: A Glitzy Image Maker," *New York Times Service* article reprinted in *International Herald Tribune,* October 4, 1989, p. 1.

67. Ibid., p. 7.

68. Howard Fineman, "Spin Doctors in Love," *Newsweek,* September 12, 1994, p. 33.

69. Morris and Gamache, *Handbook of Campaign Spending,* p. 84.

70. Mark Hertsgaard, "Electoral Journalism: Not Yellow, But Yellow-Bellied," *New York Times,* September 21, 1988, p. A15.

71. Richard L. Berke, "Image Makers Hard at Work In the Selling of a Candidate," *New York Times,* September 26, 1994, p. A1.

72. Ibid.

CHAPTER 7

1. The contestants in the election ritual must establish, first of all, that they are serious candidates who seek the office out of concern for the public good. The most obvious way to establish legitimacy is to claim expertise and original (or at least popular) ideas in certain policy areas. Policy rhetoric thus becomes both a means of attracting voting support and a basis on which to make a credible entry in the race. Candidates then link their ideas and policy positions to claims about the personal deficiencies of the other candidate or party. Personal and party competition also gives the ritualistic appearance that serious choices are offered based on free and open disagreements between the candidates. It is a small step from themes of personal competition in campaign rhetoric to the general subject of leadership. Thus, to the extent that public debate emerges in an election, the requirements of the ritual generally restrict it to (1) the policy visions of the candidates, (2) the personalities and differences of the contestants, and (3) the challenges and requirements of leadership.

2. *New York Times,* September 21, 1976, p. 1, cols. 1–2. Hereafter, the citation of dates refers to the day on which the speech, event, appearance, and so on, was reported in the *New York Times.* Unless noted otherwise, the date of actual occurrence can be obtained by subtracting one day.

3. Nationally televised speech, NBC network, March 31, 1976.

4. June 16, 1976, p. 18, col. 1.

5. Joseph Lelyveld, "The Selling of a Candidate," *New York Times Magazine,* March 28, 1976, p. 66.

6. Ibid.

7. May 13, 1976, p. 35, col. 5. This statement was made on a prior date, but it was reported in an article (William Safire's column) that appeared on this date.

8. The yarmulke clearly was part of the appeal for this elected audience. Even such details like the color (blue) of the yarmulke may reflect some calculation. Carter generally wore blue accents in his campaign attire. One of Carter's media staff revealed "I love running this guy when he's in blue. The blue gets attention. It's optically dramatic." See Lelyveld, "The Selling of a Candidate," p. 68.

9. June 7, 1976, p. 22, col. 1.

10. May 25, 1976, p. 24, col. 7.

11. May 27, 1976, p. 24, col. 1.

12. May 25, 1976, p. 24, col. 7.

13. May 15, 1976, p. 1, col. 2.

14. See Joe McGinniss, *The Selling of the President, 1968* (New York: Trident Press, 1969).

15. For an excellent account of this, see Gary Wills, *Nixon Agonistes* (New York: Signet, 1969).

16. July 2, 1976, p. 9, col. 1.

17. June 1976, p. 12, col. 5.

18. See Harvey Sacks, "On the Analyzability of Stories by Children," in J. Gumperz and D. Hymes, eds., *Directions in Sociolinguistics: The Ethnography of Communication* (New York: Holt, Rinehart and Winston), 1972.

19. See, for example, Reagan's national speech of March 31, 1976.

20. March 2, 1976, p. 9, col. 6.

21. June 2, 1976, p. 20, col. 6.
22. For example, see the *New York Times* and CBS surveys reported in the *Times* of June 11, 1976, p. 1, col. 7.
23. These quotes are from Reagan's national speech on the NBC network, March 31, 1976, p. 1, col. 7.
24. May 10, 1976, p. 20, col. 6.
25. June 7, 1976, p. 22, col. 6.
26. However, the California poll showed that Reagan may have lost as much as 5 percent of his support in California as a result of Ford's effective use of the Rhodesia statement. June 8, 1976, p. 23, col. 6.
27. May 29, 1976, p. 8, col. 2.
28. May 28, 1976, p. 12, col. 1.
29. Ibid., col. 2.
30. May 18, 1976, p. 20, col. 2.
31. At a time when his nomination was in doubt in 1952, even Eisenhower issued a few well-placed personal attacks. The 1952 Republican convention was controlled by Taft supporters; Eisenhower was the underdog. His nomination hinged on a crucial fight over the rules for seating three contested southern delegations. On the eve of this delegate struggle, Eisenhower briefly abandoned his aloof stance to accuse the Taft forces of chicanery and crookedness. He likened them to "rustlers who stole the Texas birthright instead of steers." (Texas was the largest of the contested southern delegations.) *New York Times,* July 4, 1976, p. 28, col. 3.
32. Udall. Michigan primary, May 14, 1976, p. 16, col. 2.
33. Brown. Maryland primary, May 18, 1976, p. 20, col. 2.
34. Ibid.
35. For an excellent discussion of the uses of banal language in political life, see Murray Edelman's book, *Political Language: Words That Succeed, Policies That Fail* (New York: Academic Press, 1977).
36. June 3, 1976, p. 30, col. 1; June 6, 1976, p. 1, col. 1.
37. June 3, 1976, p. 30, col. 1.
38. May 12, 1976, p. 47, col. 2.
39. May 14, 1976, p. 1, col. 2.
40. Of course, this strategy can be carried to extremes. There is a bit of political humor that recounts how Thomas Dewey, the 1948 challenger and front runner, spent so much of the campaign acting like the president that when the election was finally held the people thought it was time for a change. They voted for Truman—the incumbent.

CHAPTER 8

1. James David Barber, *The Presidential Character,* 2nd ed. (Englewood Cliffs, N.J.: Prentice-Hall, 1977).
2. Benjamin Page, *Choices and Echoes in Presidential Elections* (Chicago: University of Chicago Press, 1978).
3. See, for example, a typical day in the 1976 campaign of Mo Udall reported by Richard Reeves in *Old Faces of 1976* (New York: Harper and Row, 1976), pp. 3–4.
4. David Barber, "Characters in the Campaign: The Scientific Question," in James David Barber, ed., *Race for the Presidency: The Media and the Nominating Process* (Englewood Cliffs, N.J.: Prentice-Hall, 1978), p. 160.
5. For an analysis of this remark in the context of the debates, see Lloyd F. Bitzer and Theodore Reuter, *Carter vs. Ford: The Counterfeit Debates of 1976* (Madison: University of Wisconsin Press, 1980).

6. Lou Cannon and Edward Walsh, "War, Peace Dominate Debate," *Washington Post,* October 29, 1980, p. 1.

7. See, for example, Mark Hertsgaard, *On Bended Knee: The Press and the Reagan Presidency* (New York: Farrar, Straus & Giroux, 1988).

8. See Joe McGinniss, *The Selling of the President, 1968* (New York: Trident Press, 1969).

9. For a more extensive review of standard criticisms of election coverage, see David L. Swanson, "And That's the Way It Was? Television Covers the 1976 Presidential Campaign," *Quarterly Journal of Speech* 63 (1977): 239–248.

10. For various explanations of this dramatic license in American elections, see, among others: Walter R. Fisher, "Reaffirmation and Subversion of the American Dream," *Quarterly Journal of Speech* 59 (1973): 160–167; Edwin Black, "Electing Time," *Quarterly Journal of Speech* 59 (1973): 125–129; and John H. Patton, "A Government as Good as Its People: Jimmy Carter and the Restoration of Transcendence to American Politics," *Quarterly Journal of Speech* 63 (1977): 249–257.

11. On the importance, for social judgment, of the interplay between general norms and public actions, see, among others: Fritz Heider, *The Psychology of Interpersonal Relations* (New York: Wiley, 1958); Erving Goffman, *The Presentation of Self in Everyday Life* (New York: Anchor Books, 1959); Peter L. Berger and Thomas Luckmann, *The Social Construction of Reality* (New York: Anchor Doubleday, 1966); and Alfred Schutz, *On Phenomenology and Social Relations* (Chicago: University of Chicago Press, 1970).

12. Harold Garfinkel, "Conditions of Successful Degradation Ceremonies," *American Journal of Sociology* 61 (1956): 420–424.

13. See, among others: Erving Goffman, "The Mortification of Self," in Richard Flacks, ed., *Conformity, Resistance, and Self Determination* (Boston: Little, Brown, 1973), pp. 175–188; Erving Goffman, *Asylums* (New York: Anchor Books, 1961); and Sanford M. Dornbusch, "The Military Academy as an Assimilating Institution," *Social Forces* 33 (1955): 316–321.

14. For an extended analysis of a case from British electoral politics that is similar to Ford's series of blunders, see Charles W. Lomas, "Sir Alex Douglas Home: Case Study in Rhetorical Failure," *Quarterly Journal of Speech* 56 (1970): 296–303.

15. Tom Shales, "The Harassment of Ronald Reagan," *Washington Post,* October 31, 1980, p. C1.

16. B. L. Ware and Wil A. Linkugel, "They Spoke in Defense of Themselves: On the Generic Criticism of Apologia," *Quarterly Journal of Speech* 59 (1973): 273–284.

17. Ware and Linkugel suggest the suitability of Robert Abelson's typology of resolutions for belief dilemmas, which includes the four symbolic operations of denial, bolstering, differentiation, and transcendence (Robert P. Abelson, "Modes of Resolution of Belief Dilemmas," *Journal of Conflict Resolution* 3 [1959]: 343–352). Under some circumstances, candidates simply *deny* charges against them. At other times, they try to separate or *differentiate* an offending action from one normative category so that it can be thought of in other, less damaging terms or as a special case. Sometimes an extenuating circumstance or motive will be emphasized, or *bolstered,* in an effort to highlight a more positive interpretation. Finally, candidates may try to *transcend* the entire situation by showing that the unfortunate incident served some larger purpose or lesson. Candidate responses often combine more than one of these repair techniques, as in the case of Richard Nixon's Checkers Speech or Edward Kennedy's Chappaquiddick defense. In these notorious cases, Nixon was accused of accepting gifts during his vice presidential campaign in 1952, including a cute cocker spaniel puppy named Checkers, and Kennedy was faced with the possible end of his political career when a car he was driving went off a bridge in Chappaquiddick,

Massachusetts, and a young female companion was drowned. (For discussions of these and other examples of apologia, see Ware and Linkugel, "They Spoke in Defense of Themselves.")

18. Bernard Weinraub, "Slip and Gloom Index Rates the Candidates," *New York Times,* November 1, 1988, p. 10.

19. Murray Edelman, *Political Language: Words That Succeed and Politics That Fail* (New York: Academic Press, 1977).

20. Charles Warren, *The Making of the Constitution* (Cambridge, Mass.: Harvard University Press, 1928), p. 1.

21. Catherine L. Albanese, *Sons of the Fathers: The Civil Religion of the American Revolution* (Philadelphia: Temple University Press, 1976).

22. Karl A. Lamb, *As Orange Goes: Twelve California Families and the Future of American Politics* (New York: W. W. Norton, 1974). Both quotes are from p. 178.

23. Ibid., p. 187.

24. Ibid., pp. 185–186.

CHAPTER 9

1. Quoted in Robin Toner, "Image of Capitol Maligned by Outsiders, Insiders," *New York Times,* October 16, 1994, p. 18.

2. Charles Leonard, spokesperson for the Health Care Reform Project, quoted in Richard L. Berke, "Democrats See Voter Backlash over President," *New York Times,* June 9, 1994, p. A12.

3. Ibid.

4. Richard Lacayo, "Off to the Races," *Time,* September 12, 1994, p. 39.

5. Richard L. Berke, "Pollster Advises Democrats: Don't Be Too Close to Clinton," *New York Times,* August 3, 1994, p. A1.

6. Berke, "Democrats See Voter Backlash over President," p. A12.

7. William Schneider, remarks delivered at the conference on "The Clinton Presidency: Campaigning, Governing, and the Psychology of Leadership," held at the Graduate School and University Center, City University of New York, November 18–19, 1993. A video record of Schneider's remarks is available from the Ph.D. program in political science, attn: Stanley Renshon.

8. Quoted in R. W. Apple, Jr., "Vote Against Crime Bill Is Lesson in Clout," *New York Times,* August 17, 1994, pp. A1, A12.

9. Norman Ornstein, "Too Many 'Lone Rangers'," *Washington Post,* September 2, 1994, p. A23.

10. David Von Drehle and Thomas B. Edsall, "The Religious Right Returns," *Washington Post National Weekly Edition,* August 19–September 4, 1994, p. 6.

11. "Who's Got the Power?" *Campaigns and Elections,* September 1994, p. 22.

12. Von Drehle and Edsall, "The Religious Right Returns," p. 7.

13. Dan Balz, "For Texas Candidate, a Change of Image, But Same Goal," *Washington Post,* March 6, 1994, p. A3.

14. Dan Balz, "'New Democrats' Promise New Pressure On Clinton," *Washington Post,* December 5, 1993, p. A4.

15. Lawrence M. O'Rourke, "Demos Running away from Clinton," *The Sacramento Bee,* September 15, 1994, p. A12.

16. David Stewart, quoted in Elizabeth Kolbert, "Switching Brands," *New York Times,* November 11, 1993, p. E1.

17. Richard L. Berke, "Survey Finds Voters in U.S. Rootless and Self-Absorbed," *New York Times,* September 21, 1994, p. A12.

18. Gary C. Jacobsen, "Explaining Divided Government: Why Can't the Republicans Win the House?" *P.S.: Political Science and Politics,* December 1991, p. 642.

19. Dave Kaplan, "Incumbents Call It Quits at Record Clip," *Congressional Quarterly Weekly Report,* February 19, 1994, p. 383.

20. *All Things Considered,* National Public Radio, October 7, 1994.

21. Alissa J. Rubin, "Chances for Limited Measure Slight as Congress Returns," *Congressional Quarterly Weekly Report,* September 10, 1994, p. 2523.

22. Kaplan, "Incumbents Call It Quits at Record Clip," p. 382.

23. R. W. Apple, Jr., "For Dole and the G.O.P, a Familiar Crossroads," *New York Times,* August 30, 1994, p. A8.

24. Thomas B. Edsall, "The GOP's Variable Outlook," *Washington Post National Weekly Edition,* January 3–9, 1994, p. 13.

25. Ceci Connolly, "GOP Accentuates the Positive; Hopefuls to Sign Compact," *Congressional Quarterly Weekly Report,* September 24, 1994, pp. 2711–12.

26. Quoted in Don Balz and Charles R. Babcock, "Gingrich, Allies Made News and Impression," *Washington Post,* December 20, 1994, p. A1.

27. Judy Kosterlitz, "Brinksmanship," *The National Journal,* July 9, 1994, p. 1648.

28. Helen Dewar, "Health Care's Real Issue: November," *Washington Post National Weekly Edition,* July 11–17, 1994, p. 12.

29. See here the work of Murray Edelman, including *The Symbolic Uses of Politics* (Champagne-Urbana: University of Illinois Press, 1964); *Political Language: Words That Succeed and Policies That Fail* (New York: Academic Press, 1977); and *Constructing the Political Spectacle* (Chicago: University of Chicago Press, 1988).

30. For a discussion of how such a reading of the public mind works, see Bill Moyers' interview with Richard Wirthlin (Reagan opinion pollster and chief marketing analyst), in Moyers' Public Broadcasting Service Series "The Public Mind," Part IV, "Leading Questions," 1989. For a specific discussion of the War on Drugs as an image campaign, see Mark Hertsgaard, *On Bended Knee: The Press and the Reagan Presidency* (New York: Farrar, Straus and Giroux, 1988), pp. 156–161.

31. Jack Honomichl, "Richard Wirthlin, Advertising Man of the Year," *Advertising Age,* January 23, 1989, lead article.

32. From Michael Isikoff, "A 'Sting' Tailor-Made for Bush," *Washington Post* News Service, reprinted in the *International Herald Tribune,* Saturday–Sunday, September 23–24, 1989, p. 4.

33. Maureen Dowd, "U.S. Presidential Road Show," *International Herald Tribune,* September 26, 1989, p. 3 (from the *New York Times*).

34. Federal Election Commission, "1992 Congressional Election Spending Jumps 52% to $678 Million," March 4, 1993, p. 1; 1994 projection based on Federal Election Commission, "1992 PAC Activity Increases," January 1994, p. 1; and "PAC Contributions Track 1992 Levels," September 19, 1994, pp. 1–4.

35. Katherine Q. Seeyle, "Lobbyists Are the Loudest in the Health Care Debate," *New York Times,* August 16, 1994. p. A10.

36. Ibid.

37. Ibid., p. 51.

38. Center for Public Integrity, "Well-Healed: Inside Lobbying for Health Care Reform," July 1994, p. 75. Copies may be obtained from the Center for Public Integrity, 1634 I Street, Suite 902, Washington D.C. 20006.

39. "Well-Healed," pp. A65–75.

40. Seeyle, "Lobbyists Are Loudest in the Health Care Debate," p. A10.

41. Ibid.

42. Ibid.

43. Michael Weisskopf, "Health Care Lobbies Lobby Each Other," *Washington Post,* March 1, 1994, p. A8.

44. By May of 1994, Cooper's dominance in the money game was even more decided, for he had collected $540,145 since January 1, 1993. David S. Broder, "Upstaging the President," *Washington Post,* February 3, 1994, p. A1.

45. Ibid., p. A9.

46. Garry Wills, "What Makes a Good Leader?" *The Atlantic Monthly,* April 1994, p. 64.

47. Larry Sabato, "Political Influence, the News Media, and Campaign Consultants," *PS: Political Science and Politics,* March 1989, p. 16.

48. Jeremy Larner, "Politics Catches up to 'The Candidate'," *New York Times,* October 23, 1988, p. E23.

49. Sabato, "Political Influence," p. 15.

50. Ibid., p. 16.

51. Richard Morin and David S. Broder, "Why Americans Hate Congress," *Washington Post National Weekly Edition,* July 11–17, 1994, p. 6.

52. David S. Broder, "Can We Govern?" *Washington Post National Weekly Edition,* January 31–February 6, 1994, p. 23.

CHAPTER 10

1. For a discussion of the constitutional arguments surrounding the Arkansas term limit case, see Holly Idelson, "Term Limit Debate Moves to Congress, High Court," *Congressional Quarterly,* December 3, 1994, p. 3451.

2. Reported in an Associated Press wire story, "GOP Rethinking Term-Limit Pledge," *Charleston Post and Courier,* November 22, 1994, p. A1.

3. See Elizabeth Drew, "Watch 'Em Squirm," *New York Times Magazine,* March 14, 1993, pp. 32–34.

4. ABC News survey, September 1994, reported in Richard Morin, "They Only Know What They Don't Like," *Washington Post National Weekly Edition,* October 3–9, 1994, p. 37.

5. Ibid.

6. Data on 1960, 1970, and 1980 are from Seymour Martin Lipset and William Schneider, *The Confidence Gap* (New York: Free Press, 1983). The 1990 figure is from a *New York Times/*CBS News poll reported in the *International Herald Tribune,* November 5, 1990, p. 1. The 1994 response is from a *Washington Post/*ABC News poll that asked people to agree or disagree with the statement that "most members of Congress care more about special interests than they care about people like you." Reported in Richard Morin and David S. Broder, "Why Americans Hate Congress," *Washington Post National Weekly Edition,* July 11–17, 1994, p. 7.

7. *Washington Post/*ABC News poll, reported in David S. Broder and Thomas B. Edsall, "More Than Ever, America Sees Its Ruination in Politicians," a *Washington Post* analysis reprinted in the *International Herald Tribune,* September 17, 1990, p. 3.

8. *Washington Post/*ABC News poll, reported on the Associated Press News Wire, October 17, 1990.

9. See Morin and Broder, "Why Americans Hate Congress."

10. Although incumbent advantages have narrowed, they are still large enough to keep reform-minded candidates from enacting serious reforms after they reach office.

11. Jarol Manheim, *All of the People, All the Time: Strategic Communication and American Politics* (Armonk, N.Y.: M. E. Sharpe, 1991).

12. Reported in Richard L. Berke, "Survey Finds Voters in U.S. Rootless and Self-Absorbed," *New York Times,* September 21, 1994, p. A12.

13. David S. Broder, "Term Limits Are Dangerous Medicine," *International Herald Tribune,* October 16, 1991, p. 8.

14. Quoted in Richard L. Berke, "Defining 'Constituent Service,' " *International Herald Tribune,* November 7, 1989, p. 3 (from the *New York Times*).

15. Fred Wertheimer, "Window of Opportunity: The Climate Is Ripe for Ethics Reforms," *Common Cause Magazine,* July/August 1989, p. 45.

16. Jonathan S. Krasno and Donald Philip Green, "Stopping the Buck Here: The Case for Campaign Spending Limits," *The Brookings Review,* 11, no. 2 (Spring 1993): 17–21.

17. See Bennett, *News: The Politics of Illusion,* 3rd ed. (New York: Longman, 1996).

18. Frances Fox Piven and Richard Cloward, "Government Statistics and Conflicting Explanations of Nonvoting," *PS: Political Science & Politics,* September 1989, pp. 580–587.

19. Paul Corcoran, *Political Language and Rhetoric* (Austin: University of Texas Press, 1979), p. xv.

20. Charles W. Knepper, "Political Rhetoric and Public Competence: A Crisis for Democracy?" *Rhetorical Society Quarterly* 16, no. 3 (Summer 1986): 126.

SELECTED BIBLIOGRAPHY

Alexander, Herbert E. *Financing Politics: Money, Elections and Political Reform*. 5th ed. Washington, D.C.: Congressional Quarterly Press, 1992.
The standard reference on campaign finance reform and what it hath wrought.

Asher, Herbert B. *Presidential Elections and American Politics*. 5th ed. Chicago: Dorsey Press, 1992.
Good detailed analyses of recent elections and voting trends.

Bagdikian, Ben H. *The Media Monopoly*. 4th ed. Boston: Beacon Press, 1992.
Shows why the business end of the media matters for democracy.

Bennett, W. Lance. *News: The Politics of Illusion*. 3rd ed. New York: Longman, 1996.
A critical look at the political content of news reporting. Contrasting analysis of how reporting on politics as usual differs from election journalism.

Burnham, Walter Dean. *Critical Elections and the Mainsprings of American Politics*. New York: W. W. Norton, 1970.
A classic explanation of party systems and the history of voter alignments in American politics.

Campbell, Angus, Philip E. Converse, Warren E. Miller, and Donald E. Stokes. *The American Voter*. New York: John Wiley, 1960.
The standard reference on how a poorly informed and nonideological electorate makes individual voting decisions.

Diamond, Edwin and Stephen Bates. *The Spot: The Rise of Political Advertising on Television*. Cambridge, Mass.: M.I.T. Press, 1992.
A lively look at political hucksterism on TV.

Domhoff, William. *The Power Elite and the State: How Policy Is Made in America*. New York: Aldine de Gruyter, 1990.
No conspiracy theory here. Even more disturbing is the possibility that behind the push and pull of elite influence there lies no vision at all.

Edelman, Murray. *Constructing the Political Spectacle*. Chicago: University of Chicago Press, 1988.
A view of politics as a spectator sport with grand clashes between media-conscious leaders and constructed enemies at the center of the arena.

Entman, Robert. *Democracy Without Citizens: Media and the Decay of American Politics*. New York: Oxford University Press, 1989.
A persuasive argument that our current news and political information system discourages citizen participation.

Ferguson, Thomas, and Joel Rogers. *Right Turn: The Decline of the Democrats and the Future of American Politics*. New York: Hill and Wang, 1986.
A provocative analysis of the Democratic party being pushed to the right due to competition with the Republicans for financing with ideological strings attached.

Ginsberg, Benjamin. *The Captive Public: How Mass Opinion Promotes State Power*. New York: Basic Books, 1986.
An insightful look at how opinion polling and mass communications have tamed and standardized public opinion.

Ginsberg, Benjamin, and Martin Shefter. *Politics by Other Means: The Declining Importance of Elections in America*. New York: Basic Books, 1990.

An analysis of the decay of parties and the decline of popular participation in elections.

Greider, William. *Who Will Tell the People: The Betrayal of American Democracy.* New York: Simon and Schuster, 1992.
Why the public may have reason to be angry at both politicians and the press, and why mainstream journalists are unwilling to report on Washington politics in ways that might help those who live outside the Beltway.

Hart, Roderick P. *The Sound of Leadership: Presidential Communication in the Modern Age.* Chicago: University of Chicago Press, 1987.
A systematic analysis of the styles of presidential rhetoric.

Herbst, Susan. *Numbered Voices: How Opinion Polling Has Shaped American Politics.* Chicago: University of Chicago Press, 1993.
Suggests that faceless, isolated opinion polling may undermine the social accountability of face-to-face publics on which democracy depends.

Hertsgaard, Mark. *On Bended Knee: The Press and the Reagan Presidency.* New York: Farrar, Straus and Giroux, 1988.
A detailed account of the media management techniques used by the communications professionals behind "the Great Communicator."

Jamieson, Kathleen Hall. *Eloquence in an Electronic Age: The Transformation of Political Speechmaking.* New York: Oxford University Press, 1988.
A look at what made Reagan "the Great Communicator," contrasted with rhetorical practices of the past.

Jamieson, Kathleen Hall. *Dirty Politics.* New York: Oxford University Press, 1992.
How advertising and electronic communication techniques have corrupted communication and voter decision making in elections.

Key, V. O. (with Milton C. Cummings). *The Responsible Electorate: Rationality in Presidential Voting, 1936–1960,* New York: Vintage Books, 1966.
The classic work in the "voters are not fools" school (i.e., most people most of the time make the best sense they can out of the choices given them).

Kleppner, Paul, Walter Dean Burnham, Ronald P. Formisano, Samuel P. Hays, Richard Jensen, and William G. Shade. *The Evolution of American Electoral Systems.* Westport, Conn.: Greenwood Press, 1981.
A breathtaking sweep of elections, parties, and society in America from the rise of the Federalists and Jeffersonian Democrats to the decline of parties in the recent era.

McChesney, Robert. *Telecommunications, Mass Media, and Democracy: The Battle for Control of U.S. Broadcasting, 1928–1935.* New York: Oxford University Press, 1993.
What happened to public broadcasting in the United States and why it matters.

Makinson, Larry. *Follow the Money Handbook.* Washington, D.C.: Center for Responsive Politics, 1994.
An eye-opening look at money patterns in elections, and a guide to following the money trail in elections at all levels.

Manheim, Jarol. *All of the People, All the Time: Strategic Communication and American Politics.* Armonk, N.Y.: M. E. Sharpe, 1991.
A broad overview of how "spin doctors," handlers, public relations specialists, pollsters, and their political clients apply the arts and sciences of strategic communication.

Mauser, Gary A. *Political Marketing: An Approach to Campaign Strategy.* New York: Praeger, 1983.
A pioneering explanation of how candidate marketing works.

Mayhew, David. *Congress: The Electoral Connection.* New Haven, Conn.: Yale University Press, 1974.

The first compelling analysis of why running for office may loom larger than governing in the lives of members of Congress.

Mayhew, David. *Divided We Govern.* New Haven, Conn.: Yale University Press, 1991.

An argument that divided party government performs no worse than when the same party sits at both ends of Pennsylvania Avenue.

Morris, Dwight, and Muriel E. Gamache. *Gold-Plated Politics: The 1992 Congressional Races.* Washington, D.C.: Congressional Quarterly Press, 1994.

A gold mine of campaign finance data from congressional races.

Morris, Dwight, and Muriel Gamache. *Handbook of Campaign Spending.* Washington, D.C.: Congressional Quarterly Press, 1994.

Even more data on spending patterns, from individual races to statistical profiles.

Page, Benjamin. *Choices and Echoes in Presidential Elections.* Chicago: University of Chicago Press, 1978.

A look at the interplay of issues and candidate images in elections, and an analysis of why images become so important when issue choices are narrowed.

Patterson, Thomas. *Out of Order: How the Decline of the Political Parties and the Growing Power of the News Media Undermine the American Way of Electing Presidents.* New York: Alfred A. Knopf, 1993.

How campaign news coverage has become more negative, personalized, and less issue oriented over the last thirty years.

Phillips, Kevin. *The Politics of Rich and Poor: Wealth and the American Electorate in the Reagan Aftermath.* New York: Random House, 1990.

A convincing case that substantial amounts of wealth floated to the top during the last decade. The people should be mad as hell. But are they?

Polsby, Nelson, and Aaron Wildavsky. *Presidential Elections.* New York: Free Press, 1991.

The full view of elections from financing and party nominations to the media and voting.

Pomper, Gerald M., ed. *The Election of 1988: Reports and Interpretations.* Chatham, N.J.: Chatham House Publishers, 1989.

A collection of well-written essays examining the presidential and congressional elections with an eye to public opinion, media coverage, and historical trends.

Pomper, Gerald M., ed. *The Election of 1992: Reports and Interpretations.* Chatham, N.J.: Chatham House Publishers, 1993.

A similarly comprehensive collection of views on 1992. (Look for a companion volume on *The Election of 1996.*)

Sabato, Larry J. *PAC Power: Inside the World of Political Action Committees.* New York: W. W. Norton, 1985.

A detailed history and analysis of the world of political action committees and the power they wield.

Tulis, Jeffrey K. *The Rhetorical Presidency.* Princeton, N.J.: Princeton University Press, 1987.

A rich, readable look at the importance of rhetoric in the nation's top leadership post.

Wayne, Stephen J. *The Road to the White House: The Politics of Presidential Elections.* 5th ed. New York: St. Martin's Press, 1996.

A nuts-and-bolts treatment of the electoral system, campaign finance, party conventions, the media, voting trends, and reforms.

INDEX

activist government, 83–84
advertising, political. *See* political advertising
African Americans, 147
  1988 elections and, 38–39
Ailes, Roger, 35, 37, 51, 75, 223
Albanese, Catherine, 194
American Association of Political Consultants, 151
American Association of Retired Persons, 220
American Medical Association (AMA), 134, 220
Andreas, Dwayne, 132
anger of voters, 16–17, 48
  1992 election and, 62
  new politics and, 56
  term limits and, 226–28
Annenberg School of Communication, 219
antiwar movement, 85
Apple, R. W., Jr., 44, 238
Arledge, Roone, 34
Armey, Dick, 23, 209, 226
Atwater, Lee, 35, 36, 41–42, 75, 154
audiences. *See* political audiences

Bagdikian, Ben, 129
Baker, James, 74, 75
Baker, Ross, 142
Barber, James David, 182
Barry, Lynda, 42
Bennett, Bill, 214, 223
Bentsen, Lloyd, 30
big business
  control of news media by, 129–31
  See also money
blacks. *See* African Americans
Bloodworth, Linda, 75
Blumenthal, Sidney, 15–16
Boggs, Tommy, 132

Breaux, John, 219
Brewster, Bill, 219
Brezhnev, Leonid, 164
Broder, David, 141, 146, 224, 228
Brokaw, Tom, 132
Brown, Jerry, 72, 174
Brown, Willie, 39
Bryan, William Jennings, 82, 113
Buckley, John, 32
Buckley v. *Valeo,* 91, 232, 237
Burnham, Walter Dean, 98–99, 113, 115, 180
Bush, George, 154, 205
  1988 election and, 35–37, 179
    character, 185
    negative campaign against Dukakis, 175
  1992 election and, 55–56, 66, 74–75
    economic factors, 116, 117
    voter psychology and, 60–61
  campaign finance reform and, 232–33
  Quayle and, 223
  tax policy of, 102
  war on drugs and, 213–15
  See also elections and electoral campaigns, 1988; elections and electoral campaigns, 1992
Byrd, Robert C., 142

California, 49
  1994 Senate race in, 14–16
campaign consultants. *See* political consultants
campaign finance reform, 49, 90–91, 226
  proposal for, 231–35
campaign financing, 18–19, 22, 131
  1988 campaign, 138–39
  competition for support of contributors, 48–49

273